Repair, Maintain & Store

LAWNMOWERS & GARDEN EQUIPMENT

Richard V. Nunn

Repair, Maintain & Store

LAWNMOWERS & GARDEN EQUIPMENT

CREATIVE HOMEOWNER PRESS®

A DIVISION OF FEDERAL MARKETING CORPORATION, 24 PARK WAY, UPPER SADDLE RIVER, NEW JERSEY 07458

Manufactured in United States of America

Current printing (last digit)
10 9 8 7 6 5 4 3

Produced by Roundtable Press, Inc.

Editorial: Don Nelson

Design: Betty Binns Graphics

Illustrations: Norman Nuding

Jacket Photo: Bank Street Photographers

Jacket Tools & Equipment: Courtesy Warwick Hardware and Agway-Wadeson Home Center

The author and publisher wish to extend thanks to the many individuals and companies who so graciously provided advice, time, photographs, and store inventories (for photographs and drawings) to complete this book. Names, addresses, and individual identifications of their contributions can be found on page 159.

LC: 83-17151

ISBN: 0-932944-64-7 (paper)
         0-932944-68-x (hardcover)

CREATIVE HOMEOWNER PRESS® BOOK SERIES
A DIVISION OF FEDERAL MARKETING CORPORATION
24 PARK WAY, UPPER SADDLE RIVER, NJ 07458

Foreword

The primary purpose of this book is to save you time and money. It is not designed to make you a small-engine-repair expert or a professional horticulturist. Rather, this book anticipates through practical experience many of the problems that you, as a homeowner or apartment dweller with a lawn to maintain, will have with minor equipment breakdowns, insects or weeds, poor or nongrowing turf grasses, and storing lawn and garden tools and equipment.

You can solve many of these problems yourself—and it's easier than you may think. Most lawnmower malfunctions, for example, take little more than common sense to fix. The Number One cause of nonstarting is that the machine is out of fuel. Yet the gas tank is often the last place the operator looks when the engine won't start.

Lawnmower engine tune-ups are also easy to accomplish; you'll find all you need to know detailed in the maintenance section of this book. By making tune-ups yourself, you can save as much as $40 compared to the professional's prices. Best yet, you do the job at home—no lifting heavy equipment in and out of your car; no long waits while the pro fixes your mower; and hundreds of others. The parts that you need are readily available at many hardware stores, home centers, nursery outlets, and retailers that sell lawn and garden supplies and equipment. The procedures are frequently as simple as removing the old part and installing the new one. There is seldom anything to fix since the job is basically replacement.

To grow a handsome lawn, beautiful flowers, or abundant vegetables is not especially difficult, either. Contrary to popular belief, you don't have to have a green thumb or a farmer's luck. What you must have is patience and a little knowledge of seeds, weed and insect control, watering, and fertilizing. You'll find all the practical information you need in this book.

You also will find information on how to buy lawn and garden equipment. This alone can result in big savings in your lawn and garden operation. The expensive chrome-plated rake with the fur-covered handle or the mower with the fancy controls that resemble the cockpit of a 747 airplane aren't always the best buys—no matter how good the sales pitch on the showroom floor. Knowing a little about the basics of buying wisely can give you self-confidence; you will find those basics in this book.

There's an entire chapter devoted to the proper use and maintenance of lawn and garden hand tools, which are often crowded out by newer, motorized rivals. Much of the work you will be doing in your lawn and garden will require hand tools—rakes, shovels, pruners, hoes, saws, sprinklers. Knowing how to buy and maintain this equipment can save you lots of money and time.

I make the following point throughout the book, but it bears stating here as well. *Be careful* when you work with hand and power tools. Always remember that whirling blades and moving levers on power equipment are dangerous. *Always* follow the manufacturer's recommendations for mixing and applying lawn and garden chemicals. Protect yourself with common sense and the safety equipment (goggles, gloves, respirators) that is suggested.

—Richard V. Nunn

Contents

Troubleshooting Guide

Bluegrass, fine fescue, bentgrass, tall fescue, ryegrass

Bluegrass, fine fescue, bentgrass, tall fescue, ryegrass, Bermuda grass, zoysia

Bermuda grass, zoysia, tall fescue

Bermuda grass, dichondra, St. Augustine grass

Bermuda grass, dichondra, St. Augustine grass, bluegrass

Bermuda grass, zoysia, centipede grass

St. Augustine grass, Bermuda grass, zoysia, carpetgrass

St. Augustine grass, Bermuda grass, zoysia, carpetgrass, centipede grass

St. Augustine grass, Bermuda grass, zoysia, carpetgrass, centipede grass, Bahia grass

What grows best where? This color-keyed map will help you choose varieties of turf grass to grow anywhere in the United States.

1 Lawn Care Basics

Mary, Mary quite contrary
How does your garden grow?
With silver bells and cockle shells,
And a lot of hard work with a hoe.

This paraphrase of the familiar nursery rhyme suggests that the bottom line of any successful lawn or garden project is how hard you are willing to work at it. The chances are that your neighbor's lawn looks greener, thicker, and weed-free because your neighbor spends a lot of time and effort at it. The same is probably true of the healthy trees and shrubs and the abundant vegetables. The point is that your neighbor probably has a certain goal in mind and works hard to achieve it. The goal does not require a green thumb or even a lot of knowledge. There is really no mystery involved.

Unlike Mary with her hoe, you can avoid much of the hard work connected with lawn and garden care by using today's improved hand and power tool equipment and specially-formulated chemicals. These products are all available at hardware and home center stores, lawn and garden outlets, nurseries, and greenhouse retailers.

What goals by when?

For many Americans lawn care is a do-it-yourself job. Hiring a private gardener simply isn't within most budgets. You can hire a company (you'll find them listed in the Yellow Pages) to handle the fertilizing and mowing; this is usually less expensive than hiring a gardener. These landscaping firms do a large-volume business, and this helps keep prices in line.

Many people start out with good intentions in the spring and settle for almost anything that looks green by midsummer. But what is usually lacking at the outset—when the seed catalogs come in the mail and the shelter magazines start touting weed and insect control—is a planned approach, coupled with the proper equipment, and a lot of patience.

Total lawn management starts with planting. It then progresses to mowing, watering, fertilizing, weed control, insect control, raking, and thatching. You can follow through on any one or two of these categories of lawn management you want; for example, just keep up with mowing and watering and forget the rest. Of course, the end result will probably not be a picture-perfect lawn. That usually requires you to follow the entire regimen of proper lawn management.

In this chapter we'll discuss in detail the following aspects of lawn management:

soil analysis
seed selection
planting turf grass
fertilizing lawns
weed control
disease control
insect control
trees and shrubs

Where you live makes a difference

Climate and soil are the determining factors in deciding what types of grass you should plant and maintain. Start first by determining what variety of grass is adapted to the area in which you live. The color-keyed map will help you with the proper turf grass selection.

Consider four other factors when choosing your turf grass:

1. What type of lawn do you want? One for "show" or one for "go" (that is, for lawn tennis, a golf chipping range, baseball, badminton, or other lawn games)?

2. How much monthly maintenance is needed? Is water plentiful? Will the turf grass you select respond well to mowing and fertilizing?

3. What are the physical limitations of your lawn? Factor in such items as slope, shade, air circulation, high wind, and sunlight.

4. What is the chemical balance of your soil? Do yourself a favor and make a simple soil test; it's easy and inexpensive and it can save you plenty of time and money in the years ahead.

Soil tests

There are two ways to test soil. You can buy a fairly inexpensive soil-testing kit at a nursery or a lawn and garden outlet. Or you can take a soil sample to your county agricultural agent for testing. (This method is very inexpensive.) Some state universities also make soil tests. Do not send the sample to the U.S. Department of Agriculture; this agency does not test soil.

I would recommend that you have your test done by a county or state agency. The fee is usually less than $2, and you will obtain a higher degree of accuracy than might be available in a do-it-yourself test.

To gather soil for a test, cut the soil to a depth of 6 inches (the depth of a plant bed or the root depth of many turf grasses). Just dig with a spade to expose the various levels of soil. Then cut a 1/2-inch-thick slab of soil from the edge of the hole. If your lot is especially large (more than an acre, say), take samples from different sections of your property. Mix the samples together in a bucket and use a small sample of this mixture for a test.

What a soil test does is to measure how acid or how alkaline the soil is. The results are given on the pH scale, which is used by chemists to indicate alkalinity or acidity. The number 7 on the pH scale is a neutral rating. Any rating lower than 7 means that the soil is acid. Any number higher than 7 means that the soil is alkaline, or sweet.

Here is a pH scale and its meaning in soil testing.

If pH is . . .	the soil is
4.5 or below	very acid
4.6 to 5.0	highly acid
5.1 to 5.5	strongly acid
5.6 to 6.0	fairly acid
6.1 to 6.5	mildly acid
6.6 to 7.5	neutral
7.6 to 7.8	mildly alkaline
7.9 to 8.5	fairly alkaline
8.6 to 9.0	highly alkaline
over 9.1	very alkaline

Turf grass does best, as a rule of thumb, in soil with a pH of 6.0 to 6.5.

Changing the pH

Limestone is commonly used to sweeten the soil. It's available as finely ground stone, hydrated lime, and oystershell lime. Hydrated lime is very fast acting and should be avoided. The other types of lime act more slowly, but you will need more of these types than of hydrated to do the job. Aluminum sulfate or sulfur are the choices if you need to make your soil more acid. The accompanying charts show how the pH changes with the application of limestone or aluminum sulfate and sulfur.

pH change	limestone (lbs. needed for 100 sq. ft.)
3.5 to 4.5	3 1/2
4.5 to 5.5	4
5.5 to 7.0	5 1/2

pH change	aluminum sulfate (lbs. needed for 100 sq. ft.)	sulfur
8.0 to 7.0	4 1/2	2
7.5 to 6.5	7 1/2	3 1/2
7.0 to 6.0	5 1/2	2
6.0 to 5.5	3 1/2	1 1/2
6.0 to 5.0	7 1/2	3
5.5 to 5.0	4	1 1/2
5.5 to 4.5	8 1/2	2 1/2

Here's another rule of thumb: if the soil is sandy and loamy, use a little less limestone or chemical. But if the soil is heavy—as clay is—use a bit more limestone or chemical. And in any case, go easy. The pH should change only one unit each year. You'll be tempted to change the pH faster, but soil experts say that it's best to let the soil adjust gradually.

Lime conditions the soil; it is not a fertilizer. It helps loosen hard, clay soil, and it helps humus decay faster. Do not apply lime and manure fertilizer at the same time. The lime works chemically on the manure and the benefits are lost. Ideally, the manure should be plowed or spaded under the soil, and then the lime applied on top.

Types of turf grasses

The following descriptions of turf grasses will help you to select those that will grow best in your part of the nation. Check the map at the beginning of this chapter for additional clues. There are, of course, blends of these grasses and other strains of grasses. If you don't like what you see here, consult a quality nursery in your community.

■ **Bluegrass.** There are about 200 species of this grass, which grows best in temperate and cooler climates. It is dark green in color and has medium-textured blades.

The popular strains of bluegrass include Merion, Newport, Vantage, Victa, Windsor, Bristol, Merit, and common Kentucky.

Bluegrass requires moderate amounts of water; it may turn brownish in hot weather, but a little watering will restore its rich color.

Bluegrass diseases include leaf spot, dollar spot, stripe smut, rust, and powdery mildew. Insects that damage the grass include sod webworms, army worms, grubs, and chinch bugs. All these diseases and insects may be controlled with chemicals.

Cut bluegrass at a 1 1/2- to 2-inch height. You may even prefer to leave it at 2 1/2 inches for a carpet effect—and that cushiony feeling when you walk over it. Feed the grass during

Bluegrass

the growing season or during the fall and winter. Bluegrass loves sod that is slightly acid—6-7 pH. If you run a soil test, you may find that the soil needs a ground limestone treatment every 3 to 5 years. The amount of limestone usually required is 25 pounds for each 1000 sq. ft.

■ **Red fescue.** This is an eastern grass that likes to grow in well-drained sandy soil. Other types of red fescue are creeping red and chewing fescue. Ranier, Pennlawn, and Ilahee are varieties of this plant.

As a rule, red fescue is blended with Kentucky bluegrass to make a mixture with greater resistance to wear. It does well in shady areas, but peters out if the soil is not well drained.

Seed this variety in the fall or late summer on a fairly firm bed and cover it with approximately ¼ inch of soil. It should be watered moderately, maintained at a 2-inch height, and fertilized in early spring and early fall. The soil should have a pH of about 6.0. To maintain it, apply about 25 pounds of lime for 1000 sq. ft. annually. Red fescue is very resistant to disease, but insects such as army worms, sod webworms, and grubs can damage the turf.

■ **Tall fescue.** This turf grass is similar to red fescue. It likes cool weather, and it's a tough grass that can handle lots of work and play

Tall fescue

activities without damage.

Since the leaves of tall fescue are fairly broad, the turf should be mowed frequently to avoid a clumped look. If your soil is rich, you can keep a 1-inch height; if the soil is average, I recommend a 2½- to 3-inch cutting height to produce more body in the turf. Tall fescue has good resistance to disease; insects that like it are army worms, grubs, and sod webworms; all can be controlled by chemicals.

Fertilize this turf twice annually, in the spring and the fall. The grass likes 6.0 to 6.5 pH. You can use this seed straight or mix it with chewing fescue and Kentucky bluegrass. The best time to seed is late summer; use about 1 pound of seed for each 1000 sq. ft.

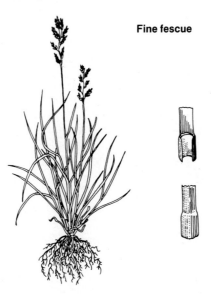

Fine fescue

■ **Fine fescue.** This is a mixture seed; that is, it is used in seed blends to make the blends adaptable to both hot sun and cool shade. For example, when fine fescue is mixed with Kentucky bluegrass, the bluegrass thrives in the sun and the fescue in shade.

Height should be kept from about 1½ to 2½ inches. Fescue tends to grow brown during hot and dry weather. Watch out for brown patch, red thread, and dollar spot; sod webworms, grubs, and army worms like the taste of fine fescue.

The best planting time is in the fall, and the turf should be fertilized

in the spring, summer, and fall. Best seed rates for planting are 3 pounds for 1000 sq. ft. If the fescue is blended with another grass seed, follow the manufacturer's recommendations on the package label.

■ **Bermuda grass.** If you live in the South and Southwest, this is the

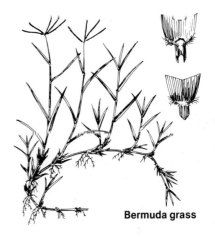

Bermuda grass

grass that grows best in your warm climate. However, Bermuda grass sometimes can be grown successfully in northern areas or where bluegrass thrives. But check a nursery before you invest.

Bermuda grass creates a very tight turf: it is cut at ¾ to 1 inch to provide a carpet effect.

Planting time is usually early summer, and you can use common seed at a rate of 2 to 3 pounds for 1000 sq. ft. Improved Bermuda grass can be sodded or planted with sprigs using from 5 to 10 bushels of sprigs for 1000 sq. ft. At the time of planting, also sow ryegrass until the lawn is established. Keep the ryegrass at a 1-inch height so it doesn't overpower its weaker cousin. You also can overseed an established Bermuda grass lawn with ryegrass when the Bermuda grass becomes dormant and brown.

The pH for Bermuda grass is from 6.0 to 7.0. The soil must be fertilized three times annually: spring, midsummer, and early fall. The grass is fairly resistant to disease, but keep an eye out for brown patch, leaf spot, dollar spot, and spring dead spot. Insects that do the most damage are sod webworms and army worms. Nematodes also can do considerable damage to the turf.

Water the turf moderately and don't become alarmed if the grass remains dormant in the spring. The temperature has to reach 60 degrees before the turf starts to turn green.

■ **Bentgrass.** If you want your lawn to look like a golf putting green and you live in the Pacific Northwest or the northeastern United States, plant your lawn with bentgrass. But be prepared to work hard to main-

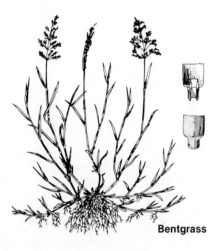

Bentgrass

tain this turf. It needs fertilizer every four weeks during the growing season, and you'll need to make frequent applications of fungicides and insecticides to protect the grass from brown patch, leaf spot, snow mold, grubs, chinch bugs, sod webworms, and army worms.

Height of cut ranges from 1/4 to 1 inch. It needs lots of moisture; and because the turf is so tight, you will have to keep it open by slicing the ground with a verticutting tool that you can rent. All thatch (dead grass) must be removed regularly as it accumulates.

Bentgrass usually is mixed with fine fescue. It takes about 1 pound of seed for every 1000 sq. ft., or you can grow it by the vegetation process, using plants or sprigs. The strain of bentgrass that does best in the Pacific Northwest and the Northeast is Colonial Astoria and Highland. But before you spend any money, go to a local golf course and ask the greenskeeper for advice.

■ **Bahia grass.** This is an excellent, tough grass that grows well in the Gulf Coast area. It thrives in warm, moist weather, but it turns brown in the winter. Usually the turf is over-seeded with ryegrass for a green look during the winter or dormant months.

Bahia grass

Bahia grass should be kept 2 to 3 inches high; cut it at least once a week and sometimes more often, especially during the growing season. The insects that like Bahia grass are mole crickets and nematodes. Brown patch is the prime disease that attacks this turf.

You can either plant the grass from seed or vegetative cuttings. You can also lay sod. The best planting time is in the spring or early summer months. Make sure the seed is scratched, since it has a waxlike covering that deters moisture from entering and results in slow germination.

If your lawn is subjected to salt air from the ocean or gulf, select another grass; Bahia grass has a low tolerance to salt.

Fertilizer should be applied four times annually to this turf: winter, spring, summer, and fall.

■ **Dichondra.** This turf grass is best suited to southern California and Arizona. It is a perennial dicot

(dicots have kidney-shaped leaves). It can be grown from plugs or from seed from March to May. You can plant it during the summer months, but you must use plenty of water to get it started.

Dichondra should be cut from 3/4

Dichondra

to 1 1/4 inches; it needs to be fertilized every other month. The plant is very prone to disease, especially alternaria and gleosporium. Cutworms, army worms, lawn moth larvae, flea beetles, and vegetable weevils all enjoy the taste of Dichondra.

■ **St. Augustine grass.** This warm-weather grass does best in Florida, around the Gulf Coast, and in California. It is easy to grow from stolons (runners) and sods.

Mowing height is from 1 1/2 to 3 inches. *Do not* cut this grass shorter than 1 1/2 inches; you can kill it.

A four-times-a-year fertilization schedule is recommended, and you should be on the lookout for brown patch during dormant seasons.

St. Augustine grass

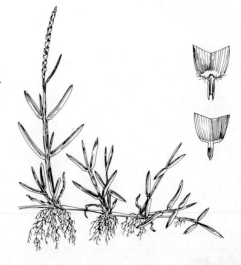

Insect trouble comes from sod webworms, chinch bugs, and, sometimes, nematodes. Since ample rainfall is common in areas where St. Augustine grass grows, you may not have to water the lawn frequently. However, this turf grass needs plenty of water, so make sure it gets it during dry spells.

■ **Zoysia.** Zoysia grows generally in the upper half of the United States. There are several varieties of zoysia: Korean, Japanese, Manila, and Meyer are examples. The grass has a fine to medium texture; it grows and greens from dormancy when the temperatures rise above 60 degrees.

Keep zoysia about ³/₄ to 1¹/₂ inches high. Fertilize it four times annually—spring, summer, fall, and winter—and give it plenty of water. This grass wants a 6.0 to 6.5 pH.

Zoysia

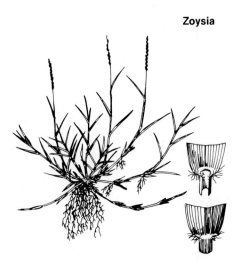

The best planting time for improved varieties of zoysia is in the warm spring months. Plant sprigs in rows that are spaced about 4 to 6 inches apart. If you are starting zoysia from seed, mix it with Kentucky bluegrass. The bluegrass helps establish the zoysia, which will overpower the bluegrass in a couple of years.

Grass seed: know what you are buying

By law, growers and packagers of grass seed must print an analysis of the contents on each seed bag. The package label usually has six classifications: purity, germination, crop, weeds, noxious weeds, and inert matter. What the label doesn't explain is what you need to know to get your seed money's worth.

Purity. The basic type of seed will be named—for example, Kentucky bluegrass—and its percentage of the total weight will be given. There may be other types of seed listed—Victa, Windsor, Merion. These improved seeds are a big value. Look for at least 35 to 40 percent purity; the higher the percentage the better.

Under the seed analysis, you will probably find two more categories: "Fine Textured Grasses" and "Coarse Textured Grasses." The fine-textured ones will be bluegrass, bentgrass, and fine fescue, including such strains as Windsor, Merion, and Victa. Under the coarse textured you will usually find a perennial ryegrass or another coarse-textured grass, such as redtop, timothy, tall fescue, or Kentucky 31. There should always be at least 40 percent of ryegrass or another strain of coarse grass in the package.

The purity percentage gives you an idea of quantity, but not quality, since even all pure seeds won't grow.

Germination. The germination percentage, usually labeled "Germ," tells you how much of the seed is *capable* of growth. If the germ figure is 85 percent, you can be fairly sure that about 85 percent of the seed will sprout. But keep in mind that this figure comes from laboratory tests under ideal conditions. Your yield may not be as high—or your yield may be somewhat higher. Remember, all seeds do not germinate at the same time. As a rule of thumb, if the germ figure is 85 percent, you can expect an 80 to 85 percent growth under normal conditions.

Crop. Look out for this one. "Crop seeds," also listed as a percentage of the total weight, means just what the name implies: crops that a farmer grows (oats, wheat, rye). Therefore, the lower the crop percentage the better. If the crop seed is more than 5 percent by weight, the label must state the name of the crop seeds.

Weeds. All seed mixtures contain some weed seed. Obviously, the lower the percentage of weed seed the better. Even 0.1 percent of chickweed in 1 pound of seed could result in 560,000 chickweed plants in a 10,000 sq. ft. lawn. When you buy a mixture with a high percentage of weed, you will also have to buy a lot of weed killer—this can cost you plenty before the season is over.

Noxious weeds. These weeds must be listed by name and by count on the label. Noxious weeds are more of a problem in farm fields than in home lawns. Also, classification varies from state to state. For example, *poa annua*, an annual bluegrass, is classified as noxious in several states. But to be on the safe side when looking for mixtures for your lawn, buy grass seed products that contain no noxious weeds.

Inert matter. Inert matter is sand, ground-up corn cobs, empty seed hulls—it is there to add weight to the package and nothing more. Of course, the more inert matter, the less seed. Read the label carefully and buy a mixture with as small a percentage of inert matter as possible.

Growers and packagers of quality seed usually offer blends of seed suitable for different lawn conditions. For example, one company offers a blend of bluegrasses to provide a deep rich color, high density, and thick texture. One blend is made especially for shady areas; another is for lawns subject to hard use (baseball, lawn tennis); still another is for covering bare spots with grass very quickly.

You can grow a very handsome new lawn by seeding it with about 2 pounds of quality seed for each 1000 sq. ft. If you are reseeding an old lawn, use 1 pound of quality seed for each 1000 sq. ft. Note the emphasis on *quality*. With the cheap seed you get lots of inert matter as well as weed seed, which you will have to control later with chemicals.

Fertilizers

Fertilizer is simply food for plants. Many turf fertilizers contain nutrients balanced for different kinds of growth. The ratios of these different formulas are indicated on the package in numbers: 5–10–5; 20–6–6; 10–10–10; 1–1–1.

The first number stands for nitrogen, the second for phosphorus, and the third for potash. When you're out buying fertilizer in a store, use this slogan to remember what the numbers mean: *Up, down,* and *all around*.

The first number means nitrogen, which makes the grass grow *up* and green. It helps the grass leaves grow and develop, and adds to the quality and thickness of the turf grasses. Fertilizer manufacturers advertise products for quick greening in the spring months. If you read the labels on these packages, you'll see that the first number in the formula is high, for example, 18, 20, 22, or 30—meaning lots of nitrogen.

The second number means phosphorus, which makes the grass grow *down*; that is, it develops the root system and rhizomes. It helps the plants to develop quickly, and it speeds up the maturing of the plants.

When the second number on the package is larger than the first number, or when it's larger than or equal to the third number, you know that the formula is designed to develop the root system.

The third number means potash, which makes the grass grow *all around*. It's designed to help the grass stay healthy and hardy. It helps in development of rhizomes and delivers amino acid and proteins to the plants.

Some fertilizers contain other chemicals to control weeds, plant diseases, and insects. These products do double duty: they fertilize the plant and control the plant's environment.

Weed control for turf grass

Lawn weeds are simply common grasses and flowers that spoil the lawn's appearance and, usually, inhibit healthy turf grass.

All the common lawn weeds are individually discussed and illustrated below, along with recommendations for controlling them. If you don't find your problem weed here, cut a sample of it and send it to one of the quality chemical and fertilizer companies in the United States. They'll identify the weed and give you suggestions about how best to control it.

■ **Dandelion**. Of all weeds, the dandelion is the most widely recognized, probably because it is so common and has been advertised as the one weed no respectable lawn should have.

Dandelions are not annuals, as is widely believed, but perennials. Since the tap roots go as deep as 3 feet (see the illustration), clipping them off at ground level does not kill them. And it really isn't practical to dig them up with a spade or dandelion fork because part of the root usually breaks off and grows again.

The best way to control dandelions is with a chemical spray or with a herbicide mixed with fertilizer. If you use either a dandelion control mixed with fertilizer or a spray, you must apply the chemical when the dandelions are actually growing—

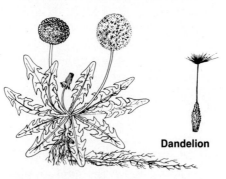
Dandelion

usually around the beginning of May.

If you live next to people who don't control the dandelions in their lawns, you will find their seed blowing over into your lawn. However, if your turf grass is thick and you apply a dandelion control once in the spring, your problems with dandelions will be minimal. It is abso-lutely true that a thick, rich growth of turf grass will choke back dandelion growth—but it won't stop dandelion growth completely.

■ **Crabgrass**. Crabgrass, known in some areas as watergrass, is a light green annual grass that appears in June and July. It forms clumps or bunches and smothers finer turf grasses.

One good way to control crabgrass is to apply a chemical and

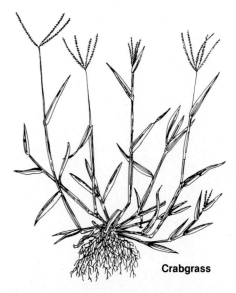
Crabgrass

fertilizer combination in early spring before the crabgrass seed has germinated. The chemical coats the crabgrass seed, preventing it from sprouting. This coating does not stop desirable turf grass from germinating.

If the crabgrass preventer is not applied in early spring, before germination, it is worthless as a crabgrass control. Other chemicals will have to be used after the crabgrass is actively growing; they can be applied with a spreader or sprayed on.

Common chickweed

■ **Common chickweed.** This weed grows almost anywhere, but it loves a moist and shady area best. Chickweed roots cover turf grasses and block their growth. Where chickweed leaf junctions touch the ground, they root and form new plants. Growth can be controlled with chemical and fertilizer combinations, such as Scott's Turf Builder Plus 2, Dicamba, MCPP, Banvel, Casoron G-4, and Sencor. Apply these products in the spring or fall.

■ **Ground ivy.** This perennial is most common in shady areas of a lawn, but does well in sunny areas, too. Although some people consider

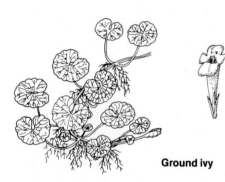

Ground ivy

ground ivy a weed, it is often used as a ground cover and encouraged to grow. If you want to get rid of it, apply Turf Builder Plus 2, Lawn Weed Control, or Dicamba in the spring and fall months.

Mouse-ear chickweed

■ **Mouse-ear chickweed.** Close mowing only stimulates the growth of this weed, which loves bright sunlight. It grows almost everywhere throughout the United States; roots form wherever the leaf junctions touch the ground. Try Scott's Turf Builder Plus 2, Lawn Weed Control, Super-D in Dichondra, Dicamba, or MCPP. Apply these chemicals in the spring or fall.

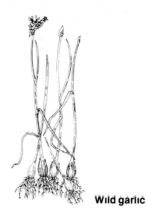

Wild garlic

■ **Wild garlic.** Wild garlic is also known as wild onion. The aboveground part of the weed looks very similar to an onion, and when you break the stem or pull up the weed it smells more like onion than garlic. To control it, try 2,4-D or MCPP in the late fall or early spring.

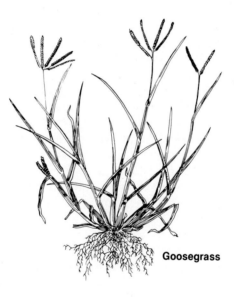

Goosegrass

■ **Goosegrass.** Goosegrass, an annual monocot, loves the sunlight and forms dark green leaves that are very tough. A lawnmower will even slow down as the blades chew through a patch of this plant. To control it, use Scott's Turf Builder Plus Halts, 2,4-D, DSMA, or MSMA in the spring and early summer.

■ **Henbit.** Henbit is a member of the mint family. You'll see this annual late in the winter or early spring, when it can be troublesome in your lawn early in the growth season. To

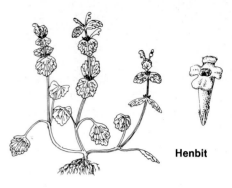

Henbit

prevent it, try Scott's Halts. To control it, use Scott's Turf Builder Plus 2, Dicamba, or Casoron G-4. Apply the chemicals in the spring and summer months.

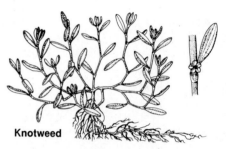

Knotweed

■ **Knotweed.** You're most likely to find this annual weed along the edges of your driveway and where the turf has been worn down. Knotweed stops the growth of turf grass. For control, use Scott's Turf Builder Plus 2, 2,4-D, Banval, or Dicamba. Apply in late winter or early spring.

Nimblewill

■ **Nimblewill**. Despite its attractive, musical name, nimblewill is a bothersome weed that destroys the appearance of quality turf grass with patches of bluish-green color. It is a perennial that is sometimes mistaken for crabgrass when it starts to turn brown in the late fall months. Applied in the spring months, Scott's Spot Grass and Weed Control along with repeated treatments of Zytron and Roundup will handle it.

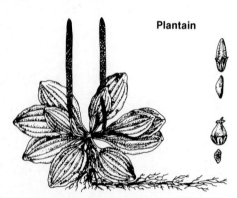

Plantain

■ **Plantain**. This perennial lies flat on the ground and stops the development of turf grasses. Rugel's plantain has purplish stems and shiny green leaves. Common plantain has a pale green stem and hairy leaves. To control both species, use Scott's Turf Builder Plus 2, 2,4-D, or Dicamba. The best time to apply it is in the spring.

Quackgrass

■ **Quackgrass**. Too bad quackgrass isn't a desirable turf grass—it grows extremely fast and spreads like lightning by means of its rhizome system. Once quackgrass takes hold in your lawn, it is very difficult to kill. Try Scott's Spot Grass and Weed Control. You can also use Dalapon, but this chemical kills all plants, so be careful with it. Apply in the spring, summer, and fall.

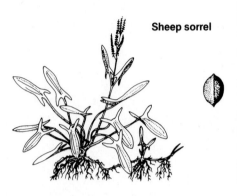

Sheep sorrel

■ **Sheep sorrel**. If you spot this weed in your lawn, get rid of it fast since it spreads like wild fire and can smother a fine turf grass lawn. You can recognize sheep sorrel by its arrowheadlike leaves. It is a perennial that spreads by means of underground roots and rhizomes. Scott's Lawn Weed Control and Dicamba are the chemicals to use. Apply them in the spring.

Seeding guidelines

You can start a lawn from scratch with seed, by planting plugs, or by planting sprigs. You can also improve an established lawn using any of these methods.

When you start from scratch, prepare the soil first. If the lawn area has lots of holes and hills—a building lot with a new house on it will have these—have a professional smooth out the dirt surface with a backhoe or blade mounted on a tractor. You can, of course, do this job yourself with spade, hoe, and wheelbarrow, but plan on spending lots and lots of time and effort. Even if you do the spade work, a final grading by a pro is still your best investment.

After leveling, remove all loose debris (sticks and stones) and prepare the soil for seeding. The earth should be tilled about 3 to 4 inches deep to loosen it. Then let the soil settle for a week or so. If it doesn't rain in this period, sprinkle the dirt with water to help settle it. But go easy; you don't want to turn the earth into a hardpan.

After the soil has settled, fertilize the entire area with a quality new grass fertilizer. New grass fertilizer has a high phosphorus content, which helps establish a strong root system.

Then sow the grass seed. Use a spreader with controls for seeding, rather than broadcasting the seed with your hands or with a whirling mechanical device. A spreader distributes the seeds evenly over the ground, giving you correct, consistent coverage without waste.

Divide your lawn into quarters and do one quarter at a time. After the seed is applied to one section, rake it down into the soil. Try to cover as much seed as possible with a reasonable amount of raking. Then do each of the other sections in the same way. It's much easier to keep track of your work this way.

Water the earth lightly with a garden hose and a nozzle on the light spray setting. You want it damp but not muddy. Keep watering daily, if it doesn't rain, until the plants germinate. Seed germination requires sunlight, moisture, and warmth. If the seeds are not watered, they can't germinate—even if the other conditions are present.

To help keep the earth moist, you can spread a thin layer of hay or straw over the newly-planted seed. If the lot slopes, stake it to prevent any erosion. To do this, place 1×2 stakes at random all across the slope.

Cut the new grass when it reaches a height of about 3 inches. Keep the mower set between 2 and 2½ inches until the lawn is fully established (about two years); then you can lower the cutting height to 1½ inches for most grass, except where noted above. From thirty to forty days after planting, use a quality starter fertilizer to fertilize the soil once again.

1. Starting a new lawn. Level the soil and rake out sticks, stones, and other debris.

2. Till the soil but don't chop it too fine; leave small pieces to prevent erosion.

3. After the soil has settled, loosen the top inch to receive the seed.

4. Seed one quarter of the area at a time, using a spreader to distribute the seed.

5. Rake the seed lightly down into the soil, covering as much as possible.

6. After the area has been seeded, lightly water the soil, using a spray nozzle.

As the lawn becomes established, continue to fertilize it, usually between February and April and again between August and October.

Overseeding established turf

The key to establishing a thicker, greener lawn by overseeding is proper preparation.

First, mow the grass shorter than 1 inch; 3/4 inch is best if you can set your lawnmower this low. Second, remove *all* old clippings, thatch, leaves, and general debris with a rake. If the lawn has low or sunken spots, fill them with topsoil, tamping it firmly so it is level with the surrounding surface.

Third, rent a slicer/seeder or have a pro slice the turf to a depth of about 4 inches. Any tool that has a slicing

1. Overseeding an established lawn. Cut the grass as short as possible.

2. Remove all clippings, debris, and thatch down to the bare earth.

3. Sow the seed with a spreader in turf sliced 4 inches deep.

action may be used; a disc cultivator pulled by a garden tractor does a good job. If the area is small, you may be able to use an aerator (this may also be rented).

After slicing, go back over the area with a rake, removing all debris. Then fertilize the area with a quality starter fertilizer. (Apply the fertilizer according to the rate chart on the package.)

Spread the new seed over the ground and follow the same watering program that you would for a new lawn.

Seeding bare spots

You can buy quick-cover grass seed to hide bare spots in your lawn. These covers consist mainly of annual ryegrass which sprouts fast, but dies out after the growing season. You can also seed with a quick cover plus a regular grass seed. The annual ryegrass helps the regular grass seed grow better because it protects the tender leaves from the sun until they become established.

1. Filling bare spots with turf grass. Rake the area clean and level any low spots.

2. Slice the soil to a depth of about ½ inch with a sharp hoe or spading fork.

3. Make sure the loose soil is ½- to 1-inch deep before sowing the seed in furrows.

4. Broadcast plenty of seed into the furrows by hand. If the spot area is fairly large, use a spreader set to the proper distribution number. Although it is not really necessary, you can cover the spot before seeding with starter fertilizer.

5. Lightly rake the soil over the sown seed; try to cover as much as possible. You won't get it all, but that isn't necessary. Then lightly water the area with a sprinkler or sprinkler attachment on a hose. Keep the area moist until the seed germinates. Cover the area with straw to help hold in moisture.

To prepare bare spots, loosen or slice the soil to a depth of about ½ inch. Then apply lots of seed to the bare area. Cover the seed by pulling the back of a rake over the area; the idea is to work the seed into the ground. Water the spot for at least a week—fourteen to eighteen days is better—to give the seed time to germinate. Water is essential. After this period, feed the area with starter fertilizer, if you haven't done so at the time of seeding.

If you are filling in a bare spot in sandy soil, you can mix the soil with peat moss to help the seed grow. Peat moss holds water; sandy soil blots it.

Plugs and sprigs

Plugging and sprigging are two ways to establish a lawn without starting from seed; sometimes, they're the only ways to establish it, depending on the type of turf grass to be grown. There are a few simple steps to follow.

First, smooth and rake the soil so that all high and low spots are leveled. Let the soil settle for a week or so; then go back over it with a rake, making sure all debris is removed. Rocks larger than golf balls should be removed; any rocks smaller than this are okay—in fact, desirable—since you want a soil mixture that has small and large particles to help prevent erosion.

After the soil is settled and raked, fertilize the soil, using a quality starter fertilizer; spread it at the rate recommended on the package.

If you are sprigging, plant the sprigs at the intervals recommended by the dealer; generally sprigs should be placed at 6 to 10 inches apart in cultivated soil.

If you are plugging, dig holes 3 inches deep for the plants at 8- to 12-inch intervals. Set the plugs firmly in the holes.

After setting both sprigs and plugs, press the soil with your fingers to compact it against the root system. Water the area frequently so the earth stays damp, but don't make it muddy. In about thirty days, cover the area with another starter fertilizer, applying the fertilizer at the rate recommended on the package.

Sodding

Putting down freshly cut sod over a cultivated ground base probably is the quickest way to establish a new lawn. It is also the most expensive. Therefore, sod generally is used to fill bare spots quickly or to prevent soil erosion on freshly graded slopes.

The first step is to cultivate the ground as you would for new seeding. Level it and remove all debris. Then fertilize the ground with a quality starter fertilizer, applied at the rate suggested on the package label.

Start the first strips of sod up against a straight edge; a 2×4 or a line stretched between two stakes will work fine. Butt the ends of the sod lengths tightly together. As you progress along the area, stagger the ends and edges of the sod strips so there are no four-corner joints. A good pattern to follow is a brick wall with a running bond configuration. On slopes, peg the sod with two 1×2 stakes for each strip to prevent slippage.

Immediately after the sod is in place, water it and keep it damp for several weeks. This gives the root system a chance to meld with the soil. It is best to overwater for the first week or so and then go to a normal watering regimen, since sod needs more water after it is first laid on cultivated ground.

When the grass has grown about one third over its length when you laid the strips, mow the grass to a 2½-inch height. After four weeks, give the sod another starter fertilizer feeding. Then follow with regular mowing and feedings.

Lawn disease controls

Lawns, like people, contract disease and must be treated chemically in order to survive. The major grass and turf diseases are snow mold, leaf spot, dollar spot, brown patch, moss, spring dead spot, and slime mold.

■ **Snow mold.** Snow mold actually looks like light powdery snow on grass leaves. Usually, a large

Gray snow mold

amount of moisture must be present for the mold to appear, and that's why you will see it in early spring as the snow melts or the rains fall. Look for it from November through most of March. You may be able to control snow mold by aerating the soil and improving drainage in the snow mold areas. To treat it chemically, use Scott's Lawn Disease Preventer, Ortho Lawn and Turf Fungicide, Thiram, Dyrene, and fungicides containing mercury.

■ **Leaf spot.** In the North, leaf spot appears as red and brown spots on blades of grass. Kentucky bluegrass is a likely victim. Down south, leaf

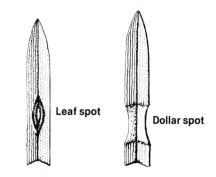
Leaf spot   Dollar spot

spot is gray and attacks St. Augustine grass. Gray circles or elliptical spots appear on leaves. Both types spread fast and kill the grass. You will find leaf spot in May and June and September through November in cool and moist weather. You can help relieve the conditions by reducing shade and improving drainage in the affected areas. You can treat the grass chemically for both types with Scott's Lawn Disease Preventer, Ortho Lawn and Turf Fungicide, PMA, Captan, Dyrene, or Fore.

■ **Dollar spot.** This disease is so named because it appears on the

lawn in round spots about the size of a silver dollar. At first, the spots are black; later, they turn brown and white. Although dollar spot affects all turf grasses, bentgrass is its favorite. Look for it from about May to mid-October. It likes temperatures of 60 to 80 degrees, with high humidity and high growth of turf grass.

You may be able to control it successfully by applying nitrogen to the soil, removing thatch, and watering the soil very deeply. For chemical treatment, use Scott's Lawn Disease Preventer, fungicides containing cadmium, Dyrene, or Ortho Lawn and Turf Fungicide.

■ **Brown patch.** Brown patch can be found in any species of turf grass almost anywhere in the United States. It is most prevalent in areas that are warm and humid. You'll recognize this disease by its irregular circular spots that range from a few inches to several feet in diameter. The disease occurs from May through September in the northern tier of states and from October through February in the southern states. Try controlling brown patch by first improving the drainage and watering the ground very deeply. Do not feed your lawn when the disease is active; fertilizer will only spread brown patch further.

You can treat brown patch chemically with Scott's Lawn Disease Preventer, fungicides containing mercury, Ortho Lawn and Turf fungicide, Tersan OM, Fore, and Dyrene.

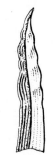
Brown patch

■ **Moss.** Moss can grow almost anywhere, not necessarily on the north side of trees. But it especially likes moist, heavily-shaded areas.

To control it, try improving the drainage. Also, cut back trees and shrubs so the area receives plenty of sunshine and air circulation. You may have to remove layers of moss with a tiling spade or other tool before the turf grass can be reestablished in the lawn.

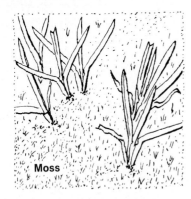

Moss

■ **Spring dead spot.** Spring dead spot looks like what the name implies: patches of dead grass in an area of healthy Bermuda grass. As the growing season progresses, the turf grass tends to cover these brown patches, but when the grass falls dormant, the patches take over again.

The best way to reduce or control the problem is by removing thatch from the lawn and by starting a good, balanced feeding program. Also, you should control pests common to Bermuda grass.

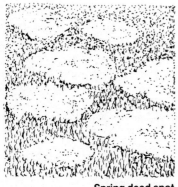

Spring dead spot

■ **Slime mold.** The name sounds worse than it really is—just a white or almost clear slimy coating on the leaves of grass.

One way to control it is to hose down the lawn with water when you are sure that a day or two of low humidity will follow. Also, use a broom rake to remove the mold from the turf.

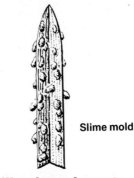

Slime mold

Controlling lawn insects

Lawn insects that harm turf grass include those that live in the soil, those that live in the thatch of the turf grass, and those that live on the stems and leaves of the plants—including grass—in your lawn. The most noxious species include ants, sod webworms, billbugs, mole crickets, chinch bugs, aphids, and white grubs.

Not only can these creatures chew your turf grass to death, but they attract animals that you may not want roaming about your lawn. For example, white grubs make excellent hors d'oeuvres for skunks, raccoons, and moles.

Here are descriptions of the more common insects and what you can do to control them.

■ **Ants.** In turf grass, anthills disfigure the turf, and the ants themselves damage the root systems of the grass plants. Harvester ants eat seed; fire ants build big mounds; leaf cutter ants actually cut paths through turf.

To control these pests, try Scott's Western Lawn Insect Control, carbaryl, and diazinon. It is best to make spot treatments with the latter two chemicals.

■ **Sod webworms.** You know your lawn has sod webworms if you see

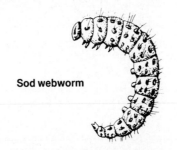

Sod webworm

grass stripped off in patches or find the grass cut in half along the leaves. Sod webworms build tunnels in thatch or debris, and they eat at night. Although all grass is vulnerable to sod webworms, bentgrass and bluegrass are favorites.

To control them, try Scott's Lawn Insect Control, Summer Insect Control Plus Fertilizer, and Western Lawn Insect Control. Or use carbaryl or diazinon. Apply the chemicals just before dark. Don't water or mow the grass for about three days after the chemicals are applied.

■ **Billbugs.** These grubs like to chew grass near the crowns. They

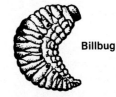

Billbug

also love to eat roots slightly below the surface of the ground; this, of course, kills the grass in large areas. You'll first notice the damage as a thinning of the turf grass.

To control this insect, use Scott's Lawn Insect Control or diazinon. If you use diazinon, you will need two applications about three months apart. Water well after application.

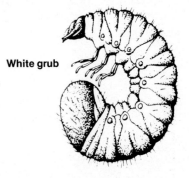

White grub

■ **White grubs.** These insects attack grass roots; as they eat the roots the turf grass dies first in patches and then in whole areas. There are many species of grubs, including Japanese, Oriental, Asiatic, Garden, and European.

To control grubs, use Scott's Lawn Insect Control, sevin, or diazinon; follow the directions on the packages.

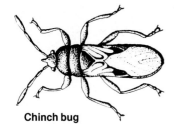

Chinch bug

■ **Chinch bugs**. When the temperature climbs above 70 degrees, chinch bugs start their dirty work by sucking the juices out of the turf grass plants and injecting a toxin into the plant system. If you don't kill these bugs immediately, your entire lawn will be ruined and you will have to reseed.

If dead grass doesn't convince you that chinch bugs are at work, try this method. Cut both the ends out of a quart can and set the can over the suspect area. Press the can straight into the soil, about half way down, and then pull it out, taking a plug of the soil in the can. Set the can and soil on a flat surface and fill the empty half of the can with water. In about 2 or 3 days you'll find the chinch bugs, if any, floating in the water.

Chemical controls include Scott's Lawn Insect Control, diazinon, and carbaryl. Water the lawn before applying the chemicals; give the lawn its first application in mid- to late May and follow with another application in approximately two or three weeks.

■ **Mole crickets**. Mole crickets eat grass roots and organic substances in the soil. They tunnel just below the soil surface, killing the plants.

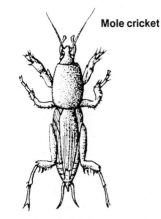

Mole cricket

To control them, try Scott's Lawn Insect Control or carbaryl.

■ **Aphids**. These insects attack plants and cause leaves to curl. They sometimes transmit virus diseases that destroy flowering plants.

For a general control, apply malathion or dimethoate spray or malathion dust.

Controlling foliage insects

This category includes tomato hornworms, May beetles, flea beetles, rose slugs, and bagworms. These are garden plant insects, and here's what you can do about them:

■ **Tomato hornworm**. It is 3 to 4 inches long with a green body with white markings. To control it, use methoxychlor, malathion, or TDE.

■ **May beetle**. The larval form looks like a white grub. Adults are red and brown or black. Control with Diazinon.

■ **Flea beetle**. This beetle is a very tiny and difficult to see. The color can be black, brown, or blue. Control with carbaryl spray or dust.

■ **Rose slug**. The bodies of these insects are tapered. They attack the

---

INSECTICIDES FOR LAWN AND GARDEN

Here's a roundup of common chemicals used in the lawn, garden, and around the house to control insects. The chemical names are generic.

This information is provided not only to help you set up an application schedule, but to give you an idea of how long to take precautions. You'd be wise to avoid contact with treated areas for the active life of the chemical—certainly keep children away during this time. And try to avoid harvesting vegetables from a treated garden until the active-life period has passed; *thoroughly* wash any food that comes in contact with chemicals.

The following chemicals have been banned: aldrin, chlordane, DDT, dieldrin, heptachlor, kepone, lindane, mirex. Any product containing these chemicals is dangerous to humans and animals and *should not* be used, even if you can still find it for sale.

Chemical	Use it to control	Active life*
allethrin	insects	short
baygon	crawling insects	long
carbaryl	insects	medium
chlorobenziate	spiders and mites	medium
coumaphos	rodents	medium
DDD	insects	long
diazinon	insects	long
dichlovos	parasites	short
dicofol	mites	long
dimethoate	vegetable pests	long
dioxathion	insects	long
endosulfan	insects	medium
fenthion	mosquitoes and flies	medium
malathion	insects	medium
metaldehyde	slugs and snails	long
methoxychlor	insects	medium
naled	insects	short
oils	insects	long
ovex	mites	long
pyrethrins	insects	short
ronnel	parasites	medium
rotenone	insects	medium
sulfur	mites	long
toxaphene	insects	long
trichlorfon	insects	long

*A short active life is considered to be three days; a medium active life, fourteen days; a long active life, thirty-five days.

Note: Many of the products listed are of the broad-spectrum type; a listing of "insects" under the heading "Use it to control" means this chemical can be used on a wide variety of insects. Check the package label.

leaves of the plant. Control with malathion.

■ **Bagworm.** You'll know you have these pests because they spin a spindle-shaped bag on leaves. The bags are about 1 inch long. Control bagworms by picking off the bags and burning them. You can control chemically by applying carbaryl or toxaphene spray.

Insecticides

When using chemicals, you always run the risk of destroying those insects that are beneficial to plant life and growth. Therefore, it is important to follow the directions on the packages and to use the chemicals *only when necessary*.

All-purpose insecticides almost always contain three chemicals: methoxychlor, malathion, and dimethoate is one combination; malathion, methoxychlor, and carbaryl is another.

Insecticides for specific pests are often single chemicals; some are outlawed in various states and localities. This is usually true if the chemical has a very high toxicity rating. For example, aldrin is very high in toxicity while carbaryl is low.

The safer chemicals include: DDD (TDE), diazinon, dimethoate, malathion, methoxychlor, pyrethrum, and toxaphene.

Highly toxic chemicals include aldrin, demeton, dieldrin, nicotine sulfate, parathion, phosdrin, rotenone, thimet, and trithion.

Be responsible when you apply chemicals. While many of the chemicals on the market are safe, there is certainly a good deal of controversy. So find out as much as you can about a product *before* you apply it. Read the entire label, check the chart for additional information, and take all safety precautions as described here.

SAFETY FIRST WITH CHEMICALS

Liquid or powdered herbicides and pesticides always present possible danger, and you would be wise to take safety precautions. Buy premixed chemicals rather than mixing the chemicals yourself. You are safer, and the chemicals are more convenient to use.

■ *Always*—no exceptions—store chemicals where children cannot get at them.

■ Keep children away from the yard when you apply chemicals.

■ Obey any instructions printed on labels, such as "store in a cool, dry place," "keep away from heat," "mix in a metal container," and so on.

■ Wear a cartridge respirator when you mix and apply chemicals (a dust mask is not enough). And since chemicals are easily absorbed through the skin, it's a must that you wear safety goggles, leather gloves, a buttoned long-sleeved shirt, and trousers (no shorts).

■ If you must mix chemicals, do it outside.

■ If you spill a chemical on yourself or your clothing, remove the garment and wash the skin thoroughly with soap and water.

■ Do not smoke while you are working with chemicals.

■ Clean the equipment as soon as you finish the application.

■ Take a shower or bath immediately after any chemical application.

■ Wash any clothing worn when applying chemicals separately. Don't mix these clothes in with the family laundry.

■ *Do not* apply chemicals on a

windy day. The overspray or dust can be airborne throughout the immediate area, endangering others in the vicinity.

■ When applying two or more chemicals, use two or more different sprayers or spreaders. If this is impossible, clean the sprayer or spreader *thoroughly* before you load it with a different chemical. *Mixing chemicals is dangerous.*

■ If any chemicals are left for the next day's work, package them and store them where children can't get at them. *Do not* leave them under the porch or out in the yard.

■ Chemicals formulated to destroy all vegetation really do destroy it. Make sure that you apply these chemicals according to the manufacturer's instructions.

■ Follow any cautions on the label about applications in drainage areas. Rain water can carry chemicals to other areas of your lawn or garden—or to your neighbor's.

■ If you have any doubts about the effects of any chemical on people, contact your regional Poison Control Center.

Where to write. Safety equipment is manufactured by many companies throughout the country. The most important piece of safety equipment for you to buy is a Type BE cartridge respirator; this will mask out organic vapor, fumes, dust, and mist. The following companies should have an outlet in your area. Write them or check your telephone directory for a supplier near you.

Mine Safety Appliances Company
400 Penn Center Boulevard
Pittsburgh, PA 15235

3M Company
3M Center
Building 230-B
St. Paul, MN 55101

2 Buying Power Equipment

Traditionally, the best time to buy power equipment—lawnmowers, weed trimmers, edgers, and chain saws—is late fall and the winter months because retailers like to clear out this inventory to make room for more seasonal merchandise and the new models that are bound to come for next spring's selling season.

So it is not far-fetched to shop for a lawnmower in December or January with 8 inches of snow on the ground. In fact, you will probably find a better deal then than in the spring when the grass starts to grow. Even if the retailer has put the stock in the back room at the close of the season, don't be reluctant to ask for a demonstration and a price. And be sure to try several different stores before you make a decision.

Here's where you are most likely to find power lawn and garden equipment:

home center stores
hardware stores
nursery outlets
general catalog stores
discount chains
drug stores with home departments
lawnmower repair shops
farm implement stores
large chain grocery stores

Choosing the right lawnmower

The best buy is a brand-name lawnmower. You should always buy as much quality in a lawnmower as your budget can afford. A poor-quality product will be a troublemaker from the outset—you can count on it. If you shop around, however, you will find that quality equipment costs only a few dollars more than poorer quality merchandise. Quality lawnmowers also offer other benefits and features.

■ Replacement and repair parts are usually readily available for brand-name lawnmowers. Dealers carry these parts and so do most repair shops, in case the equipment has to be repaired by a professional.

■ Full warranties covering parts and labor are part of the package with a quality lawnmower; if the lawnmower malfunctions during the warranty period, it will be fixed free.

■ Service contracts are sometimes available for heavy garden equipment, but you'll have to pay for it. Basically, the contract provides for regular maintenance and, in the event of a breakdown, repair of the equipment. This is a good benefit to have, especially if you live in a rural area where transporting the equipment to a repair shop is difficult. With a service contract, the repairman comes to the equipment, or at least picks it up and delivers it after repair.

■ Professional repair persons prefer to work on brand-name equipment because the manufacturers standardize their parts. Therefore, the pro doesn't have to scout about the countryside trying to find a replacement part for a no-name lawnmower or other piece of lawn and garden equipment.

■ Components that have to be replaced regularly, such as lawnmower blades, filters, spark plugs, wheels, throttle assemblies, mufflers, and nylon string, are easy to locate through regular retail channels.

For example, if you buy a lawnmower with a two-cycle engine, the oil that you mix with the gasoline is readily available at many outlets (even some grocery stores), so if you're caught short late Saturday afternoon when the dealer's shop is closed, you can buy the oil elsewhere without having to wait until Monday morning.

■ Brand-name equipment is sold at many stores; thus comparison shopping for better prices and, sometimes, service and warranties is easy. No-name equipment generally is poorly distributed, and this makes comparison pricing difficult.

■ Credit may be a consideration—especially if you are buying heavy, costly equipment. Many dealers and general catalog stores have special payment plans that a drug store or grocery store doesn't have.

There is a case, of course, for no-name equipment—especially lawnmowers; they are generally priced lower than brand-name mowers. And no-name mowers usually have a brand-name engine—Briggs & Stratton, for example—which is a plus feature. The catch is that the engine may be too small for the job you want it to do. Be careful to get the facts before making a selection.

Your first consideration is power

Expect to pay from about $150 to $200 for a very good quality 3.5 hp lawnmower. At this price it most likely will be a stripped-down model without fancy hubcaps and control consoles. As with automobiles, the price goes up as you add extras.

Don't be blinded by the showroom shine. Your very first consideration should be power: how much horsepower does the engine have? Your power needs are directly related to the size of your lawn and to the nature of the lot—is it hilly or flat?

I've tested many different types of lawnmowers and my recommendation in a few words is simply this: *buy a little more power than you think you might need.* The cost is not prohibitive, and the added power will add years to the life of the equipment.

The following guidelines are based on lot size and character. If you live on a city-size lot, that is, about 75 feet wide by 180 feet deep, a 3 or 3.5 hp gasoline-powered mower will provide plenty of power. Also consider an electric or motor-driven mower. Electric mowers are described by their amp rating, not horsepower. The horsepower-to-amp formula is this: the more amps the more power. A 12-amp motor is about the equivalent of a 1½ to 2 hp gasoline engine.

If you live on a ⅓ to ½-acre lot, a 3.5 hp engine is enough power *if* the mower is a walk-behind push type and the lot is flat. If the mower is self-propelled and the lot has slopes or is a bit hilly, buy a 4 or 5 hp engine.

If you live on 1 acre and the lot is fairly flat, buy a 4 hp walk-behind mower. Go with a 5 hp engine if the mower is self-propelled and the lot is somewhat hilly.

The 1-acre lot is a breakpoint between walk-behind and riding mowers. If the lot is highly landscaped and has a garden, a large patio area, and so forth, the self-propelled or walk-behind push mower probably is the equipment to buy. However, if the lot is mostly turf grass, you may want to consider a riding mower. I recommend that the engine have at least an 8 hp capacity; 10 hp is better.

Unless you like exercise and have lots of time, 2- to 5-acre lots require a rider or tractor mower with at least a 16 hp engine. An 18 hp engine is even better; don't overlook a 20 hp unit, especially if you need the power to operate accessories. If this large lot is at all hilly, you must buy the larger-capacity equipment. The workload simply is too great for a smaller engine; although it may perform smoothly at the outset, breakdowns will soon become commonplace.

Lawnmower types and features

Reel and rotary are the two basic types of lawnmowers, whether they are walk-behind types or tractor types. Rotary mowers are considered the workhorses of turf grass cutting; reel mowers are more delicate and are best suited for fine turf grasses and smaller lots.

The characteristics and variations of both types that you will want to consider before making a buying decision are listed below.

If you own a very small lot, a good push reel mower is the tool to buy. If the reel mower has an engine, it is known as a power reel mower. The engine should turn out at least 5 hp. It is more complicated mechanically than an engine-driven rotary mower, and you can expect to pay more for it than a standard rotary mower.

Power reel mowers have from five to seven cutting blades. The blades overlap the turf grass and pull it against a cutting bar at the bottom of the mower. Then a roller, or series of rollers, smoothes and compacts the clippings as the mower goes over them. The big advantage of power reel mowers is quality of cut. The blades snip the turf grass like scissors. The result is a very fine cut—almost a manicured look. The greens on a golf course are a good example of reel-cut grass.

Reel mowers are better suited to flat lawns that are planted with fine turf grass such as fine fescue, zoysia, and Bermuda grass. Grass cutting with reel mowers must be fairly

Safety throttle control

Gasoline engine rotary mower   Height setting

frequent; these mowers have a difficult time with heavy and tall grass.

Hilly lawns are also difficult to cut with reel mowers because the mower tends to scalp the high ridges of the uneven ground. You have to adjust the cutting blade constantly to make allowance for the uneven ground, and this can be troublesome. Also, the grass is cut unevenly with the adjustments and the manicured look disappears.

On the plus side, power and hand-pushed reel mowers usually outlast rotary lawnmowers if they are used to cut fine turf grasses. In fact, on a flat lot and fine turf grass, a quality reel mower should last a lifetime provided it is properly serviced and maintained.

Rotary mowers (all power driven) are extremely powerful even with a small engine. With a rotary mower you can cut thick, heavy, wet grass and weeds. The blades will even whack fairly large stalks with ease. In short, you can treat a rotary mower with less caution than a powered reel mower.

Rotary mowers offer a selection of blade widths, whereas a reel mower usually has a standard 18-inch width. Rotary mowers have 18-, 19-, 20-, 21-, and 22-inch blades; the ones on tractors go even wider with the cuts—up to 60 inches.

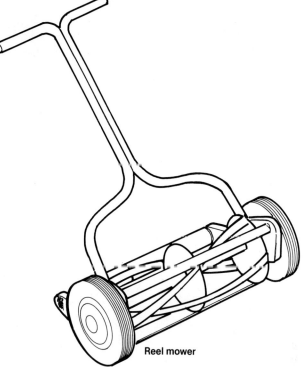

Reel mower

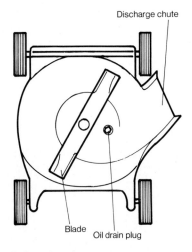

Discharge chute

Blade   Oil drain plug

Bottom view of rotary mower

If your lawn measures about 5000 sq. ft., I recommend an 18-inch blade for a rotary mower. If the lawn is over 10,000 sq. ft., the 21- and 22-inch blades work best and will save you some cutting time.

What the names mean

Push-type mowers. These are either (1) reel mowers without motors, (2) walk-behind powered reel mowers, or (3) walk-behind rotary mowers. In the first case, hand reel mowers, you furnish all the power. With motor- or engine-powered reel or rotary push mowers, you furnish the forward and reverse power; the power plant turns the blade.

Push mowers are usually the lowest-priced members of the lawn-mower family. The range is approximately $80 for the no-name units to about $200 for basic models with, perhaps, one or two features such as a foldaway handle and a three-position throttle control lever.

Rear-bagging mowers. These mowers have blades that are especially designed to lift or vacuum the cut grass off the surface of the ground and into a grass-catcher bag.

These mowers may be stamped "High-Lift" or "High Cut," and you might be able to tell the feature by the considerable depth of the mower deck—4 inches or so.

Mulching mowers. Mulchers are designed to lift the grass cuttings up under the bottom of the deck, where they are double-cut by the blades into very small pieces. The small clippings then sift down into the turf grass and become mulch.

A word of caution about mulching mowers: with this equipment you *must* cut the grass on a regular basis —usually twice a week, but at least once a week. If the grass grows beyond an inch or so, the blades and the deck lose their mulching efficiency.

High-wheeled mowers. If your lawn is uneven, rough, or hilly, and the grass generally is difficult to cut regularly, a high-wheeler could be the solution. The mowers have bicycle-type wheels with the engine mounted aft and the deck mounted forward. The wheels, usually 16 inches in diameter, roll over ruts and bumps easily. For lawn mowing, the 4

High-wheeled mower

Rear-bagging mower

Gasoline engine reel mower

Electric rotary mower

hp engine is adequate; for field mowing, buy the 5 hp unit.

Some features worth having on the high-wheelers include folding handles for transport and storage, underdeck baffles for grass-bagging power, and kink- and rust-resistant control cables.

Self-propelled mowers. The engine powers both the cutting blades and the wheels of this type. The power drive will be either on the front or rear wheels. We find that the front wheel drive is easier to operate on flat lawn surfaces, while the rear wheel drive is best if the lawn slopes or is hilly. Don't buy a self-propelled unit with less than a 3.5 hp engine; a 4 hp unit is recommended.

You can expect to pay about 25 to 40 percent more for a self-propelled lawnmower. Make sure that it includes such features as a foldaway handle for storage and zoned controls (drive control throttle, clutch) at your fingertips.

Electric mowers. If you have a small lawn that is fairly free of obstructions that can catch power cords, consider an electric lawnmower. The electrics offer these desirable features: quiet running, easy maneuverability, low maintenance, and easy repair. The only problem—and it is solved by learning how to handle it—is the extension cord, which always seems to be in the cutting path.

When buying an electric mower, be sure the power cords are No. 12 or No. 14 gauge wire in order to supply adequate power to the motor. Choose a mower with double insulation to make it shock-proof. The electrics have the same features as their gas-powered cousins, including mulching ability, grass catchers, foldaway handles, handle power switches, and so on.

Riding mowers. If acres are involved in your lawn-cutting chores, a riding mower is almost a must, along with a hand-powered reel mower or a gasoline- or electric-powered walk-behind mower to trim where the rider can't go. Rider mowers are powered by either gasoline or diesel engines; the diesels are newcomers on the market, but so far there haven't been serious complaints about their performance.

Most riders offer a truckload of accessory options, including gang reel mowers, sickle bars, lawn rollers, spike aerators, lawn vacuums, pickup sweepers, brushers, rakes, sprayers, plows, disc harrows, spreaders and seeders, planters, scrapers, log splitters, loaders, and snow-removal attachments.

Most consumers make the mistake of buying rider mowers without enough horsepower. Riders used on large lots take a great deal of abuse, and if you add accessories to the load (a gang reel mower, for example), the need for extra power is critical. If your lot requires a rider, begin your considerations with a 16 hp engine—and go up from there.

Features of rider mowers worth noting include these:

■ If your lot is fenced and is covered with trees, shrubs, and other low obstructions, the mower with a low profile may be the best buy. Maneuverability around obstructions is important and saves plenty of time in trimming.

■ The mower must have a cutting-height adjustment that can be quickly changed as mowing conditions change. Quality rider mowers usually have an easily-reached lever control for making cutting height adjustments.

■ The configuration of the mower and the accessories should be arranged so you can service the battery, check the oil, and change the plugs and air filters without lots of hand contortions. The mower should have handy equipment mounting bars that are easy to use with a minimum of hitching mechanics.

■ Flexibility in accepting accessories is important if you want the mower to do many jobs.

■ Narrow turning radius is very important if you have many obstructions in your mowing area. Rider mowers don't have power steering, but the steering wheel should be very responsive to your touch. Take a test drive, if at all possible, to check the ease of steering and the turning radius.

■ Is the mower built with wide-set wheels for stability on hills and slopes? Also, a wide tire tread contributes to weight distribution so the rider doesn't rut the turf.

■ Is the seat comfortable and positioned so you can reach all the necessary control devices? Is the seat movable back and forward? Do you sit in the seat or on the seat, straddling the machine? The quality mowers have seats that you sit in.

■ Look for an engine with sufficient horsepower, a large-capacity fuel tank, mufflers and other devices that reduce engine noise, a seat safety switch, headlights, and practical engine gauges such as amperes, oil pressure, water temperature, and a maintenance minder.

■ Transmissions are available in three ranges. A low-range transmission is a good, all-purpose unit. It has plenty of torque for most cutting and accessory projects. A medium-range transmission provides more speed, but less torque, while a high-

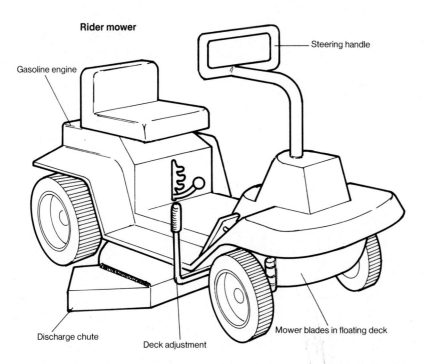

Rider mower

Gasoline engine

Steering handle

Discharge chute

Deck adjustment

Mower blades in floating deck

What to look for in power mowers

Starter rope pull. This part must be mounted on or near the push handle (instead of on the motor), as now required by law on walk-behind lawnmowers.

Mufflers and exhausts. These components should include a spark arrestor, and should be mounted above the lawnmower deck. The muffler on this model is on the lower right side of the motor.

Turn the demo model on its side. Check the blade mounting bracket. Is the blade easy to remove, replace and sharpen? On this model you need to remove only one bolt. Also look for baffles surrounding the blade (on the right side above). They help force the grass into the discharge chute instead of clogging the underside of the deck.

Commercial lawnmowers. These units are often sold in retail outlets. The large fuel tank on this commercial two-cycle engine model saves constant refilling.

Check riding mower controls. Make sure you can reach them easily while comfortably seated. Try them out in the store. If not, try another model until one suits you.

Check the mowing deck. It should adjust easily. You can raise or lower the blade on this model simply by pulling out a large pin (center) and inserting it in a different hole.

range transmission will furnish some torque, but mostly speed.

Most riders, whatever the transmission range, have three- or four-speed transmissions, with two or three speeds forward plus reverse, similar to a car. Some transmissions feature a hydrostatic drive, with a single-lever speed control that operates as an automatic transmission in an automobile does. With this

transmission, you don't manually change gears; moving between forward and reverse usually is done with a foot pedal or lever.

■ The extras—rider manufacturers can load the basic tractor with lots of niceties. On quality riders, some of the niceties are standard, while most of them are optional. If your budget permits, buy a keyed igni-

tion, a transmission with a neutral gear, an engine with power take-off (PTO), and a design where all moving gears, belts, and chains are safely covered.

Lawnmower features

Lawnmower manufacturers and salespeople tout a wide variety of features in order to sell equipment. Some of the features are outstand-

What to look for in power mowers

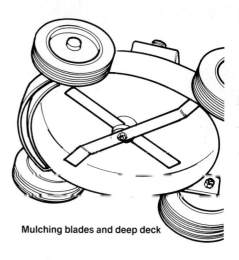

Mulching blades and deep deck

Comfortable seats are essential. Try different seat designs before you buy. A spring seat, like the one shown here, should be stiff enough to give you a firm ride.

Hitches should operate easily. This mower has a power take-off (PTO) for accessories (center).

wet, the cloth bags tend to sag. When the weather is cold, the plastic bags may crack.

Mulching blade. Mulching mowers (see above) are usually rotary mowers that have two crossed blades. Since the blades cut the grass at least twice, the mower doesn't need a grass catcher. The cut grass, in fact, becomes lawn mulch. Mulching blades work best in fine grass. They don't work as well in high and wet grass.

Mower deck. Choose a deck that has a low profile so you can push the mower against or under obstructions. The best buys (although more costly) are aluminum and magnesium decks. Steel decks are satisfactory, but you *must* take very good care of them: hose them out after every use; spot-prime chips and breaks in the metal with metal paint to prevent rust. Steel decks are more durable than their nonrusting counterparts as far as cracking and breaking are concerned, but you must avoid objects that can dent the steel. Aluminum and magnesium decks crack if struck hard; when that happens they must be replaced.

Exhaust system. Exhaust systems on walk-behind mowers are mounted either under or above the deck. The top-mounted muffler is easier to change and doesn't become clogged with grass. The bottom-mounted mufflers can damage the turf grass with excessive heat if the mower is stopped and left running. Mufflers

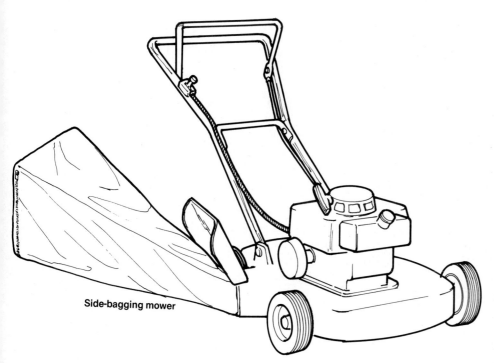

Side-bagging mower

ing; many are just gimmicks. Here are the worthwhile features that you should consider, your budget permitting.

Grass catcher. Grass catchers are standard on some models, optional on others. The catchers may be side- or rear-mounted on the mower; I recommend the rear type because it doesn't get in the way of such

obstructions in the lawn as shrubbery, trees, fences, and outbuildings. With a side bagger, of course, you can reverse the travel of the mower to cut close, but this can be a headache to do frequently.

Some catchers are made of plastic or a similar material; others are of cloth. The plastic ones don't absorb water; the cloth ones do—even if they have been waterproofed. When

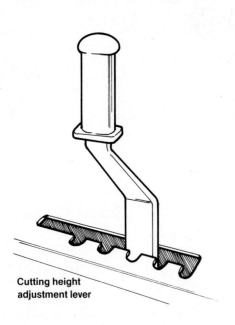

Cutting height
adjustment lever

usually are decibel-rated to indicate their sound-deadening ability.

Blade adjustment. *Do not* buy any lawnmower that lacks a means to adjust blade height. It is important that the height of turf grass be maintained (see Chapter 1) for proper growth. On less expensive mowers the height adjustment usually involves repositioning four bolts in holes provided in the frame of the mower. Changing these bolts when they become rusty and debris-encrusted can be a problem. Quality mowers have wheel-adjustment levers: you simply move the levers backward or forward to adjust the wheels to the cutting height you want.

Safety devices. To meet the safety standards of the Consumer Product Safety Commission, all walk-behind rotary lawnmowers made after 1982 must have a hands-on control that will stop the blade completely within 3 seconds after the control is released. The control also serves as a power switch; the mower cannot be started until this control is activated. Although the device adds about $50 to the price of the mower, it will lower the injury rate.

A safety device worth having is a discharge chute, which directs the grass clippings and other debris downward as they're thrown out from under the mower housing. All discharge chutes *must* deflect down. If not, debris such as a rock can be thrown 50 yards or so at the speed of a bullet.

A keyed ignition system or a locking system is recommended, especially if you have children. Machines that can be started easily by children are *dangerous.*

On the new models, the starter for the mower is located at the rear of the deck, not at the side or front. With an easy-starting engine you no longer have to put your foot on the deck to hold down the mower while you crank the engine with the pull rope.

The new federal standards have resulted in some higher-quality motor parts. Electronic and solid-state ignitions are now standard equipment on many quality mowers. Improvements in carburetion now produce better operation at both high and low temperatures.

Power grass trimmers

You can buy an electric- or gasoline-powered nylon string grass trimmer or a trimmer with a round saw blade. The no-frills electric models are so inexpensive that you can't afford to be without one. And when the unit breaks down it is usually cheaper to buy a new one than to repair the old one. The gasoline-powered trimmers, of course, are more expensive; they are designed for heavy grass and weed cutting in areas that can't be reached with a tool or an extension cord.

The gas-driven trimmers require an oil and gas mixture since the engine has two cycles. Maintenance is fairly simple (see the chapter on two-cycle engines).

You can also buy battery-powered (cordless) trimmers, but their cutting capacity is smaller than that of the other types because the batteries need frequent recharging. These trimmers are fine for small trimming jobs, however. A transformer is included to recharge the batteries on household electricity.

Electric trimmers require almost no maintenance. Nylon line for all

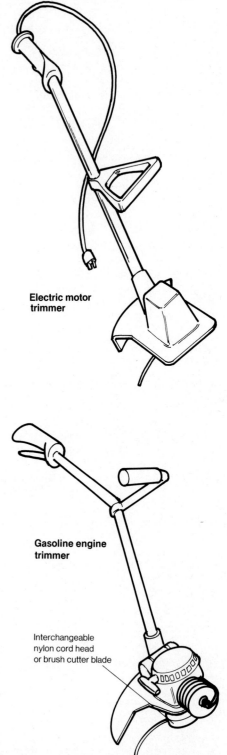

Electric motor
trimmer

Gasoline engine
trimmer

Interchangeable
nylon cord head
or brush cutter blade

models is plentiful and can be found in most general merchandise stores.

All trimmers are fairly simple mechanically: a motor turns a length of nylon or a round blade at a very high speed. On the string type, the nylon feeds off a spool and clips weeds and grass down to the roots or

What to look for in clippers

Safety devices. Look for safety controls on hedge clippers, such as this on/off switch (top) that controls power to the trigger (below).

Plastic shield. This model has a shield to protect your hand against debris thrown back by the cutting bar.

Shoulder strap

Gasoline engine brush cutter

Electric motor edger

to any height; you control the height by positioning the head of the trimmer. Some models have an automatic string feed; you tap others on the ground to release more string from the spool.

Some larger and more expensive models are multipurpose, with hoe, edger, and power snow shovel attachments available.

Trimmers are rated by width of cut —from 7 inches up to 20 inches. The weight between motor and cutting unit is usually well distributed, but some models—the brush cutters, for example—have extra handle and strap accessories for easier handling.

I recommend at least a 12-amp motor for a 9-inch blade or a 4-amp motor for a 6-inch blade; gasoline engines should be 3.5 hp. These are minimum requirements. When the blades must take big, deep bites out of the turf more power is necessary.

Don't buy an edger unless it has an adjustable front wheel for depth of cut, fingertip controls with a throttle lock, easily removable blades for sharpening, and comfortable tool balance. If the edger can be converted for use as a trimmer, make

sure the conversion can be made easily; otherwise you'll spend hours tinkering with nuts and bolts. If you do lots of edging, consider the professional edgers that have a greater depth-of-cut and power range.

Power hedge clippers

The most efficient clipper is one that can handle a wide range of stalk, limb, and branch sizes. Specifications on the tool will provide you with this information; use it to buy a tool

What to look for in chain saws

Chainsaw chain brake. The white lever, above, is a safety device that stops the chain quickly in case of emergency.

Control positioning. Are the controls within easy reach when the chainsaw is in operation? The stop/start buttons, locks, and the throttle should be only a finger's length away, as they are on this model.

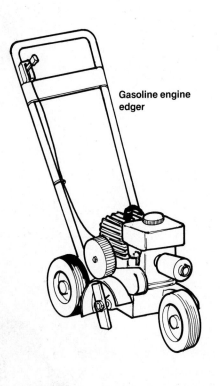

Gasoline engine edger

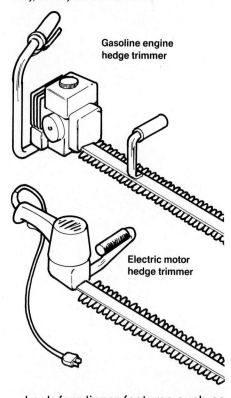

Gasoline engine hedge trimmer

Electric motor hedge trimmer

that's up to your cutting requirements.

Minimum blade length should be 13 inches; otherwise you can't trim with any assurance of squareness. For light to medium trimming, an electric trimmer should have at least a 2.2-amp motor with a 3000 spm (strokes per minute) capacity.

Look for clipper features such as double insulation against shock, double-edged blades, a friction-type clutch that helps protect the motor and the blades when the blades jam, devices that prevent the plug from pulling out, and comfortable weight and balance of the tool. Get a demonstration if possible.

To protect your eyes and hands wear safety goggles and a pair of heavy leather gloves when you use a power clipper.

Power garden tillers

A garden tiller is a specialized tool. If you do lots of gardening and your budget permits buy one. It will save you many hours of hard labor; and with care, it should last for years and years.

Quality garden tillers have at least eight tines and a 20-inch ground-breaking width. You need plenty of power. The engine should be at least 4 hp for simple tilling and at least 5 hp if the tiller is used with attachments. Attachments that you can buy include cultivators, snow blowers, log splitters, and soil graders.

Ask for a demonstration and take this opportunity to steer the tiller. If you can't get a demonstration, at least run the tiller down an aisle so you get the feel of the tool. The weight should be balanced near the tines so you gain the advantage of the engine weight pressing downward.

If your budget permits, consider a tiller with a chain-drive transmission (which provides more power), self-sharpening tines (often standard equipment on quality tillers), vertical and horizontal adjustments for the steering handles, and an electric starter.

Rear-tine tillers cost more than front-tine tillers because they're heavier, but your choice depends on the type of ground you are tilling. If the ground is usually hard and compact, you need the rear-tine tiller's extra weight. If the ground usually is loose and workable, a front-tine tiller is adequate for the job.

There are three basic tine designs: bolo, pick and chisel, and slasher. The bolo tines are for digging and mulching. Pick and chisel tines are for working in hard and rocky soil. Slasher tines are for cutting through thick vegetation. You generally get bolo tines as standard equipment, but you might be able to switch to one of the others. Ask the retailer. If your budget permits, I suggest that

Front-tine tiller

you buy the bolos and the slashers for a good working combination.

Power lawn blowers

To work efficiently, a lawn blower should blast air out at 100 mph velocities, and even more is better for jobs such as clearing away leaves, grass, snow, and general lawn and garden debris. So when choosing a unit remember: the more power, the more wind.

You have a choice between electric- and gasoline-powered blowers. The electric units are limited only by the length of the power cord. If this will be a problem, your best buy is the gasoline unit. If you're considering an electric unit, a 6-amp motor that produces a 245 cubic feet per minute wind velocity should be your

Gasoline engine backpack blower

minimum requirement. You don't have to worry about the gasoline-powered unit size; all those I've tested are more than adequate to handle the job.

Multipurpose blowers also are available with 5 hp gasoline engines. You usually get a combination of vacuum, blower, and shredder in a single machine.

Look for features such as light weight and good balance, trigger locks, variable speed controls, double insulation, and devices that prevent the cord from unplugging on the electric models. The gasoline models should have safety-grip clutch drive levers, large wheels, a front swivel caster for maneuverability, adjustable nozzle height, and a warranty.

A word of caution: make sure you have an area into which debris can be blown—a fenced corner is fine for this. Otherwise the debris will sail over your lot and onto your neighbor's, and this is bad for community relations.

Power snow removers

More than any other lawn and garden tool, snow blowers should be carefully matched to the type and amount

of work they have to do. If you're in doubt as to the quantity and weight of the snowfall in your area, call the National Weather Service for your district.

Snow blowers are virtually the same tool as the leaf and debris blowers described above. Snow blowers are not designed to handle drifts, but they are effective against thin layers of snow. You have to work with them almost as the snow is falling. A blower with a 200 mph wind velocity is a good selection.

Power snow shovels have a rotor that tosses snow about 10 feet. You can tackle drifts with a power shovel, but expect to spend some time at the job. Shovels cut approximately 12-inch-wide paths with one or two passes. They are available in both electric and gasoline models. The

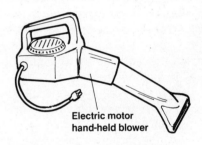

Electric motor hand-held blower

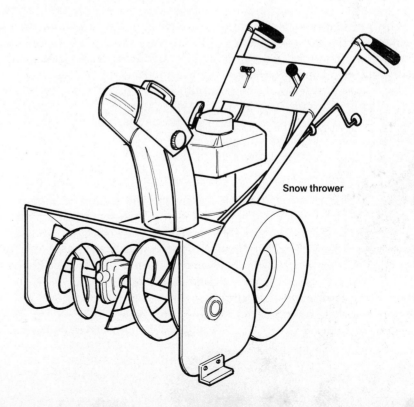

Snow thrower

electric ones are almost maintenance-free, and you don't have starting troubles on cold days. You are, of course, restricted by the length of the power cord. The extension cord should be at least No. 12 or No. 14 wire.

If you're considering the electric model, look for comfortable total weight and good balance, an ignition lock, double-insulation against shock, and a gear drive transmission.

Gasoline shovels have a recoil rope starter and two-cycle engines. You have to mix the gasoline with oil. Test the unit for weight and balance, and check for the possibility of adding attachments—a grass trimmer, an edger, a hoe.

Both electric and gasoline units should have a warranty. Ask about local service centers you can turn to when the warranty no longer is valid.

One-stage snow throwers are designed with an auger (like a horizontal post-hole digger) that either throws the snow from the cutting path or pushes the snow aside. A model with a 22-inch clearance should have an engine with a minimum of 3.5 hp.

Two-stage throwers also have an auger, but the auger feeds the snow into an impeller that throws the snow out of the machine. The average clearance is from 24 to 28 inches; engine size ranges from 5 to 10 hp. Buy as much power as your budget permits.

The gasoline engine usually is matched to the machine's snow capacity but check to be sure. If you are considering a larger gasoline model—one with about a 32-inch width capacity, for example—the engine should be at least 10 hp. If not, the equipment and you will have to work much harder than necessary.

Two-stage thrower equipment features should include:

rotating discharge chutes or spouts that turn at least 160 degrees

electric starter to get the machines started on very cold days

key (or childproof) ignition

skid shoes adjustable from ground level to about 1½ inches

shock-resistant power train

tire chains

windproof operator cab

On the larger, more expensive models, look for a limited-slip differential and two-stage auger systems for both loose and packed snow. The big models usually have five forward speeds and a reverse gear. Speed is not important. In fact, the slower speed models usually have more torque and thus provide better traction in snow.

If you already own a lawn tractor or riding mower, you may be able to add a snow brush or blade. You should also consider an electric starter if your equipment doesn't have one. As a rule of thumb, riding tractors and mowers with blade and brush attachments are best for removing light snow that falls infrequently and has a rapid melt rate. Blades and brushes just won't do a super cleaning job in heavy, wet snow.

Choosing the right equipment
If the snow in your area is light and falls in 2-inch layers or less, the best power tool to use is probably a power shovel. You can also use a lawn blower on a very light snowfall.

If you live in a garden apartment or townhouse, a power snow shovel with a 6- to 8-amp motor probably will be adequate to remove snow from decks, patios, porches, steps, and short walkways.

If your snowfall is light and falls in about 2- to 6-inch layers, a walk-behind snow blower or a one-stage snow thrower should be adequate.

If you live in a three-bedroom home on an average lot, a one-stage thrower with a 3.5 hp gasoline engine and a 22-inch clearing width should be about right.

If your snowfall is wet, heavy, and falls in 2- to 6-inch layers, buy heavy-duty equipment that includes a rotating chute and a transmission built to withstand the shock of ice and packed snow as well as the stopping

power of buried stones, bricks, logs, rocks, and the edges of walks, driveways, and uneven paving.

If you live on a large lot with lengthy driveways and walkways to clear, consider a 6 hp unit with a two-stage blower.

If you live in the northern tier of states where the annual snowfall runs to 30 inches or more, you'll need a two-stage thrower with capacity to handle the snowfall and an engine powerful enough to drive it.

Other factors to consider
The size and cost of snow removal equipment you have to buy may be modified by many factors. Consider these:

■ Is it possible to put up a snow fence or drift-inhibiting barriers in the neighborhood? Fences can save a good deal of snow removal labor.

■ How much snow removal does your local tax provide? If municipal snow removal crews leave high mounds of snow blocking driveways after the roads in your area are cleared, talk with your neighbors. You all may be able to buy a tractor and blade or heavy-duty snow blower cooperatively. Each person can pay an equipment fee and share in the labor.

■ If your taxes provide adequate snow removal, you may be able to get by with a power shovel. Of course, the least expensive tool for the job is the old-fashioned scoop shovel!

Power tools for cutting and splitting wood
This category includes electric and gasoline chain saws and power-driven firewood splitters. Electric models, as a rule, are best suited for light cutting and splitting; the gasoline models are designed for handling big timber.

Chain saws. For pruning, cutting small (diameters of 2 to 3 inches) logs, and cleaning out brush, an electric chain saw is powerful enough. I

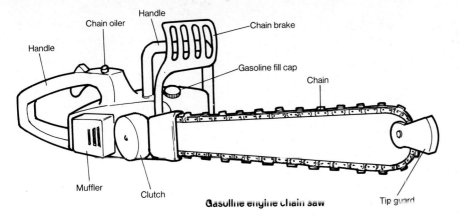

Handle
Chain oiler
Handle
Chain brake
Gasoline fill cap
Chain
Muffler
Clutch
Tip guard

Gasoline engine chain saw

recommend a longer blade (sizes range from about 8 to 16 inches) with the power capacity to match (about 10 to 12 amps).

Electric chain saws are quiet, lightweight, and fairly inexpensive. As with other electric tools, you are limited somewhat by the length of the extension cord (get No. 12 or No. 14 wire). Maintenance is low with the electric models; they need little care, and starting in cool or cold weather is seldom a problem.

Gasoline-powered chain saws have two-cycle engines that are rated by cubic-inch displacement, not horsepower. The more displacement, the more powerful the engine; sizes range from 1.6 cubic inches to 8.3 cubic inches. For example, you'll find the 1.6 engine with an 8- to 12-inch blade; a 60-inch blade takes an 8.3 engine. If you cut mostly firewood, I recommend a 4.5 cu. in. displacement engine with a 20-inch blade. Anything larger than this belongs in the lumberjack category, and most homeowners simply don't need this much tool power to cut firewood.

Gasoline chain saws (and some electric ones) have important built-in features; some are standard equipment, others optional. Either way, these are worth your consideration:

■ A chain brake is a safety device that is built into the front handle of the saw. The brake is cocked, like the hammer on a gun, before the saw is started. If the nose of the chain bar hits a hard knot or obstruction, the front handle releases and snaps the brake shut, stopping the chain instantly.

■ An anti-kickback nose guard looks like a curved piece of metal over the tip of the chain blade. It prevents objects from striking the tip of the chain, causing kickback. There are limitations with the guard: you can't make pocket cuts in materials; you can't go through a saw kerf with the end of the bar; and you are limited to logs of certain diameter. But by planning, you can go around these limitations. Therefore, I highly recommend that you buy a saw with this safety feature.

■ A reduced kick chain limits, but doesn't entirely eliminate, chain kickbacks. It is a good investment.

■ A left-hand guard protects your hand from the whirling chain in case the chain breaks during operation.

■ Shock absorber devices reduce the vibration of the saw. Pick up a chain saw with these devices and the handles seem to be loose and wobbly. This feeling is caused by the shock absorbers mounted between the handles and the housing of the saw.

■ An automatic oiler provides the lubrication the saw needs. In order to operate properly, the chain has to float along in oil. Most oiling systems also have a pushbutton override in case the saw needs more oil than the automatic system provides.

■ An easy-start device is a type of compression release that lowers the compression in the cylinders when the starter rope is pulled.

■ An automatic chain sharpener is a great help if you do light cutting. Many users of chain saws, however, prefer to sharpen the cutters themselves with a sharpening tool that may be purchased where saws are sold.

■ Nose sprockets are mounted at the tip of the chain bar and turn with the chain; their purpose is to reduce friction. The sprockets must be kept lubricated for best results. Some saws do not have nose sprockets.

■ Electronic, or solid-state, ignition does away with breaker points and condensor in the engine, and thus eliminates the expense and labor of periodically replacing them.

■ Most brand-name chain saws have at least a one-year warranty against defective materials and workmanship. When you buy equipment also find out about repair procedures, such as where to take or send the saw in the event of a breakdown.

Log splitters. Electric and gasoline power has replaced sledge hammers and muscle power for splitting firewood and logs. The electric splitters are amazingly efficient. Some exert more than 7 tons of thrust using a fairly small motor; this is accomplished with reduction gearing.

Gasoline model splitters are sold separately or as an accessory to another garden tool (a tiller, for example). In either case, they should have at least a 5 hp engine, and the splitter should be operated with a chain drive, not a belt drive. Belts tend to slip and burn if the log load is too great.

Features to consider include log capacity (26 inches is standard), splitting time (a cord of wood in two hours is about standard); weight, portability, and a drive train (belt or chain) with clutching devices. Don't overlook warranties and ask about local repair outlets. Since some units weigh more than 100 pounds, transporting them to and from a repair shop might be troublesome.

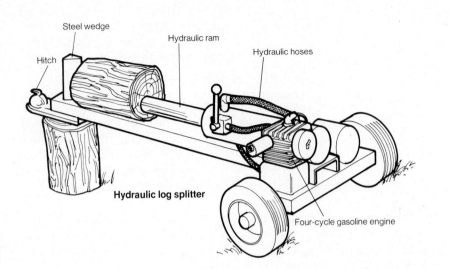

Steel wedge

Hydraulic ram

Hydraulic hoses

Hitch

Hydraulic log splitter

Four-cycle gasoline engine

Whether you split your own firewood or buy it from a dealer, you should know the formula for a cord of wood.

■ A *full* cord of wood is a stack of wood that measures 8 feet long by 4 feet high by 4 feet wide.

■ A *face cord* is 8 feet long by 4 feet high by the length of the wood, which may vary considerably. The average length is about 16 inches.

■ A *stack* of wood is about the same amount as a face cord.

■ A *truckload* of wood depends on the size of the truck. Pick-up trucks (a standard truck bed) hold approximately one-third of a cord of wood.

By *weight*, a ton of firewood equals about half a cord, if the wood has been air-dried after being cut. Hardwoods burn hotter and longer than softwoods. Dried wood burns better than freshly cut, or green, wood.

Tool safety

Many power tools you can buy for lawn and garden projects have built-in safety devices to protect you against injury. For example, lawnmowers may have a deadman lever to stop the blade quickly. Chain saws have anti-kickback devices; trimmers have guards over the nylon string.

But even if your tools have these devices, you should always be careful when using the equipment and wear appropriate safety apparel.

Lawnmowers. Wear heavy work shoes. An old pair of leather golf shoes makes excellent lawnmowing shoes because the spikes prevent slipping, especially on slopes.

Refuel lawnmowers out in the open, *never* inside a storage shed or garage. Avoid spilling gasoline on the engine during refueling and do not refuel while the engine is hot.

When starting a lawnmower, keep your hands and feet away from the blade area. Never place hands or feet near the blades while they're running.

Chain saws. Wear heavy leather gloves, safety goggles, and heavy shoes (those with steel-reinforced toes are best). If you are felling trees or cutting brush with a chain saw, wear a hardhat.

Chain saws are very noisy. I recommend that you use ear plugs (silicone rubber is the best buy) or headphone-type sound deadeners.

Clothing should be fairly tight fitting, especially trouser legs and shirt sleeves; keep sleeves buttoned.

Trimmers and edgers. Wear gloves, safety goggles, and a respirator. Trimmers and edgers raise lots of

dust which can be uncomfortable and, sometimes, dangerous.

Dusters and sprayers. Be extremely careful when mixing chemicals; keep all chemicals out of reach of children. *Always* wear a respirator when applying chemicals with a spreader or sprayer. Don't spread or spray on a windy day.

Axes, weed and brush cutters. Wear leather gloves and heavy shoes. Work with sharp tools. A dull tool is dangerous.

Blowers. On gasoline models, the muffler becomes extremely hot. Keep your hands away from the muffler. Wear safety goggles even if you're removing snow or rounding up leaves. Blowers pick up rocks, sticks, and other debris from under the snow and leaves.

Tillers. A tiller works best when the ground is slightly moist. You should cut away as much vegetation as possible, since weeds and grass tend to jam the tines.

Wear heavy shoes and gloves when tilling, and let the tiller do the work. Don't push it along, just steer it.

Cultivators are similar to tillers, and the same working and safety rules apply.

Snow throwers and blowers. Since it's cold outside the heavy clothing you wear offers good protection. But be very careful to keep clear of the area where the snow is being thrown; the equipment can pick up small rocks and other debris under the snow. Wear safety goggles while operating a snow blower or thrower. Keep children away from the machine and the snow piles.

Power log splitters. Wear heavy shoes, gloves, and safety goggles.

Overhead jobs. For overhead cutting with any tool, wear leather gloves and safety goggles. A hardhat is a good idea, too. Be careful in positioning ladders, especially stepladders. Lean a stepladder whenever possible. Have a friend hold an extension ladder as you work on it, and keep your hips within the rails as you work. *Don't reach.*

Equipment storage

The ideal spot to store lawn and garden equipment is in an outdoor shed with a lock on the door. Plans for building a simple storage shed are presented in Chapter 3; you also can buy prefabricated sheds. The prefab models are available in wood and metal. Prices range from about $200 to $800, depending on the material and size. Wood is the more expensive; metal is less so. Sizes range from small sheds to full-sized garages.

Double, *locking* doors with a low threshold are *must* features for the prefabs. The locks are for protection, of course, but more important, they deter children from entering the shed and playing with tools and chemicals. The low threshold lets you roll in equipment easier. The doors should be mounted with top rollers since bottom tracks tend to clog with dirt and debris.

If you set up a lightweight prefab, you should use an anchoring kit, which consists of auger-type stakes and wire.

When buying or building outdoor sheds, make sure you follow local codes as to size and, especially, height. Some communities restrict height—and even design—of these outbuildings.

Other storage areas to be considered are your garage, a walk-in basement, or a carport storage area. There's usually room in these areas for lawn and garden equipment and supplies, although at first you may not think so.

The key is space planning, and here are several ideas that you can apply:

■ Small, lock-equipped metal cabinets are excellent for storing chemicals. Place them in a garage in front of your car or at the side of it. Space in a basement or carport usually is not critical.

■ Between-the-stud shelves create storage space in garages, carports, and basements. The shelves are the depth of the studs—3½ inches—but there is plenty of room for single and side-by-side items. In fact, storing products just one item deep is to your advantage; you never have to hunt behind things to find the one you want.

■ When you buy equipment, consider foldaway handles so the storage can be more compact.

■ Perforated hardboard (I recommend ¼-inch tempered hardboard nailed over studs or furring strips) offers plenty of hanging room for hand tools. The metal hangers made for perforated hardboard are available in many configurations to match tool shapes; they are fairly expensive, but worth the investment.

If you paint hardboard, be sure that both sides are sealed. Otherwise, the material may warp.

Additional tool storage ideas may be found in Chapter 3 and throughout the book.

Labels and literature

Outdoor power equipment is usually labeled with a tag that bears the seal of the Outdoor Power Equipment Institute (OPEI). This seal means that the equipment has been tested by an independent laboratory and has met all the safety standards set by the U.S. Consumer Product Safety Commission or the American National Standards Institute. You'll also find a date on the seal since safety standards are updated constantly. The seal is an important form of safety protection for you or anyone who uses the tool.

The UL (Underwriter's Laboratory) seal is usually found on electrical equipment. UL is not a government agency, but rather an independent testing laboratory. Its seal indicates that the product will perform as the manufacturer says it will.

As you go shopping for lawn and garden equipment, make use of the manufacturer's literature that usually is offered free. It is a valuable source of information on tool performance and features, and it makes a wonderful comparison-shopping reference. Since you invest considerable amounts of money when you buy major equipment, comparing brands and models is one of the best ways to get your money's worth.

Lawnmowers, tillers, blowers, trimmers, chain saws, etc.—all come with an owner's manual that explains operation and troubleshooting. Retailers often have problems in keeping owner's manuals with the tools; shoppers pick them up and walk away with them. Therefore, many store owners keep the manuals back in the office and sometimes forget to include them with the sale. Be sure that you remind them.

Hand and power tool retailers usually are listed in the advertising pages of the telephone directory. If you need a special part or tool, you often can find the information here.

3 Building a Storage Shed

Providing adequate storage and repair space for lawn and garden equipment can cramp living quarters, especially if you live in a small house. One good answer to this problem is to erect an outdoor shed. You can buy ready-built, completely assembled sheds, made of wood or metal. You can also buy prefabricated units that you erect yourself. A third alternative, which is described in detail in this chapter, is to build a shed from scratch to your own specifications. The cost, surprisingly, is about the same for any choice.

The prefabs and ready-builts take much less time and effort to set up, of course, than building a shed from scratch. The advantage of building yourself is that you get a structure designed to meet all of your needs—such as storage, a specialized workshop, dimensions suited to location requirements, and personal preferences.

Function and efficiency are the determining factors in the shed design described in this chapter. Its 8 × 10-foot floor area is large enough for a small repair or potting bench along one wall. The 10-foot height at the front of the shed provides enough room to store long pieces of wood and plywood, and the lowest height—8 feet—still leaves plenty of head room for lighting and overhead storage. By adding several collar beams (2 × 4s) that span the width of the shed and by laying 1/2- or 3/8-inch-thick plywood sheets over the beams, you can provide overhead storage for seasonal items and a place to put chemicals where small children can't reach them.

Best of all, the simple design of my shed can be easily modified to suit your own needs. I built the shed illustrated here using a 4-foot module to take advantage of standard-size building products. The result is a big savings on material costs, since there is little material cutting required and, consequently, little waste material.

The shed can be square, rectangular, or even L-shaped. A rectangular shed is preferable to a square configuration, if you intend to include a workbench along one end.

Height is an important consideration. A minimum roof height of 6 feet is required at the low wall. A minimum of 8 feet is required at the high wall. If the roof is any lower, you simply won't have enough head room to work. The difference in the height of the two walls determines the pitch of the roof. On my shed, the pitch is 1 in

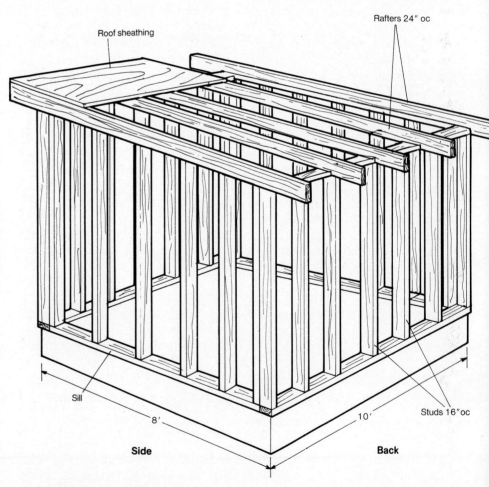

Framing diagram for storage shed

Roof sheathing

Rafters 24″ oc

Studs 16″oc

Sill

Side

Back

8′

10′

4 (3 inches in each foot)—fairly steep because of heavy winter snowfalls in my area. Also, this height adds considerable overhead storage room, an important asset often overlooked in shed design.

Community considerations

Before you build or buy any outdoor shed, you must check the local building codes; they may restrict the type and size of building you may erect. Retailers who sell prefabricated and ready-built sheds usually know these code restrictions. If your dealer is in doubt, check the building department of your community government. Check to see if you need a building permit to erect a prefab unit or build your own shed.

Another consideration is your neighbors' reactions. It's a good idea to tell them what your plans are before you start building. Your shed could block a view or cause your neighbors planting or drainage problems.

Laying out the job

Before you start buying materials or digging earth, read the remainder of this chapter to give yourself an idea of what building a shed from scratch involves. It's a good idea to sketch the project on graph paper first, drawing each wall and the floor plan to scale. If you decide to modify the dimensions given here, these drawings will prove helpful as construction proceeds.

When you've decided on the size of your shed, make a trial layout of the perimeter (length and width) with four 1×2 wooden stakes and a ball of twine. You'll also need a tape measure for this job. The string outline will show you how much space you'll need; you may relocate the layout several times before making a final decision.

Tools and materials

Complete lists of tools and materials needed to lay the concrete foundation and erect the wooden shed are given here. The basic shed design uses standard sizes of framing, sheathing, siding, and roofing materials. The easiest way to modify the plan is by increasing or decreasing the lengths and widths of standard materials in 2- or 4-foot increments. You can, of course, use odd-sized materials, but this will increase your costs.

If, for example, you decide to make the higher wall 9 foot instead of 10 feet, you will still have to buy 10-foot-long 2×4s because 9-foot lengths are not sold. The 1-foot length you cut off each 2×4 will be throw-away scrap, since it is too short even to use as stud blocking.

TOOLS NEEDED TO BUILD THE OUTDOOR SHED AND WORKSHOP

Note: Some of the tools listed below may be rented from a rental outlet at reasonable cost. All will be useful for future home maintenance and improvement projects.

Tools

16-ounce claw hammer

Carpenter's level (3/5-inch bubble)

Carpenter's square or combination square

7 1/2-inch portable electric circular saw

Crosscut handsaw

Sledge hammer

50-foot tape measure

Hacksaw

8-foot stepladder

16-foot extension ladder

Caulking gun shell

Rake

Shovel or spade

Pick

Tamper

Chalkline and chalk

Garden hose

2-gallon plastic bucket

Adjustable wrench

Butt chisel

Wooden mallet

Wooden concrete float

Marking pencils

Optional Tools

Sabre saw

Miter box and back saw

Outdoor lawn and garden shed. The adaptable design can be enlarged or scaled down to fit your needs by simply changing the measurements. Building the shed requires three weekends of work, from placing the concrete slab to adding the trim. Standard-size building materials and simplified building construction techniques are used throughout.

Extension cord (No. 12 or 14 wire)

Paintbrush

Steel trowel

Broom

Graph paper

MATERIALS NEEDED FOR THE OUTDOOR SHED AND WORKSHOP

Materials	Quantity
2 × 4 × 10s (straight as possible)	39
2 × 4 × 8s (straight as possible)	8
1/2 × 4 × 8 C-D sheathing	4
3/8 × 4 × 8 A-C plywood (for soffit)	1
Texture 1-1 siding (3/8 × 4 × 8)	11
1 × 6 × 8 pine (straight as possible)	5
1 × 4 × 14 spruce or pine (straight as possible)	9
15-pound building felt	1 roll
Prehung door unit (any size you want)	1
Prehung window unit (any size you want)	1 or more
Asphalt shingles	1 square
Cedar shingle shims	15 pieces
Lock set	1
Roofing cement	2 cart.
Caulking compound	3 cart.
Glazing compound	1 small can
16d box or common nails (hot-dipped or coated)	15 pounds
10d finishing nails	2 pounds
Galvanized roofing nails	3 pounds
8-inch sill or carriage bolts, with nuts and washers	10
Exterior finish	3 gallons
Exterior trim finish	1 gallon
Concrete for 8 × 10 × 5 slab (check your dimensions)	2 yards

Optional Materials

4 × 4 posts, 3 or 4 feet long (3-foot lengths preferable)	2
Interior hardboard finish	2 quarts
Interior bench finish	1 quart
Quarter round for stud/ shelf trim	10 feet
1/4 × 4 × 8 tempered perforated hardboard	1
3-0/6-8 solid core door (for the workbench)	1

The foundation

Lay out the perimeter of the foundation with stakes and string. Then place the inside faces of the 2 × 4s that will be used as forms lightly against the string.

1. Building the foundation. Lay out the slab plan using 2 × 4 (or larger) form boards and pointed stakes. If you are in doubt as to where the slab should go, use string and stakes to set up a trial layout. The forms must be level and square; nail the stakes to the outside of the forms.

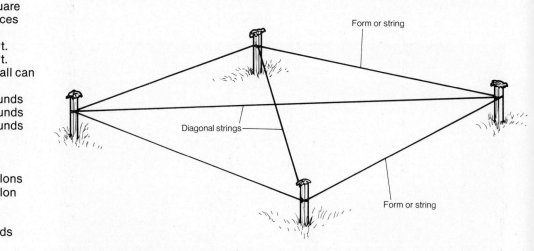

2. Are the forms square? The best way to find out is to run two lengths of string diagonally from inside corner to inside corner. If the diagonal strings are exactly the same length, the forms are square. It's not necessary for the 2 × 4 forms to be in place to make this test. Once the strings show a square layout, set the forms to the string.

Using a carpenter's level, put the top edges of all four forms in a fairly level position. You don't have to be especially accurate at this point. What you are trying to do is estimate how much earth will have to be moved to level the forms. You don't have to excavate for the foundation if you don't want to, but it must be placed on level ground. If considerable earth will have to be removed, you may want to relocate the founda-

tion to save digging.

After you decide where the foundation site will be, the perimeter edges must be set out accurately and perfectly square. The best way to do this is with stakes and string. Refer to the diagram that explains how to square the layout using the diagonal string method. When the string outline is square, set the forms against the string.

For an 8 × 10-foot foundation, a 5-

inch-thick foundation slab is adequate. If the slab is larger than 8×10-feet, it should be reinforced with wire mesh. Instructions for this are given on page 42. An integral footing (see illustration) may be used to give additional support to larger structures. The footing is placed at the same time the slab is placed; a wider form (2×12, instead of 2×4) may be necessary.

Use 2 foot long 2×4 stakes to hold the 2×4 forms in position. Sharpen the stakes with a saw and drive them next to the outside face of the forms, so that the top of the stake is slightly below the top edge of the form. If this is difficult to do, drive the stake as deep as you can (so that it is fixed solidly in the ground), set the form, and then saw off the top of the stake.

You need stakes at each corner (2 stakes per corner, one on each side) and stakes spaced about 30 inches apart along the sides of the forms. You don't need to overstake; the amount of concrete that you are placing will not exert a great deal of thrust. Just make the forms solid, so that they don't collapse when the concrete is placed.

Make sure each form is level along its top edge, and—using the diagonal string method and a carpenter's square—make sure the corners are perfectly square. Then nail through the outside of the stakes into the outside face of the form boards.

If you have to remove dirt at the high spots inside the forms, use it to build up the low spots. If there are no low spots, the excess dirt should be tossed outside the forms and used for backfill, if needed later.

On the other hand, if you need fill —e.g., for a steep-sloping area—you can usually buy it from a landscaping outlet. Determine the amount that you need by measuring the volume inside the forms. Then double this figure, since fill compacts to about one-half of its original volume. Spread the fill in 4-inch layers, tamping each one down. You can rent a hand tamper for this, or use a lawn roller if the area is large enough to accommodate it.

As you add fill, spread it by running a straight 2×4 screed across the top of the forms. This will help you keep

3. Square the corners at each end, and drive the form stakes even with or slightly below the top edge of the forms. If this is difficult to do, drive the stakes deep enough to hold the forms firmly, and then cut off the top of the stakes (using a crosscut handsaw) level with the top of the forms.

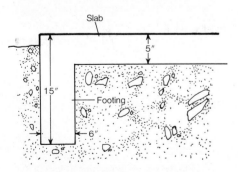

Foundation footing. If the foundation needs extra support to prevent frost heaving, dig a trench around the projected perimeter of the slab for an integral footing. The concrete slab and the footing are placed at the same time. The footing should extend below the frost line. Ask the National Weather Service for the depth of the frost lines in your area.

4. When the forms are in position, but not finally set, level the ground, lowering the high spots and filling the low spots. Run a 2×4 straightedge along the top of the forms to determine the depth of the slab; measure from the bottom of the straightedge to the ground. This will show you where to remove dirt and where to fill. The ground should be fairly level, free of grass, leaves, sticks, and other debris, and tamped firm. If you fill with gravel and/or sand, the surface must be tamped.

the fill level and even.

Although the surface over which you place the concrete should be generally level and firmly tamped, a few shallow holes won't hurt. The concrete will simply fill these depressions. Sometimes it is easier to fill them with concrete than to level them with dirt, stone, bricks, or gravel.

When you're finished filling, recheck the square of your form corners and double-check your measurements.

Special filling

If the ground on which the concrete is to be placed is firm and solid, no extra filling will be needed. But if the ground is not solid and stable, you should add a gravel fill base and a sand fill over the gravel. If you are in doubt about whether you should do this, ask a concrete contractor in your community; most of them will give you a straight answer, even though you are doing the job yourself. Retailers that sell concrete and cement also should know.

A standard gravel and sand fill consists of 4 inches of gravel and 2 inches of sand. It's a good idea to excavate enough earth to hold this fill. Moisten both materials after they are in place, and tamp them down to form a solid base for the concrete. If you use this method you may have to increase the width of the forms from 2 × 4s to 2 × 8s—or whatever it takes to hold both the fill and the concrete.

If an integral footing is going to be placed along with the foundation slab, dig a 12-inch-deep ditch around the perimeter of the slab. The width of the ditch should be about 6 inches. Fill the bottom of it with about 2 inches of gravel, and tamp the gravel firm. The sides of the ditch can serve as the forms for the concrete if they are made straight and smooth.

The concrete

My 8 × 10-foot slab had an average depth of 5 inches. It took just under 2 cubic yards of ready-mixed concrete to fill the forms.

Ready-mixed concrete is sold by the cubic yard or "yard" for short. If less than 5 cubic yards are ordered, you usually have to pay a premium, since the cost of hauling the material to the job site can be considerable. However, the additional price may be worth it; concrete mixing is hot and tiresome work, and, by the time you buy the gravel, sand, and bagged cement and haul it home, the difference in price is usually very small.

In any case, the way to estimate the number of yards of concrete needed is to multiply the width by the length by the depth—all in feet. Divide the answer by 27 (since there are 27 cubic feet in a cubic yard). The concrete estimating chart in this chapter will help you figure the amount you need. An easier way is to give the concrete company the dimensions of your slab (length, width, and depth), and they will figure the amount for you.

Estimating concrete
(Cubic feet needed to make a slab)

Length × width	Thickness in inches		
	4	5	6
6 × 8	16	20	24
8 × 8	21	26	32
8 × 10	26	33	40
10 × 10	33	42	50
10 × 12	40	50	60
12 × 12	48	60	72

If you decide to mix your own concrete, you must rent a concrete mixer for the job. A good formula is one part cement to two parts gravel to three parts sand. Blend these parts together thoroughly; then add water until the mixture is about the consistency of whipped cream.

If you start with one bag of cement (80 lbs) in the formula above, and add 160 lbs of gravel plus 240 lbs of sand and sufficient water, you will get about 1½ yards of concrete.

There are several types of cement available; I recommend Portland Cement Type I or IA. The aggregate (sand and gravel) should be clean. "Coarse aggregate" is gravel or crushed stone that is more than ¼ inch in diameter and smaller than 1½ inches in diameter. Water should be clean.

Reinforcing the concrete

Wire mesh (welded wire fabric) is often laid in concrete to help compensate for the expansion and contraction of the concrete during temperature extremes. Otherwise, the slab is liable to crack. You can buy wire mesh at some home centers and at hard materials dealers. The cost of the small amount of mesh you will need for a shed slab is reasonable. If you decide to reinforce the slab, use welded wire fabric (WWF). Here are the specifications:

Size/Type	Slab Thickness
6 × 6-in. #8/8 WWF	4 inches or less
4 × 4-in. #8/8 WWF	5 inches or less
4 × 4-in. #4/4 WWF	6 inches or less

The mesh should end up in the middle of the slab. The simplest way to do this is to fill the forms half way—about 2½ inches deep for a 5-inch slab. Then insert six or eight pieces of brick or stone into the wet concrete so that they rest on the ground. Lay the mesh on top of these supports and place the rest of the concrete. Work carefully, so that the mesh stays in position.

Concrete placement

The key to successful concrete pouring is to have everything ready when the truck arrives or when you dump the concrete out of your mixer. The working time for concrete is so short that you simply don't have time to reset forms, build new forms, or run to the store for a forgotten tool. Make sure the area is free from vegetation and is properly compacted. You'll need a friend to help you operate the opposite end of the screed (the 2 × 4 straightedge that levels the concrete between the forms) and install the sill bolts. If you use a ready-mix company, the truck driver may volunteer to help, but don't count on it.

As the truck arrives, or just before you dump the mixer, lightly sprinkle the ground with water from a garden hose. This helps to prevent the water in the concrete from soaking too quickly into the fill.

Ask the driver to make the pour in small amounts—about ¼ of the slab

5. When the concrete truck arrives, lightly water the area inside the forms. Then, as the concrete is placed, screed (level) the surface with a 2 × 4 straightedge, filling in any low spots in the concrete. Work the screed back and forth across the surface in seesaw fashion. Let any extra concrete fall over the end form; then bunch it in a pile with a shovel. Don't worry if the concrete inside the forms bulge slightly higher than the top edges of the forms; it will settle and shrink as you continue to work with it.

6. Screed the surface a final time. If you find low spots, fill them with the extra concrete you piled at the end of the form. Just pitch it onto the surface with a shovel, and then level it with the screed. When the surface has been screeded level with the top of the forms and is fairly smooth, remove the heap of excess concrete from outside the forms. One way to dispose of it is to nail together a square of 2 × 4s and fill it with the excess to make a stepping stone or splashblock.

7. Set the sill bolts about 1½ inches in from the edge of the concrete. Place the bolts about 18 inches from the corners; they must not match the stud locations. Two bolts on the short dimension and three bolts on the long dimension is enough support for this 8 × 10 foot structure. Dig the holes for the bolts in the fresh concrete with an old screwdriver. Use a combination square to make sure the bolts are vertical. Pack the concrete around the bolts, as shown, and smooth the surface with a piece of wood or a trowel.

at a time. After the first pouring, screed the surface level, filling in low spots with shovelfuls of concrete.

Continue to pour, screed, and shovel until the forms are full. Then, with a friend holding the other end of the 2 × 4 screed, carefully smooth the concrete so that it is level with the top edge of the forms. Work the 2 × 4 back and forth with a see-saw motion to level the surface, while simultaneously moving it from one end to the other.

The sill bolts

Immediately after the slab has been screeded, install the bolts to hold the sill or bottom plate of the shed. (The shed's super-structure will be fastened to the sill.) You can use 6- to 8-inch sill bolts or regular carriage bolts with nuts and washers. Hardware and home center stores sell them. Space the bolts about 4 feet apart and bury them in the concrete about 1½ inches in from the edge of the forms so that the threads project about 2 to 2½ inches above the surface of the concrete. Use a square to make sure that the bolts are absolutely vertical in the concrete.

Once the bolts are set, you can smooth the concrete surface around the bolt shanks with a float or trowel. Turn the nuts down on the threads when you are finished. This way the threads will be clean of concrete and other debris when the nuts are turned off to accept the sill.

It is possible to anchor the sill with concrete nails. Since the concrete is "green" (soft), the nails are easy to drive with a baby sledge hammer, and they hold tight. However, I recommend the sill bolt method since it is easy and ensures a tight joint between the sill and the concrete.

Finishing the concrete

When you have finished screeding, so that all voids have been filled and all high spots leveled, stop work and wait until the concrete surface is shiny. Then work over the surface with a wooden float. The float looks like a steel trowel, but it has a wooden base and handle. Use the float to force any visible pieces of

8. When the concrete surface looks shiny, smooth it with a wooden float. Keep the float flat on the surface; don't press on either edge. Fill in any low spots and push any pieces of aggregate below the surface. If you have to get onto the concrete to float it, use a piece of plywood as a kneeling board; then float away any indentations the board makes.

9. If you want a non-skid concrete surface, as shown here, drag a kitchen broom or push broom across the surface, after it has been floated. Just let the weight of the broom lightly rough up the concrete.

gravel below the surface of the concrete, and to smooth over slight imperfections left by the 2 × 4 screed.

After the area has been floated, it is time to finish the surface. If you want a smooth finish, go over the concrete's surface with a steel trowel, using a back-and-forth motion. Keep the flat of the blade on the work. If you tilt the trowel, you'll get a scored, washboard appearance. Go over the surface at least three times with the trowel, waiting 5 to 10 minutes between each session. If you want a non-slip surface, work the concrete with a broom. A broom finish is much easier to make than a trowel finish: just drag a push broom or regular kitchen broom (flat side down) across the floated surface. Whichever method you choose, you will have to work quickly from the time of the pour to the final finishing. Concrete is a fast-hardening material, and, once hardened, it can't be satisfactorily finished.

Concrete must be cured after it is finished. After the material has hardened for several hours after the finishing, moisten the surface with a fine spray from a garden hose, and keep the surface wet for several days. This can be done by covering the area, after sprinkling, with plastic sheeting to hold the moisture, or by sprinkling the surface three times a day for 3 to 5 days.

Form stripping

Let the slab cure and harden for at least 5 days before you strip the forms from the concrete. If you pry the forms carefully away from the concrete and wash them off thoroughly, you can use them for framing the shed.

You can pull the forms before you set the sill, or set the sill and then pull the forms. I left the forms in place since their straightedges can help guide the layout of the sills.

Fastening the sills

Use 2 × 4s that are as straight as possible for the sills. If you can obtain it, use pressure-treated lumber to deter rot. If you can't find it, coat the sills with a wood preservative before setting them. Buying pressure-treated 2 × 4s saves this messy procedure.

Mark and drill holes in the 2 × 4s for the sill bolts. It is best to set the two longer dimension sills first, then fill between them with the shorter ones. You get a tighter, more accurate fit this way.

Use the diagonal string method to square up the sills. The sills *must* sit square on the slab, even though the slab may be slightly out of square. To ensure a square fit, you can adjust the sills with shims as you bolt them down. The edge of the sills should be flush with or about 1/4 to 1/2 inch over

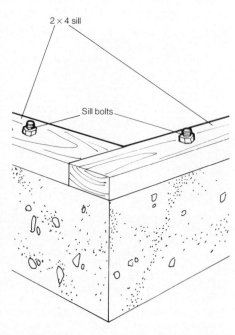

Sill installation. Drill holes in the 2 × 4 sills to match the sill bolt locations, and bolt the sills to the foundation.

the edge of the slab. The siding drops down over the sills and over part of the slab when it is nailed to the framing.

Once the sills are properly drilled, set, and squared, fasten them to the slab with the bolt washers and nuts.

Wall framing

The wall framing, which is made with 2 × 4s, is set 16 inches on center (oc), that is, the vertical 2 × 4s—called studs—are 16 inches apart, measured from the center of one 2 × 4 to the next.

Front and back walls. The best way to lay out the front and back walls is to position the top plate of each next to the sill plate. The length of the 2 × 4 top plate should match the length of the sill perfectly. (Read the section on Door Framing below before continuing.)

Starting at one end, mark the stud locations 16 inches oc on both plates —the top of the sill plate and the bottom of the top plate. If you do both at the same time, the marks will match.

If you are using 4 × 8-foot plywood siding, mark both plates at the point where the edge of the siding will fall when it is nailed in place. The edge of the siding should split a stud—that is, overlap the stud about half its width. If the stud mark—the center of the stud—*does not* match the edge of the siding, you will have to cheat the studs slightly one way or the other so you do have a match.

Be sure the stud location marks on both the top plate and the sill plate match exactly. An easy way to this is to mark the stud location on the ends of the top and sill plates. Then measure out 48 inches (the width of the siding), and mark this point. Then mark the stud location at the 48-inch mark, so that the stud splits the mark —half the stud for the first piece of siding, and half for the adjoining piece of siding. Then go back along the 48 inches and mark the remaining stud positions on both the top plate and the sill plate. They should be as close as possible to the 16-inch oc spacing, but it's all right if they are slightly off.

Nail the studs to the top plate, as they lie on the ground, using the marks for position. Nail down through the top plate and into the studs.

Tip the stud and plate assembly

2. After the sills are in place, mark the stud locations on them and on the top plates at the same time. Then nail the top plate to the studs, as shown here, to make the front and back wall frames. (The side wall studs cannot be prefabricated like this, since they must be cut individually—at an angle—at the top plate.) After nailing the front and back wall studs, have a helper lift the framing into place and hold it while you toenail the bottom of the studs to the sill plate at the marked locations. Be sure each stud is plumb. When one wall framing has been nailed in place, brace it with a length of 2 × 4 until you can tie it to the other wall.

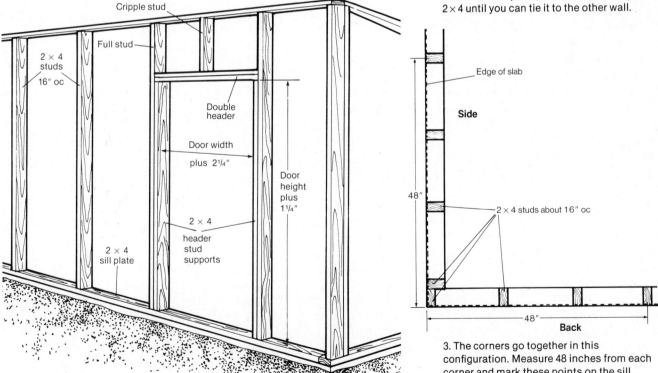

Cripple stud

Full stud

2 × 4 studs
16″ oc

Double header

Door width
plus 2¼″

Door height plus 1¼″

2 × 4
header stud supports

2 × 4
sill plate

Edge of slab

Side

48″

2 × 4 studs about 16″ oc

48″

Back

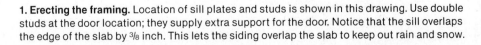

1. **Erecting the framing.** Location of sill plates and studs is shown in this drawing. Use double studs at the door location; they supply extra support for the door. Notice that the sill overlaps the edge of the slab by ⅜ inch. This lets the siding overlap the slab to keep out rain and snow.

3. The corners go together in this configuration. Measure 48 inches from each corner and mark these points on the sill. They indicate the vertical lines where the edges of the siding will fall. Reposition the studs at these points so that, in each case, the edges of the siding split the stud.

up onto the sill and toenail the bottom of the studs to the sill at the marks. You will need a helper to hold the wall while you nail it in place. When you have finished nailing, brace the wall with a couple of 2 × 4s while you construct the other walls —which you mark, assemble, and fasten in the same way.

Door framing. The door can be installed in any wall in any spot you choose. It's a good idea to space the studs for the door as you assemble that wall. (The windows can be cut into a wall after it has been assembled.)

The specifications call for a prehung door—that is, a door mounted in a complete frame—but you can use a standard door that isn't prehung, if you wish.

If the door is prehung, measure the width of the door and the jambs. Add 1 inch to this measurement. The additional inch allows ½ inch on each side for leveling and plumbing the door in the framing.

If the door is not prehung, measure the width of the door. Add the width of the jambs (¾-inch a side or a total of 1½ inches), and allow an additional inch for leveling and plumbing the door—½ inch per side.

Then lay out the wall framing, maintaining the stud spacing mentioned above and placing the door framing where you want it, even though the door framing may shorten the distance between the last stud and the door studs. (The door itself is not installed at this point.)

The door framing uses double studs on each side. Use one full stud on each side of the door—one that extends from the sill to the top plate. (You can use one of the wall framing studs as part of the door framing.) The second stud should be the height of the door plus the width of the top jamb plus a ½-inch leveling allowance. The second studs are nailed inside the full studs, and a double 2 × 4 header is then nailed on top of the second, shorter studs. See the illustration of this framing.

A cripple stud is nailed between

4. To frame the side walls, cut the side-wall corner studs at a 10° angle so that the side-wall top plates will butt against the front- and back-wall top plates. The back-wall joint is shown here. Nail the corner studs in place, and then cut the top plate to fit the angle cuts at both corners, as shown here. Nail into the ends of the corner studs through the face of the top plate.

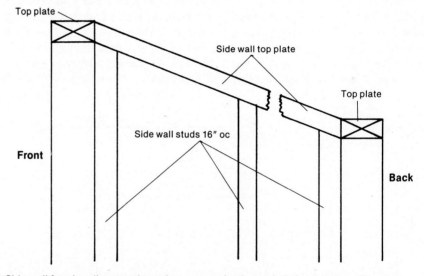

5. Side-wall framing diagram shows how you make the roof pitch angle by nailing the side-wall studs to the front- and back-wall studs and then cutting the top plate to fit.

the door header 2 × 4s and the top plate. It strengthens the door opening and gives you a nailing point for the siding.

The back-wall framing is shorter than the front-wall framing, which produces the roof pitch. In the plan provided, the front wall is 10 feet from sill to top plate and the back wall is 8 feet from sill to top plate. You can modify this height any way you want, but you should maintain at least a 6-inch difference so that the roof will drain. Remember to use the module concept.

Side-wall framing. The side-wall framing has to be cut on top at an angle. The angle in this plan is 10 degrees.

To frame the side walls, set the studs at each end, nailing them to the front and back wall framing. Then cut the side wall top plate to fit between the front and back wall top plates. Nail it in place. Then mark the side sills for stud locations, as you did the front and back walls.

The marking of the siding for stud position is important. Set a stud at one corner and measure out 48

6. The rest of the side wall framing is measured, angle cut, and nailed into position one stud at a time. Set each stud in place, plumb it, mark the angle of the cut against the top plate, and cut the stud to fit. Toenail the stud at the bottom sill plate, plumb it, and then nail into the end of the stud through the face of the top plate. The siding was tacked on in this photo to show the angle of the side-wall top plate.

inches—the width of the siding. The stud at this point is used as a nailer. The siding should split this stud. If the wall is longer than 96 inches, mark each 48-inch increment along the sill and top plate, and place a stud at each marked point. The other studs should be set about 16 inches oc between the 48-inch marks. If you are off the measurement just slightly, it doesn't really matter because you can cheat the nailing points somewhat.

The same measuring system would be used for lap or drop siding. You want to stop and start two lengths of siding on the same split stud. If you prefer drop siding to plywood sheets for your exterior, you should use 3/8-inch C-D plywood sheathing underneath the drop siding. In either case, your measurements will be the same.

With a helper, set the studs plumb (vertical) on the sill marks and mark the cutting angles on the edge of the studs where they meet the top plate. Mark each stud separately, and double-check the measurement to make sure each stud is plumb as you make the mark. Then make the angle cut; the stud should fit the space between sill and top plate perfectly.

Toenail the studs to the bottom plate. Fasten the studs at the top plate by driving the nails down through the plate into the studs.

The stiffeners. When you have completed the wall framing, nail pieces of siding to it at opposite corners. This will stiffen the structure, so that it won't wobble so much.

Roof framing and sheathing

Measure and mark the 2×4 rafters that form the roof framing. For my shed, I used 2×4×12s to give a 2-foot overhang at the front and a 1-foot overhang at the back of the shed.

Climb up on a ladder and square and mark the first rafter for the bird's-nest cuts that are made where it meets the top plates of the front and back walls. Double-check the measurements and the cutting angles. Saw the cuts as nearly perfectly as you can. Then test the rafter by inserting the cut rafter over the top plates. Put a square on the top plate and rafter. If the fit is somewhat sloppy, use a butt chisel to make the cut fit the plates. When you're satisfied with the fit, use this rafter as a template for cutting the other rafters. Do just one rafter at a time, and test each for fit; nail each one into position on the top plates. The spacing should be 24 inches oc. Drive the nails down through the narrow side of the rafter, through the cut, and into the top plate.

After you have set two or three rafters and nailed them, cut another rafter without bird's-nest notches and fasten it to the outside edge of

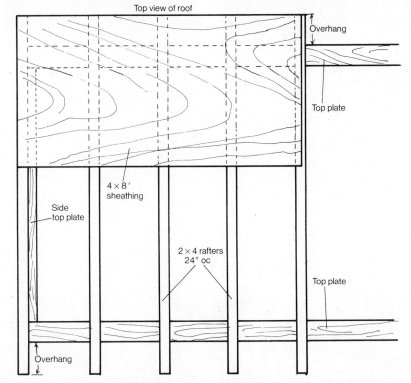

1. Rafters and roofing. Roof diagram, with the walls in position, shows rafter and sheathing location. The 2×4 rafters are set 24 inches OC. The rafters overhang at the front and back of the shed. The overhang can be as wide as you want it; here it is 1 foot at the back and 2 feet at the front.

2. This is the angle cut made in a rafter at the place where it meets the top plate of the *back* wall. It was cut with a portable electric circular saw, but you can use a crosscut handsaw or even an electric sabre saw. Keep the cut as square as possible.

3. This is the bird's nest cut made in a rafter at the place where it meets the top plate of the *front* wall. The straight cuts were made with a crosscut handsaw, and the bottom cut with a sabre saw. Keep the bird's nest cut as square as you can.

the top plate on the end wall. Be sure this rafter is level with the inside rafters. Position a sheet of sheathing lengthwise across the rafters, butting one edge against the outside edge of the rafter that you nailed to the outside of the top plate. Move over to the other edge of the sheathing and make a mark on the top plate. This is the nailing point for the next rafter in the series; two pieces of sheathing should split this rafter. You now can measure from this rafter to the other end wall for the remaining rafters.

Finish notching and nailing all the rafters, and mark and cut the last rafter to fit on the outside edge of the top plate on the far side of the shed.

The rest of the roof sheathing is now nailed to each of the rafters; the

outside edges of the sheathing overlap the outside rafters. (See illustrations.)

Cover the roof sheathing with 55-pound building felt (tarpaper), overlapping the edges by about 6 inches. Use roofing nails. Cut the paper on the ground to the correct length and have it passed up to the roof. This is easier than trying to unroll and cut the paper on the sheathing.

The roofing

Since the roof is a simple construction, without valleys, stacks, or chimney, you can start the roofing by laying a single row of shingles upside down along the bottom edge of the sheathing.

If you wish, you can nail a drip edge along the edges of the sheath-

4. Test both rafter cuts by positioning the rafter on both top plates. Use a carpenter's square to check the angle between the face of the rafter and the edge of each top plate. If the cuts do not fit to your satisfaction, trim them with a chisel. When the cuts are correct, use the rafter as a cutting pattern (template) for all the other rafters. After you cut each rafter, test it against the top plates, and trim the cuts with a chisel to make the correct fit. When all rafters have been properly cut and fitted, nail them to the top plates.

5. The notched rafters are nailed to the top plate. Nail through the top edge of the rafter and into the face of the plate.

ing. Drip edges are extruded from plastic or metal; they help prevent water from flowing backward under the shingles. (See drawing.)

The shingles are laid in overlapping rows beginning at the lower end of the roof. Stagger the shingles within the rows. You can cut them to fit before you nail them, or you can cut them along the edges of the sheathing after all courses are nailed. Use a utility knife for cutting.

Each shingle takes four nails; the nailing points usually are marked on each shingle. If possible, avoid exposing the nailheads; the shingles should cover them. Drive the heads of the roofing nails just flush with the top surface of the shingles; don't crack shingles by driving nail heads

below the surface. The nails should be driven below the adhesive or self-sealing strips.

After the shingles have been nailed and trimmed, cover any exposed nailheads with daubs of roofing compound. You can buy the compound in cartridges that allow application with a caulking gun shell.

The siding

The siding is nailed to the studs, sill, and top plate. At the sill and at the top plate, space the nails about 3 inches apart. Along the edges of the siding, space the nails about 3 inches apart where they are driven into the studs. Space the nails about 6 inches apart where they are driven into intermediate studs, fire block-

ing, cripple studs, headers, and jambs.

On the front side of the building and at both sides, you will have to cut the siding to fit. Use a straight cut on the front, and mark the angle cuts on the sides. You can hold the siding in place while a helper marks the angles. Use a straightedge or chalkline to make the cutoff mark.

Nail a piece of 2×4 blocking between the studs where the horizontal edges of the siding join. This blocking provides a second place to nail in addition to the studs. It's also a good idea to place a line of caulking compound along the edges of the fill siding, just before you set the siding and nail it. The caulking forms a waterproof seal between the joints.

6. The end rafters are not notched, but are nailed to the top plates of three walls. Before nailing the rafters, you should nail some of the siding to the corners to strengthen the framing. The rest of the siding can be applied later. Nail the plywood sheathing to the rafters. Cut the plywood sheets so that you can stagger all the joints between sections. Run the grain of the sheathing horizontally. Start nailing the sheathing at the back wall and work up to the front wall. This gives you a working platform.

7. Use shingles laid upside down along the edge of the sheathing as a starter course. Then start the first shingle course at the low end of the roof, nailing it on top of the starters. Although you can buy self-sticking shingles, it's a good idea to apply daubs of roofing cement under the edges.

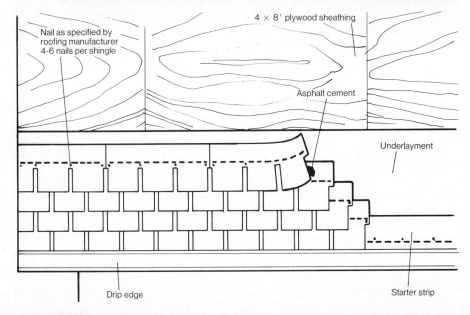

Nail as specified by roofing manufacturer 4-6 nails per shingle

4 × 8′ plywood sheathing

Asphalt cement

Underlayment

Drip edge

Starter strip

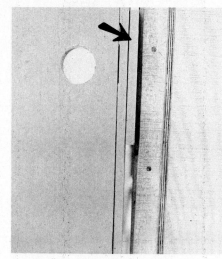

1. Installing the door. Cut the sill plate at the bottom of the door flush with the studs to make room for the door framing. You can use a handsaw or a sabre saw (if the blade is long enough). Cut the sill to just above the slab. Then knock out the length of wood with a hammer. Any rough edges will be covered by the door jamb.

2. Fill the space between the door jambs and the framing. For this, I used scrap from the roof sheathing and the 'packing' board from the bottom of the prehung door. The door must swing in the opening freely. Be sure you level and plumb it before you final-nail it into place.

3. Set the door jamb (right) out from the framing (left) by the thickness of the siding, so that the siding will fit flush with the jamb.

The door

Installing a prehung door is simple: just fit the jambs and header jamb between the studs, and nail the door through the jambs to the framing.

The door has to be plumbed (leveled), so that it opens and shuts easily. The door should open outward, to leave more space within the shed.

To install the door:

■ Remove a section of the sill plate, as shown in the photos. Nail the sill to the slab next to the door opening, using concrete nails, if the sill bolts do not hold the sill tightly at this point.

■ Insert the door in the framing, between the two double studs and beneath the header.

■ There should be about ½ inch of space between the side jambs of the door and the framing, and between the top jamb and the framing. Cut short pieces of ½-inch-thick plywood from the roof sheathing scrap, and block in the space between the jambs and framing, plumbing the door as you go.

You may need a couple of cedar or pine shingles for use as shims. The shims, wedged between the blocks and the jambs, will allow leveling adjustment. Just tap the shims between the blocks and jambs until you get a level fit. Then saw off any projecting wood, so that the shims are flush with the edges of the jambs. Cover the framing, the edge of the siding, and part of the jamb from the front of the door with a trim strip.

The ½-inch spacer blocks don't have to be butted together; just stagger them around the jambs, so that the jambs are solid.

Nail into the framing through the jambs and blocks. Use finishing nails, and countersink the nailheads.

If you decide to install the door before installing the siding, be sure the door jamb extends far enough out from the framing to enable the siding to fit flush with the front edge of the jamb. (See photograph.)

Doors tend to warp very quickly—even doors made for exterior use. Seal the door with the same finish you intend to use on the shed. Coat the front, back, and all edges of the door, as well as the door jambs and header.

■ Install the lock set. Most prehung doors are prebored for the locks, and the jambs are mortised for the strike-plate. The lock set package will have installation instructions to follow.

■ Trim the door. The specifications call for 1 × 4s mitered together, but you can butt-join the corners if you want; butt joints are easier, and you won't see the joints after they are stained or painted.

If you want a fancy trim, you can buy casing moldings, and miter the corners.

The door frame inside can be left untrimmed, or if you plan to hang gypsum-board, you can use a trim molding to finish off the entrance.

The window

A prehung window is very simple to install. The window comes complete with brick molding, and the lights are even glazed and secured with glazing compound.

Have a helper hold the window against the siding at the spot you want the window located.

Make sure the window is level and plumb; then trace the outline of the window on the siding. Use the inside window framing as the tracing edge. When you are finished, doublecheck your measurements, and follow these steps:

■ With a sabre saw or circular saw, carefully make a pocket cut in the siding, running the sawblade along the marks. Easy does it; you're cutting through the siding and *part-way* through one or two studs. Your power saw will have enough zip to make this cut, but don't force the saw through the wood.

■ When the cut is made, finish the corners with a handsaw.

■ Go inside the shed and finish sawing through the stud(s) with a

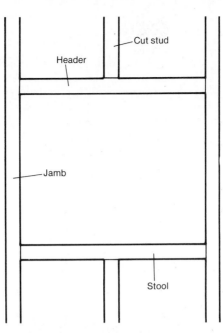

2. Window framing diagram calls for only single header, stool, and jambs because very little weight is involved in this superstructure. You can double the studs at the side of the window and the header at the top of the window if you wish.

handsaw. Then knock out the hole with a hammer. The cut piece should pop right out; you shouldn't have to force it.

■ Shorten the sawed stud(s) another 1½-inches—the thickness of a 2 × 4.

■ Toenail two sill-to-top plate studs at the edge of the opening you cut.

■ Cut a 2 × 4 to make a header for the top of the opening; then cut a 2 × 4 to make a stool for the bottom of the opening. Nail these 2 × 4s to the two sill-to-top plate studs and to the cut-off studs. The opening is now framed with 2 × 4s.

1. Installing the window. In this construction, the window was located after the siding was on; this was accomplished by drawing the outline of the window on the siding, using the prehung window as a pattern. Then a pocket cut in the siding was made with a portable electric circular saw. The corners of the cut were made with a crosscut handsaw. The top and bottom cuts were made through a stud, and the final stud cuts were made inside the shed with a crosscut handsaw. The studs and headers were fitted into the space.

3. The window framing inside the shed. Since the window frame did not fill the space between three studs, a jamb stud was added along the right side of the window. The header and the stool extend from stud to stud.

4. The finished window. The prehung window slips into the pocket cut and is nailed to the framing with countersunk 10d or 12d finishing nails. Fill the nail holes with glazing or caulking compound. Use high-quality caulking compound to seal the window frame where the moulding joins the siding; fill the top crack completely.

■ Insert the window into the opening from the outside. It should fit perfectly. If it doesn't, find out where it's binding and use a chisel to remove enough wood from the 2 × 4 frame to free the window.

■ Level the window in the opening by inserting cedar or pine shingle shims between the 2 × 4 frame and the sides and top of the window (jambs). Cut off any excess material.
    Nail the window through the jambs and into the 2 × 4 framework. Use finishing nails, and countersink them.

■ Nail a thin strip of wood over the small crack at the bottom of the window, where the window framing meets the siding; this seals out the weather.

■ Caulk around the window where the brick molding meets the siding. Caulk the top first; then work down the sides and across the bottom. Work the caulking into the cracks. It is critical to keep out moisture at these points.

In conventional construction, double framing headers and jamb headers are installed for doors and windows. They are not used in this shed, however, since there is little weight on either the door or the window frame. (The extra studs handle the brunt of the weight.) You can, however, provide for double framing by adding one more 2 × 4 × 10 to the materials list.

The soffit and fascia

Measure, mark, and cut the ¼-inch plywood sheet for the soffit, which is nailed to the underside of the overhanging rafters at the front and back of the shed.
    You will have to splice the soffit board on both front and back. Measure the pieces of the soffit so that they meet in the middle of a rafter, splitting it for a nailing surface. You do not need a soffit at the sides of the structure.
    The fascia is a piece of 1 × 6 that you measure, mark, and nail to the

Installing the soffit and fascia. Measure, cut, and nail the plywood for the soffit to the undersides of the rafters. Then measure, cut, and nail the fascia boards to the ends of the rafters, covering both the edges of the plywood roof sheathing and the soffit. The butt joints of the fascia should be caulked. The fascia is also nailed to the face of the end rafters so that the fascia matches all around the shed. For a final trim, nail 1 × 6 boards to the siding where it meets the soffit (not shown here).

Corner trim. Trim the corners with 1 × 4s lap-joined together. Nail through the trim, into the siding, and into the corner framing pieces. Caulk the joints between the siding and the trim pieces.

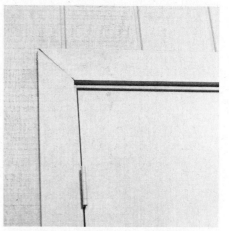

Door casing. Use 1 × 4s, either butt-joined or mitered, as shown here, for the door casing. Use finishing nails to attach this trim; countersink the nails, and fill the holes with glazing or caulking compound. If you mis-cut a miter joint slightly, just fill the joint with caulking compound. Caulk the joint between the trim and the siding at the top and side jambs.

vertical ends of the rafters. Do not nail it to the edges of the soffit board. Install 1 × 6 fascia on both sides, so that the roof line trim is the same all around. You will have an angle cut to make at each end of the side fascia boards. Just hold each board in position and mark it for the cut. Gutters are not used in this design, but you can install a gutter at the back of the shed if you want to. Gutter hangers are fastened under the first course of

shingles; the back of the gutter hangs against the fascia. Give the fascia two coats of finish before you hang the gutter. Caulk any butt joints along the length of the fascia.

Trim and blocking

The shed, for all practical purposes, is now finished.

The corners are trimmed with lap-jointed 1×4s that are nailed to the siding.

The 1×4 boards also may be used as trim pieces under the soffit, front and back. The ends are squared with the edge of the siding.

At this point, if you are building the shed described here, you should have less than half a sheet of siding left and some end pieces of 2×4s. The siding can be cut into strips and used for shelving inside the shed; the 2×4s can be cut and nailed between the studs for additional framing support and for between-the-stud storage.

Finishing the shed

Plywood siding should be finished with either pigmented stain or a high-quality exterior paint. The specifications call for a pigmented stain because plywood usually is plugged with synthetic patches that do not absorb regular stain as wood does. Use the same type of finish on the trim; it may be applied with brush, roller, or spray gun.

The inside workshop

The workshop inside the shed, like the shed itself, follows a simple design. It extends along one wall and is made from a single sheet of perforated hardboard, a 3-0/6-8 solid-core door as a workbench, and two pieces of 4×4.

Use ¼-inch-thick, tempered, perforated hardboard for the tool storage board. Let it extend from the top plate of the shed to the sill, and nail it directly to the studs.

To set up the workbench, first cut the 4×4-inch posts 34 inches long and nail them to two corners on the long side of the solid-core door to act as leg supports. Drive the nails through the face of the door and into the leg supports. Nail a 2×4 that is the same length as the door horizontally across the studs and through the hardboard, so that its top edge is 34 inches from the floor. This 2×4 is a ledger strip on which the back edge of the door will rest. Set the door on its leg supports and on the 2×4 ledger; then nail through the face of

A small prefabricated shed. This galvanized steel outdoor shed has a sliding metal door; the 5×4-foot size provides 16 square feet of storage space.

A large prefabricated shed. A gabled roof and double-doors are features of this metal shed; it's available in sizes from 6 × 5 to 14 × 14 feet. Heights run from 69 to 83 inches; areas from 30 to 175 square feet.

the door and into the 2×4 ledger strip. This provides a rock-solid workbench. However, you can remove the workbench whenever you wish by simply pulling the nails in the ledger.

When the workbench becomes worn, cover it with a sheet of ⅛-inch-thick tempered hardboard nailed to the door face. When the hardboard surface becomes worn, pull the nails, turn the hardboard sheet over, and use the clean side.

Between-the-studs storage space can be created by toenailing the scrap 2×4 ends, which were cut from studs and rafters, horizontally into the studs.

My work area was finished with a sunny yellow flat paint on the tool board and a light blue on the storage shelves and workbench. These colors reflect light from the window and the open door and from overhead lighting mounted on the collar beams.

Another tool storage plan would involve cutting the perforated hardboard in half and mounting the half pieces side-by-side to the studs. This would fill one complete wall of the design offered here.

If a shed is not in your plans at the moment, you still can assemble the workbench at the end of a garage or along a wall. The bench takes up only 30 inches of floor space.

Prefabricated sheds

You can buy two types of outdoor shed: ready-built and ready-to-assemble. The ready-builts usually are made of galvanized steel. High-quality metal sheds feature double roof beams at the roof's ridge for added strength, hot-dipped galvanizing to resist rust and corrosion, and one-piece doors for sturdiness.

The models that you erect yourself are cut from chipboard or plywood and have solid wood doors and trim. Wooden sheds have a long-term, nonrusting advantage over many metal units.

Sizes of both types of shed run from 4×2 feet up to garage size. Some models meet the National Standards for Storage Buildings, which are listed by the American Society for Testing and Materials (ASTM).

Most shed manufacturers design their sheds to conform to standard local code requirements as to building size and construction design that prevail throughout the nation. However, before you invest in a prefab or ready-built shed, be sure to learn the specific code restrictions for your neighborhood. Remember to lay out the plan of the building on the ground with stakes and string before beginning to erect it. It is easier to move the string than the building.

The tools you'll need

For a ready-made building, you'll need screwdrivers (both standard slot and Phillips head), pliers, a sledge hammer, a shovel, a tape measure, and a carpenter's level.

For a prefabricated building, you'll need the tools listed above plus a crosscut saw, chisels, and an adjustable wrench.

If you decide to place a concrete foundation for a prefab or ready-built shed, you will use the same tools and procedures as were specified for the build-it-yourself plan described earlier in this chapter. Most manufacturers of outdoor sheds and buildings include a foundation plan with their

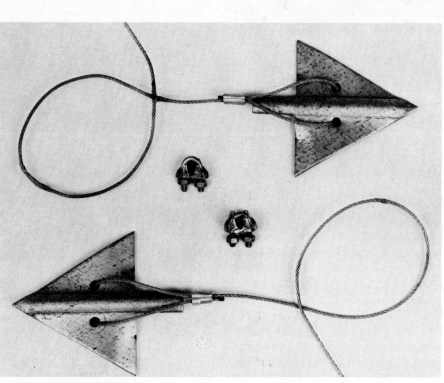

Anchoring devices. Prefabricated sheds can be secured to the ground with anchor kits. Some anchors are arrow-shaped; others have augers on the ends that twist into the ground.

products. Some buildings are set on bare ground and staked into place. Others require concrete block footings, plywood floors on block footings, steel floors, or concrete slabs. Some designs include anchoring devices, which are usually auger rods with screweyes at one end. In such models, the augers screw into the ground, and metal cable is secured to each screweye and through or over the building. Installation instructions are furnished by the manufacturer. Don't leave the store without them.

Metal shed maintenance

To maintain a metal shed, hose it down twice a year, apply a coat of quality paste wax to the metal surfaces after each hosing, and buff the surfaces. If the shed has a metal floor, be sure to keep it clean and waxed, too.

If you discover any rust spots, remove the rust with steel wool, and then cover the bare spots with two coats of metal paint of the same color as the rest of the shed. If the shed needs repainting, use a high-

quality metal paint or a latex paint that has been formulated especially for metals. The paint container's label gives this information.

Paint wooden buildings with latex, alkyd, latex/acrylic, or oil-based paint. If you are repainting over a deep red, blue, or green color with a lighter-color paint, expect to apply two coats of paint for a satisfactory covering job.

If your shed has fiberglass panels, you can keep them looking new by washing them with household detergent and water. Rinse after soaping. If you want to paint the fiberglass, you may be able to use a paint formula tailored for marine use. Check with a retailer who sells marine supplies or with an auto parts store that sells auto finishes. Most home centers and hardware stores don't sell marine coatings.

Ninety percent of any successful paint job is a matter of correctly preparing the surface for paint. Scrub the surfaces to be painted with a stiff brush and buckets of clean water and household detergent; then rinse well with a garden hose.

Work from the bottom of the building to the top. If you work from the top down, dirty detergent and water will streak the unwashed surface. Washing the surface removes dirt and the normal chalk dust from old paint, and reveals where scraping and repair jobs will have to be done.

After the wood has dried, remove all peeling paint, spot-prime the bare spots, and fill all cracks with a good exterior caulking compound.

General storage

Storage space is where you find it. It can be in front of your car in the garage, in an outdoor carport storage area, in a crawl space under a porch or split-level house, overhead in a shed, overhead in a garage, in a basement room.

Perforated hardboard is ideal for hanging storage. You can buy an array of hooks for the holes that can hold anything from light containers to sledge hammers. Buy the 1/4-inch-thick, tempered material; it provides better support. Also, it's a good idea to paint the hardboard on all sides and edges before installing it. The finish deters warping and delamination, an especially desirable protection in damp locales.

Hardware and home center stores sell a wide variety of shelving components. You can use regular shelf brackets with 1 × 6 (or wider) boards fastened to the brackets, or you can buy adjustable shelving with metal runners and clips to hold the shelves in place. Ready-made steel shelving is also a good buy, and there are designs for garage and utility room storage that can accommodate almost anything you want to set on the shelves.

Steel cabinets with door locks make excellent storage places for chemicals and sharp tools. Office-supply retailers stock them.

Kitchen cabinets also make ideal workbenches and storage areas. You can sometimes buy used cabinets for little or nothing at remodeling sites. Phone a few contractors in your area and ask them about it. Also

Garage storage. Simple but extremely functional steel shelving creates garage storage tailored to the front end of a car. The shelves are weight-rated; they'll hold hundreds of pounds. Sold knocked down, the units can be assembled quickly with just a wrench and a screwdriver.

Hanging wall shelves. Most hardware and home center stores stock many sizes of shelves made of metal, wood, simulated wood, plywood, and plastic, that can be hung almost anywhere.

check home improvement outlets that sell cabinets. These retailers may be able to steer you to a customer who is replacing old cabinets, and you may be able to buy them at a good price.

4 Lawnmower Maintenance

This chapter discusses reel lawnmowers, rotary mowers (including electric mowers), self-propelled walk-behind mowers, and small lawn tractors (rider mowers). Gasoline engines, both two- and four-cycle, and pull starters are discussed separately in Chapter 5.

REEL LAWNMOWERS

Known in some parts as an "Armstrong," the push-type reel mower, without engine, is still one of the simplest and best grass-cutting machines available. Because it has to be pushed, it may not be the most efficient machine to use for cutting large expanses of turf grass. But for small townhouse and garden apartment lots, this equipment does the job with a fine manicured look.

Power-driven reel mowers are more complicated because of the engine. You'll find information on servicing and repairing small gasoline engines in Chapter 5. The other parts of both push and powered mowers are discussed here.

Reel mower problems

The mower is hard to push

The handle of a push mower may be made of wood or metal with a T crossbar for hand grips. If the handle is loose or broken, it will sit too high or too low, making the mower difficult to push. If it's too high, the force on the handle will be downward into the ground and not forward. If it's too low, the force will be upward, slightly

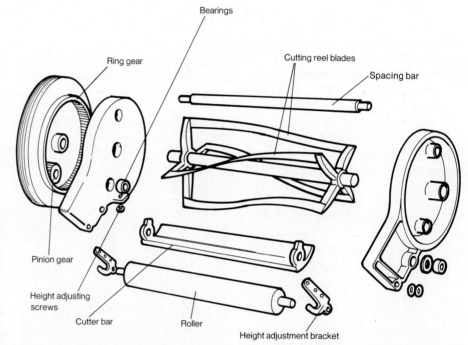

Anatomy of a hand reel mower. The two main problem areas are the cutting reel blades and the roller. Both need constant adjustment, sharpening, and maintenance.

tipping the mower back on the roller. Ideally, the forward thrust should cause the mower to plane across the turf grass.

If the handle is wood, the T is fastened to the handle with a bolt and nut assembly that is tightened by turning a nut recessed into the underside of the handle. If the T is broken and you can't find a replacement part, you might be able to have it duplicated at a cabinet or millwork shop. The handle from the T to the mower may also work loose or break at the mower connection. This connection is critical since it determines the angle of the handle.

Looseness results when the bolts that run through the metal bracket that is fastened to the handle enlarge the holes in the wood. If this happens, buy several metal ferrules (sold for gutter spikes at hardware or home center stores). Cut the ferrules with a hacksaw to the width of the handle and insert them through the holes in the handle. Assemble the bolts and nuts and tighten them. Use flat washers under the heads of the bolts and nuts to distribute the tightening pressure.

If this make-do trick doesn't work, the handle will have to be replaced. If a replacement can't be found, you

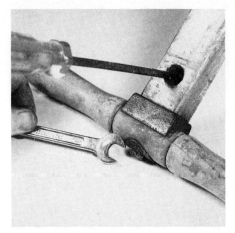

Adjusting the handle. To remove or tighten the handle on a hand reel mower, you usually have to wedge the nut recessed in back of the handle and turn the square nut on top of the handle. Use a screwdriver for a wedge.

1. Maintaining wheel gears. Access to wheel ring and pinion gears is easy. Just remove the bolts or cotter keys holding the wheel together. Mark the holding fasteners and keep them together so you can return the fasteners to the same wheels.

2. Dirty and grit-filled grease causes several problems with ring and pinion gears. Clean away this grease at the start of each mowing season and replace it with a nonfibrous, heat-resistant grease.

may be able to fashion a handle from 5/4 stock cut to the width needed; use ash, hickory, or oak. Or have a cabinet or millwork shop duplicate the handle for you. The shop (see the Yellow Pages of your telephone directory) will need the old handle for a pattern, so take it along.

If the mower is difficult to push, the problem could be string or debris gathered around the axles of the roller or the wheels. If this isn't the hang-up, make sure that:

the blades on the cutting reel are properly bypassing the cutting bar

the drive chain is clean and lubricated

the clutch control rod is engaging the clutch assembly properly

the drive belt (if not a chain drive) is tight on the pulleys

the adjusting knob for the roller height is properly tightened

the cutting blades are not bent

the roller and the cutting bar are in straight alignment

The gears are sluggish

This problem occurs on both hand-pushed and engine-driven reel mowers. Look for trouble first in the wheel gears of the manual model

and in the wheel, pinion, and ring gears of the power model.

The wheels of a hand-pushed model are held to an axle with a bolt and cotter key or just a bolt that turns off counterclockwise. The wheel is shaped like a clam shell; the gears for the cutting blades mesh with gears along the inside rim of the wheel in many models.

These gears seldom break because little torque is put on them. What does happen is that dirt accumulates in the lubricating grease on the gears, which causes the gears to become sluggish and hard to turn.

Try cleaning the gears outdoors with gasoline applied with a throw-away paint brush. When the gears are flushed clean, relubricate them with cup grease (not too much) and reassemble the wheels.

On power models, look for trouble in pinion and ring gears, which are located next to the drive wheel. Like those in hand-pushed mowers, these gears can also become clogged with dirt-filled grease, causing them to be sluggish. Use the same gasoline and brush technique to clean them; lubricate them according to the manufacturer's recommendations and reassemble the parts.

Look also at the chain drive, where the lubricant may be causing the mower to be sluggish. The drive may be cleaned with gasoline or WD-40,

then lubricated and reassembled. Techniques for this are shown later in this chapter (see under Self-Propelled Walk-Behind Mowers).

The blades bind

The cutting bar across the bottom of the mower on all reel models should be adjusted so it just touches, or bypasses, the blades on the cutting reel. If this adjustment is just a tad off, the blades will bind. In fact, you may not be able to turn the cutting reel at all.

The adjustment is made at the cutting bar, not at the reel. Try tightening or loosening the screws along the edge of the bar to correct the binding.

If adjusting the cutting bar or repositioning the cutting reel at the frame or housing doesn't help, the binding may be caused by bent blades, since both the cutting bar and the cutting reel are stationary.

Blades are bent when a hard object—a stick, a rock—jams between the cutting reel and the cutting bar. You often can straighten a minor bend by tapping the blade lightly with a hammer (see illustration).

If the blades are badly bent, replace the cutting reel with a new one. It is very difficult, even for a professional, to straighten badly bent blades satisfactorily.

Out-of-balance blades usually are caused by bent blades that put the cutting reel out of round. If the cutting blades are out of balance, replace the reel. Straightening generally isn't satisfactory.

On power mowers, broken or badly aligned pinion or ring gears sometimes can cause the blades to bind. This is not a common cause, but it's worth checking if bent blades are not the problem. Remove the gear cover and the drive wheel for inspection, and replace any broken parts that you find.

Adjustments to reel mowers

Sharpening blades

The following technique is really a touch-up procedure and is not a substitute for a professional sharpening job.

The best way to touch up the cutting reel blades and the cutting bar is to use auto valve grinding paste and a trick called backlapping.

First make sure that the cutting blades and the cutting bar are in alignment and that the two components just bypass each other all along the cutting edge. If they do not, the trouble is probably a bent blade. Straighten it (explained above) or take it to a pro.

Use a single- or double-cut flat file (double-cut is best) to remove any nicks or metal burrs along the cutting edges of both the blades and the bar (see illustration).

Next cover the blades with a thin coating of grinding compound. You can use your fingers for this. Spread out the compound evenly on the cutting surfaces.

Prop up the mower so you can turn the reel with the wheels. (If the mower is engine-powered, be sure to disconnect the spark plug.) Turn the cutting reel slowly *backwards*, so that the grinding compound is squeezed between the cutting blades and the cutting bar. The grinding compound sharpens both cutting edges at the same time as they pass each other.

When you think the blades are

Straightening blades. Try to straighten a bent cutting blade by tapping it lightly with a hammer on the flat side of the blade near the cutting edge.

Smoothing blades. You can remove nicks from the cutting bar with a smooth or double-cut flat file. File away from the edge and keep the file flat along the surface.

1. Sharpening blades. You can sharpen reel blades at home; the process, called backlapping, uses automobile valve grinding compound. Smear it along the blades and the cutting bar, then rotate the blades *backward.* You will have to repeat this treatment several times. Make sure the entire blade touches the cutting bar as the reel is rotated. Remove the compound after sharpening.

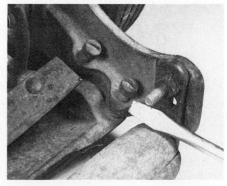

1. Adjusting cutting bars. The cutting bar is usually adjusted with screws so that the cutting blades move across it in a uniform slice. Rotate the reel very slowly as you make the cutter bar adjustment. You will have to test each blade. If one blade is off more than another blade, you will have to make a compromise setting. Just try to get the bar even.

2. To test the sharpness after backlapping the reel, insert newspaper between the blades and the cutting bar and rotate the reel forward. It may take several trys before you get the newspaper in the right position. The blades and cutter bar should cut the paper as cleanly as a good, sharp pair of scissors would.

2. Some cutting bars have a stiffening bar mounted along the grass side of the bar. If this bar is screw-mounted, the screws may loosen, causing the mower to drag and catch on debris. If possible, tighten these screws. If you can't and you are having a problem, have a machine shop run a smooth welding bead along the joint between the stiffening bar and cutting bar.

sharp, wipe off the compound so the blades are clean. Then adjust the cutting bar so the bar and the cutting blades just meet along the entire length of the blades. Test for blade sharpness (see illustration).

If this grinding compound treatment doesn't work, it's likely that the blades, cutter bar, or both are so dull that touch-up is impossible. Take the mower to a professional for sharpening.

Warning: Do not take the cutting reel off the mower and try to grind the blades sharp on a power grinder or a sharpening stone locked into the chuck of a power drill. What almost always happens is that the grinding takes the temper out of the metal or ruins the straightedge. When this happens, both the reel and the cutting bar must be replaced.

Adjusting mower cutting height

To adjust the height of cut on a reel mower, move the roller up or down. To raise the cutters, that is, to adjust the mower so that the grass is cut taller, you actually lower the roller. To cut the grass shorter, you raise the roller.

This adjustment can be tricky since there are two bolts, nuts, or handles to loosen and tighten on each end of the roller. If the roller is not level across the width of the mower, the grass is cut at a slight angle. Worse, the cutting blades and bar are put into a bind, and both could be damaged.

Make all height adjustments on a smooth, level surface such as a concrete garage floor. Doublecheck the level of the roller and then check the mower cut on grass. If the cut is not level, readjust the roller.

Rollers may be in one or in three pieces; they may be made of metal or wood. They require little maintenance. However, the roller axles should be kept clean and lubricated, and the roller surfaces should be cleaned if they become encrusted with dirt or mud.

Wood rollers tend to split where the axle is inserted into the roller. This is usually caused by misalign-

1 **Setting rollers.** Rollers must be set parallel with the cutting bar on reel mowers. The roller shown here was purposely off-set. The right side would cut grass high; the left side would probably scalp the grass.

2. Rollers are adjusted by loosening screws or handles at the roller brackets or bar position and moving the roller up or down. Here the roller is in its highest position; the grass will be cut as short as possible.

ment of the roller with the cutter bar, which throws the roller into a bind.

There is no satisfactory way to repair a split roller. Wire wrapped around it will put the roller out of alignment with the cutter bar. Wood plastic or adhesives will hold for a short time, but water and chemicals will soon undo this repair.

A new roller is the only answer, and it may be very difficult to find one. The best solution is to have a new roller turned on a lathe at a cabinet or millwork shop.

General lubrication

Unless otherwise specified by the manufacturer, a heat-resistant grease is recommended for wheel gears of both power and push reel mowers. Rollers should be oiled with No. 20 or 30 motor oil before the mower is used. Use a lightweight oil

Regular lubrication. Once a month put several drops of SAE 20 or 30 oil in the holes marked "oil" on hand reel mowers and power reels.

Maintaining rollers. Apply linseed oil to wood rollers with an old cloth at least once a month or, better, after each use. Clean metal rollers with water, oil them lightly with a cloth after each use.

(No. 10) on chain drives and keep the chain clean. Other working parts, such as throttle and clutch assemblies, should be lubricated occasionally with No. 10 oil. (Maintenance procedures for gasoline engines may be found in your owner's manual and in Chapter 5.)

General maintenance

Reel mowers, like any other piece of lawn and garden equipment, are subject to dampness and the chemicals used on lawns.

After each use, hose the mower clean and wipe it dry. Wipe the metal parts with an oily cloth so a thin film of oil covers the metal parts, especially the cutting reel blades and the cutting bar.

Lubricate the wheel gears a couple of times during the cutting season and sharpen the blades at the start of each season. The rollers need an occasional scraping with a putty knife to remove caked mud and other debris.

If the mower is old, protect the metal parts by spraying them with metal paint after removing all grease and rust completely from the metal surfaces. A good rust remover (Naval Jelly) and steel wool do an excellent rust-removal job. Mask the parts you don't want painted (the cutting edges, the roller) before spraying.

Where to write for parts. Finding parts for a hand reel mower may be difficult. Your first stop should be a lawnmower repair shop. For bushing and bearing parts, an automotive parts outlet may have what's needed.

Below are the names of three reel mower sources that may be able to help you find parts and answer any specific questions that you might have. Write to the Consumer Information Director of these companies.

MTD Products, Inc.
5965 Grafton Road
Valley City, OH 44280

McLane Manufacturing, Inc.
7110 East Rosecrans Boulevard
Paramount, CA 90723

Outdoor Power Equipment Institute
1901 L Street N.W.   Suite 700
Washington, D.C. 20036

ROTARY LAWNMOWERS

Rotary mowers use a large blade mounted horizontally that whirls at several thousand rpm. At that speed, the blade just whacks the grass off; it's not actually clipped between blades as it is by a reel mower. Walk-behind rotary mowers have one blade; common sizes range from 18 to 22 inches in diameter. Larger rider mowers frequently mount two blades side by side.

Rotary mowers are powered by either a small gasoline engine or by an electric motor. Electric motors are discussed below. (See Chapter 5 for a discussion of two- and four-cycle engines.)

General maintenance

Prevent rust and corrosion by cleaning the mower after each use. Protect

metal parts by wiping on a thin film of oil. If any rust appears, remove it and repaint. Lubricate the wheel axles during the cutting season. Sharpen the blade at the start of the season (this technique is described later in this chapter).

Electric lawnmowers

The electric motor, driven by house power, has a driveshaft to which the cutting blade is bolted directly. And that's all there is to the power supply and cutting mechanism; nothing could be simpler or so care-free.

Most electric lawnmower motors are double-insulated to prevent shock. Double insulation is a motor-mounting technique that isolates the power parts and circuits from the metal parts of the mower; thus, if you touch any part of the mower, there is no chance of getting an electrical shock. A three-wire system (positive, negative, and ground) is usually not used with double insulation.

Electric mower configuration. The motor of an electric-powered lawnmower is located under a housing on top of the mower. The housing is usually removed by backing out several screws or bolts from the bottom of the mower.

Electric mower problems

If the motor doesn't run, there are only three possible causes: the motor isn't receiving power, the brushes in the motor are burned out, or the electrical wiring is short-circuited.

No power

If the motor is not receiving power, make sure the switch to the mower is

on, and that the power cord is connected to the extension cord. Check the main electrical service entrance to your home; a fuse might be blown or a circuit breaker tripped. If this is not the problem, try plugging the extension cord into another outlet.

Trace the power cord to the motor. Is the cord in good repair and properly connected to the switch and the motor? These connections may be loose or dirty; a frayed power cord may be causing a short circuit in the system.

To solve these problems, remove the old wire and install a new wire of the same size, connecting it in the same way as the old one.

Removing a power cord is simple. Long screws with nuts and washers hold both the switch and the motor housing together. Turn the screws counterclockwise to loosen them. There may be terminal connectors on the wire ends. If so, you can solder new terminals to the wire or resolder the old ones. Use noncorrosive solder and a soldering gun or iron; *do not* use a propane torch for this job.

You may be able to replace the cord with a complete cord assembly sold at dealers who inventory your make and model of electric mower.

Extension cords for motor-driven mowers should be at least No. 14 gauge wire; No. 12 gauge wire is better. Smaller wire (No. 16 or No. 18) can cause severe power loss and so damage the motor. Smaller wire can overheat and cause a short circuit or even an electrical fire. If the extension cord is cut by the mower blade, replace the extension; *do not* try to mend it. Splices in the wire can be dangerous.

If the mower motor runs but seems to lack power, the problem may be a power shortage caused by a small-gauge wire extension cord, a loose connection along the power line supply, or a partly-tripped circuit breaker at the main power entrance to your home.

If the mower has a deadman safety switch, check it to make sure it is engaged properly. The mower may have a safety device at the grass catcher hook-up. Unless the grass catcher is firmly locked into position, the motor will not start.

Worn brushes

Most mowers have a universal motor, which has carbon brushes mounted at one end of the motor shaft. These brushes press against a commutator to complete the electrical circuit. Brushes are made of soft metal, and they wear down during normal use. When they are worn they tend to spark; this is the warning that the brushes should be replaced.

The brushes are held against the commutator by springs with a screw cap or by a clip (see illustrations on page 121). Replacing the brushes is just a matter of removing the mower housing and perhaps the motor housing in order to get at the screws or clips.

If the motor has a screw cap arrangement, back out the screws carefully and remove the springs with a tweezers or the tip of a small screwdriver. Then remove the brushes by tipping over the motor. The brushes should fall out of the slot.

If the brushes are held by clips, you may be able to remove them with your fingers; just pull straight up and out. If this does not work, try inserting the tip of a screwdriver under the brushes and prying gently.

Insert the new brushes (make sure they match the old ones) and secure them with springs and screw cap or clips.

Short circuits and other problems

Most motors on lawn and garden equipment are permanently lubricated at the factory. However, you might look at the motor to see if there are oiling holes. If so, lightly oil the motor with No. 30 nondetergent oil several times during the season. A couple of drops of oil is plenty. Don't overlubricate.

Motor parts, such as the bearings, armature, and shaft, can wear out, causing shorts and no-run troubles. Take the motor to a professional for repairs since special equipment is necessary. But get a repair estimate

first. A new motor—or even a new mower—may be less costly than the repair of the old motor.

Worn control switches

The on/off switch on a motor-driven mower works like a toggle light switch. If the switch is worn or short-circuits, replace it with a new one. The cost is not prohibitive. The procedure is simply to remove the power wires on the old switch and connect them the same way to the new switch.

Replacing cutting blades. An electric lawnmower blade can be removed by blocking the blade with a tool or a chunk of wood so you can turn the nut that holds the blade in position at the center.

Vibration

Although a motor-driven mower runs very smoothly and quietly, vibration can sometimes be a problem.

Vibration is usually caused by a cutting blade that is not in balance. Touching up the cutting edges of the blade with a file usually causes this problem. Remove the blade and have it sharpened and balanced by a professional. Or better, buy a new blade; it will probably be less expensive than repair.

Vibration also can be caused by loose motor-mounting bolts. Tighten them clockwise with a wrench or socket.

The bend doesn't have to be severe; even a slightly bent motor shaft can cause considerable vibration. Bending is usually caused by the blade hitting a hard object. If a

bent shaft is the problem, the motor will have to be replaced, a job for a pro.

Sharpening and replacing rotary blades

Even though you're careful, lawnmower blades become dull and nicked. When they do, the grass cut is ragged, or worse, the lawnmower becomes out of balance and vibrates, which can cause serious damage to the engine and other parts of the mower.

Before each mowing season and twice during the season, you should check the condition of the mower blade. If the cutting edge is just lightly nicked or dulled, you can touch up the blade with a flat metal file with a medium cut.

Keep the file flat on the cutting surface and file toward the cutting edge.

Cleaning the deck. Before you remove the blade for sharpening or replacement, clean the under side of the mower deck with a scraper or putty knife.

Removing the blade. Use a socket or adjustable wrench to remove the blade, if you have a wrench big enough. If not, use a pipe wrench, but be careful; the jaws are powerful. Block the blade with a length of wood so you can turn the nut.

Removing a blade housing. Some blades are held in a housing to prevent the blade from whirling on the engine shaft when it is turning. Remove the blade nut and lift the blade off or out either end of the housing. If the housing is bent or damaged, replace it.

Sharpening a blade. Remove any small nicks on the angled cutting edge of the blade with a flat file, and then sharpen the blade. Take the same number of file strokes along each cutting edge to maintain blade balance.

Take the same number of file strokes on each cutting edge. If you take more metal off one edge than off the other, the blade will be out of balance.

If the cutting edges are in bad condition, have a professional sharpen the blade. But remember, a new blade may be less expensive than a professional sharpening.

Some manufacturers require that blades be resharpened at an angle different from the original. If your owner's manual calls for this different angle and you don't own a power grinder, have a professional do the sharpening.

Most lawnmower blades are sharpened at a 25-degree angle with

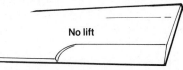

No lift

This blade has lost its lift and won't pick up grass. It must be replaced.

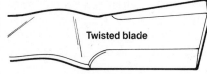

Twisted blade

This blade is twisted. Junk it and install a replacement blade.

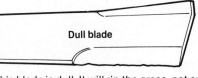

Nicked blade

This blade is badly nicked. Replace it with a new blade.

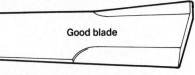

Dull blade

This blade is dull. It will rip the grass, not cut it. Sharpen the edge.

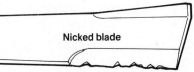

Good blade

This blade is in good condition. No sharpening or reshaping is needed.

Blade evaluation. Blade condition determines whether you should resharpen it or replace it.

a dulled edge, not a knife-sharp edge.

When you have to replace a rotary blade, consider installing a set of thin nylon strips (see illustrations).

SELF-PROPELLED WALK-BEHIND MOWERS

There are two basic drive assemblies for self-propelled lawnmowers. One utilizes a chain drive from the engine to the front wheels; the other utilizes a belt from the engine to a gear box pulley arrangement at one of the wheels, usually the back.

Troubles with either type drive are usually caused by a dirty or stretched chain, a worn or stretched drive belt, or dirty or worn gear connections at the wheels.

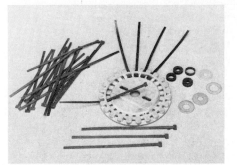

1. Nylon strip blades. Flexible nylon blades held in a metal hub are designed to cut grass but not injure you should you accidentally stick your foot under the mower deck. The strips are pulled through the hub, which is attached to the mower engine shaft like a regular blade.

2. Installed, the nylon blades look like this. Cut the tips of the blades with scissors to clear the mower deck.

Chain drive problems

A chain drive from the engine sprocket to the wheel sprocket doesn't slip. If you are getting slippage in the drive make sure that the sprockets are tight on the axles and that teeth in the sprockets are not broken. The sprockets are usually held with Allen screws driven into the hub of the sprocket.

If the chain is noisy, the problem is a loose chain. It should deflect only about 1/4 inch between the sprockets. You may be able to loosen the engine and move the engine back and forth in the slotted holes to loosen or tighten tension in the chain. If not, the chain will have to be shortened.

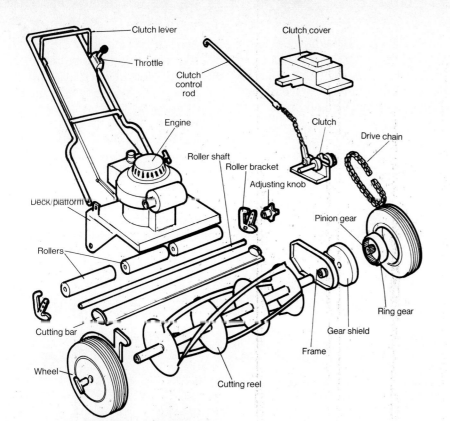

Clutch lever
Throttle
Clutch cover
Clutch control rod
Engine
Roller shaft
Roller bracket
Adjusting knob
Clutch
Drive chain
Pinion gear
Ring gear
Gear shield
Deck/platform
Rollers
Cutting bar
Wheel
Cutting reel
Frame

Anatomy of a power reel mower. The design is basically that of a hand reel mower to which an engine and a clutch assembly have been added.

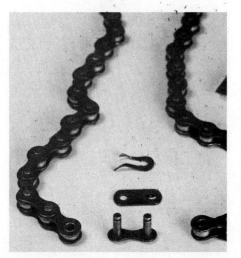

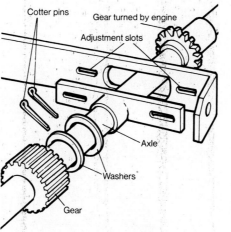

Cotter pins
Gear turned by engine
Adjustment slots
Axle
Washers
Gear

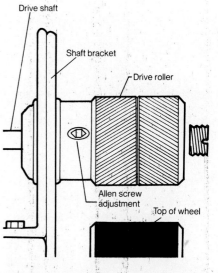

Drive shaft
Shaft bracket
Drive roller
Allen screw adjustment
Top of wheel

Removing drive chains. Drive chains may be disjoined at the master link (center). This link is held by a keeper (above) that is thicker than the ones on other links. Remove this keeper by inserting a screwdriver between the side plates and twisting the keeper off.

To take up the slack, find the master link in the chain. Then pry the strap off with a screwdriver and punch out the connecting link pins. Remove the link next to the master link. You will have to file or grind the pins holding this link flush to the tie strap. Then punch out the pins and connect the master link to the last link in the chain.

Gear-wheel drives. Some self-propelled lawnmowers use gear assemblies to move the wheels. This one has a gear that is driven by a chain from the engine. The teeth on another gear mounted on the same axle engage matching slots in the mower's hard-rubber tires.

If you have trouble finding the master link, remove one of the chain sprockets by loosening the screw on the hub of the sprocket; you may be able to pull it directly off the shaft or axle. You now may be able to remove the chain and lay it flat so that you can find the master and remove the second link.

A slack chain is usually caused by

Adjusting roller drives. Improperly adjusted roller drives can strain the engine and may even slip so that the equipment doesn't move. Tighten all bolts and screws. Then check the clearance between the roller and drive wheels; it should be about 1/4 inch on most models.

worn wheels or the plastic gear that drives the wheels. By replacing either, you may not have to take up the slack in the chain. To replace plastic wheel gears, remove the cotter pins holding on the gears. Then, pull off the gears, which probably have thin washers on both sides of the gears. Replace the washers with the new gears.

Belt drive problems

To replace a belt on a belt-driven self-propelled mower, disconnect the spark plug wire from the spark plug. Then remove the belt cover, which is screwed or bolted to the deck. Tip over the mower so it is not resting on the grass chute. From underneath the deck, slip the old belt off the pulley at the blade. Slip the new belt over the blade and onto the pulley. Then run it out through the slot in the deck to the drive wheel.

Set the mower on its wheels. Slide

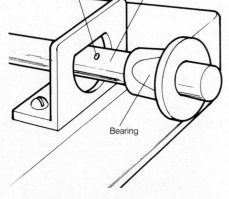

1. Replacing drive belts. The upper drive belt on many engines is easy to replace by removing the roller, bearing, and/or wheel on the drive shaft. These parts are fastened by a recessed Allen screw in the shaft.

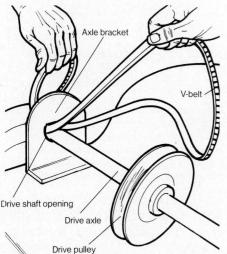

2. The belt slips in through the drive shaft opening, as pictured, and around the pulleys. Make sure the belt is aligned with the pulleys so the belt doesn't wear and bind the engine's operation. As you fit the belt through the hole, also loop it around the drive shaft.

the old belt off and the new belt onto the gear box pulley. Make sure the belt is not twisted. It should be seated in both pulley grooves. Then replace the housing and spark plug wire.

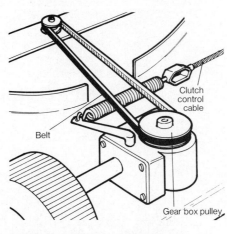

1. Belt drive adjustment. To tighten a belt-driven gear box self-propelled lawnmower assembly, first remove the deck housing. The belt goes around the cutter bar and the gear box pulley.

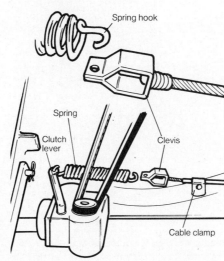

2. When the housing is off, adjust the clutch lever and cable to take up any slack (see text).

Clutch control problems

If the control wire from the handle to the clutch drive is not tensioned properly, the mower may not pull itself along. See illustration for adjustment procedure.

To adjust the control cable with a spring and clevis, unscrew the cable clamp from the mower deck. Then disconnect the clevis from its spring

and slide the spring cover off, if it has one. Pull the spring so that the clutch lever is as far as it will go toward the clevis. At the same time, pull the clevis as far as it will go toward the spring.

Now turn the clevis until the hole in the clevis is aligned with the hook on the spring. Hook the units together.

Finally, attach the cable clamp to the mower deck. The cable control should now be perfectly adjusted.

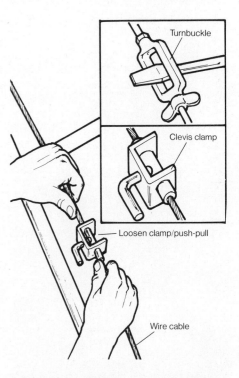

Adjusting the clutch. Clutch control rods or metal wire may be tightened or loosened by turning a turnbuckle or a clevis clamp in the linkage. The rollers should have about an 1/8-inch gap between their surfaces and the wheels.

SMALL LAWN TRACTORS

There are many different makes and models of small lawn and garden tractors. The engines range in size from 10 to 16 and larger horsepower. Features include lift systems for plow blades, four-speed transaxles, hydrostatic drives, and all kinds of accessories. The most common accessory is the rotary mower, but you can also attach lawn sweepers, lawn vacuums, sprayers, plowers, tillers, cultivators, planters, and so on.

Basic maintenance of tractors

It would take a book the size of a New York City telephone directory to discuss the maintenance and repair of all of this equipment. So, in this section, I've kept these procedures to the basics; I'll cover those parts that are common to most tractor models. The procedures may vary somewhat from tractor model to tractor model. But you'll be able to see how the steps given here apply to your tractor.

Always follow the owner's manual or repair guide for your model. These pamphlets may be obtained from the dealer, usually at no cost, or by writing to the manufacturer. If there is a charge, it will be nominal.

A typical lawn and garden tractor has a one-cylinder, four-stroke engine that is air-cooled. Maintenance and repair of this power plant is similar to that for any four-stroke engine and is discussed in Chapter 5.

Most tractors have rubber V belts that drive the mower blades, tillers, and other equipment. The engine furnishes power to the wheels through a chain to the rear axle. Some accessories are driven hydraulically; others are driven by chains.

Transmission problems should be left to a professional. Problems affecting drive belts and chains, clutch, steering, brakes, and the battery and starter—all of which can be handled by the owner—are discussed here. Regular lubrication is also your responsibility.

General lubrication and cleaning

Your tractor probably has two types of oil fittings: a hole for SAE 30 non-detergent oil, which is filled from an oil can, and a fitting for a grease gun. Unless otherwise specified by the manufacturer, use only a lithium automotive grease in these fittings.

Points that require oil include lever and spring assemblies, the steering rods, the clutch and brake rods, power take-off (PTO) levers and springs, and shift levers.

Points that require grease include the axles, the clutch assembly, and the brake assembly. You can recognize all the grease ports by their external fittings, which dovetail with the fitting on the end of the grease gun. Attachments must also be oiled and greased.

Before starting the tractor, be sure to check the engine oil and add more if it's needed.

The following lubrication and cleaning program should be followed after the tractor has been driven for twenty-five hours, if not earlier.

1. Change the engine oil every twenty hours.

2. Clean and re-oil the air filter.

3. Oil both ends of the steering wheel shaft, that is, at the steering wheel and at the gear assembly.

4. Oil the front spindles at the axle.

5. Oil the front wheel bearings or repack them with grease (see illustration).

6. Check the battery fluid level (see illustration).

7. Check the air pressure in the tires. Standard inflation is from 12 to 15 pounds for most tractors.

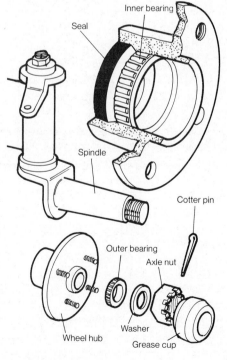

1. Wheel bearing maintenance. Jack up the wheel, remove the bolt that holds the grease cap and then remove the nut locked with a cotter pin.

2. Clean and lubricate the bearing assembly. Replace worn bearings and also the seal, if possible.

Headlight replacement. Most riders have sealed beam headlights. The two connections for each light are usually spade terminal fittings. Two brackets hold the lights in position. Loosen the screws holding the brackets to remove the headlight.

Oil check. Before you start a rider mower engine, check the oil. If it's low, fill the crankcase with SAE 30 (unless another grade is specified by the manufacturer). Change the oil after every 20 hours of engine operation, regardless of other instructions.

8. Use a paper clip or a short length of wire to clean the vent in the fuel tank cap. This vent must be kept fully open at all times to prevent a vacuum seal in the tank.

By following this routine maintenance regimen, you can save many repair headaches later. The professional repair shops all agree: lack of maintenance is the Number One cause of problems with lawn and garden equipment.

The battery

The electric starter on your tractor is probably powered by a wet battery similar to the battery in an automobile. The battery may be closed (you will not be able to add water to it) or you may be able to unscrew the caps on the top of the battery to check and correct the electrolyte level.

Check the battery every month if it's not sealed (see illustration).

SPECIFIC GRAVITIES AND THEIR MEANINGS

Specific gravity	Charge number	Meaning
1.260–1.280	100	fully charged
1.230–1.250	75	well charged
1.200–1.220	50	half charged
1.170–1.190	25	weakly charged
1.140–1.160		very low
1.110–1.130		discharged

Use a hydrometer every month to check the specific gravity. The hydrometer is a very inexpensive tool that you can buy at any auto parts outlet. A range of specific gravity, which indicates the strength of the sulfuric acid in the electrolyte, is shown above. For every 10 degrees above 80 degrees, add .004 to the figures in the left-hand column; for every 10 degrees below 80 degrees, subtract the same amount.

If you notice that the specific gravity changes more than .025 as you make the test, the battery should be replaced.

Keep the battery terminals clean (see illustration).

1. Battery maintenance. Dirty battery terminals can prevent the engine from starting. Remove the cables frequently (disconnect the engine cable first) and clean the connections with steel wool. Clean the terminal posts on the battery with a mixture of baking soda and water applied with a brush; flush the battery with water after the soda and water mixture stops bubbling. Use steel wool to shine the terminals and then coat them with petroleum jelly.

2. Check the battery electrolyte frequently (if the battery is not sealed). If the weather is hot, check it before you use the mower. The electrolyte level should be at the level of the rings inside the cells. Use distilled water to fill the cells. Don't smoke while you work on the battery, and keep your face away from the battery.

Coil maintenance. If the ignition system has a coil, keep it and its connections clean. If the coil windings short out, or the wires break the engine won't start. Inspection is easy: you can see the wires going to and from the coil. Unscrew the caps and examine the ends. If you notice any damage, replace the wires.

Caution: when working with a battery, *do not* smoke or work in an area where sparks are present. Work in an area that is well ventilated and wear safety goggles.

Electric starters and alternators

Most rider mowers have electric battery-driven starters that spin the flywheel to start the engine. The starter unit also disengages the flywheel immediately after the engine starts or the power supply goes off.

The starter is usually permanently lubricated at the factory, but you should lubricate the gear splines and the engaging gear. A couple of bolts hold the starter in position. After removing these bolts by turning them counterclockwise, take the starter off the engine. You can then lubricate the gears with SAE 30 weight oil, with No. 2 lithium grease, or with whatever the manufacturer recommends.

If the starter is malfunctioning, do not try to repair it yourself. Instead, remove it from the engine and take it to a professional for repair.

To manufacture electricity to run the mower and keep the battery fully charged, the mower may have a generator or an alternator. Another possibility is that the starter will serve as generator/alternator. Most starters and generators are sealed at the fac-

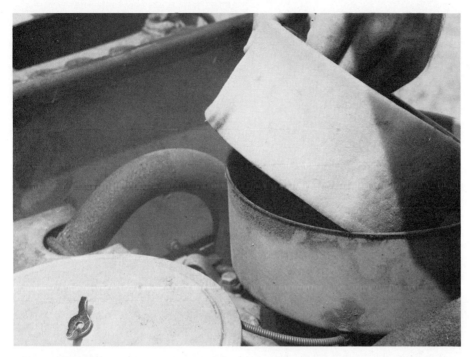

1. Filter maintenance. Air filters on rider mowers may be washable, or they may be paper filters in a canister. If the filter is washable, like the one shown here, use household detergent and water to clean it. Then rinse it and lightly oil it. If it's paper, tap out the debris and use the filter for a few more hours of operation. Then replace it.

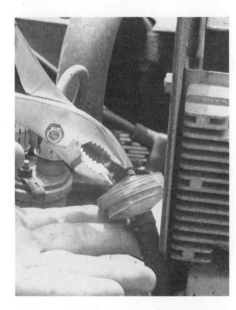

2. The fuel filter is mounted in the fuel line between the fuel tank and the engine. A clamp holds the filter to the fuel line. Remove the worn or spring clamps and wash the filter in nonflammable fluid. If the filter has been in service for a mowing season, replace it.

3. This crankcase filter is connected to a hose on one end and a metal housing on the other. To get at the filter mesh, remove the hose clamp, cover, screen, O-ring, and another clamp. The screen and the mesh should be cleaned with nonflammable grease cleaner. If the O-ring washer is damaged or worn, replace it.

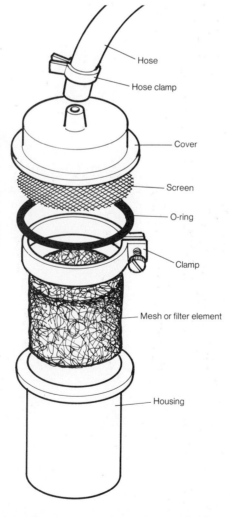

Hose

Hose clamp

Cover

Screen

O-ring

Clamp

Mesh or filter element

Housing

tory, but if either unit has oil ports, squirt in about four drops of 30 weight oil before, midway through, and at the end of the mowing season. If repairs are needed, you should take the unit to a professional. But get an estimate first. The cost of a rebuilt unit may be less than that of repair.

Cleaning filters

If your tractor has a dry air filter, clean it after every twenty-five hours of engine operation, more frequently if conditions are dusty (see illustration).

Most tractors have fuel filters located in the fuel line between the gas tank and the carburetor. Keep this filter clean by washing it out with fresh gasoline. If the filter can't be cleaned, replace it.

If the tractor has a crankcase breather (mounted on the crankcase) it probably has a filter element that should be cleaned every month during the mowing season. Use detergent and water or a noncombustible cleaner made especially for grease and oil. Behind the filter will be some sort of reed valve that controls the air flow. Keep this passage clean and open.

Another type of crankcase breather is mounted at the top of the engine.

The transmission oil cooler is another type of filter that must be clean. Keep the cooling fins or vents free of dust and debris since any clogging can cause the tractor to overheat quickly. Compressed air is the best way to clean the fins; second best is a brush or whisk broom. You also can use a garden hose with the nozzle turned to full blast. To get under and behind the cooler, unscrew the bolts holding the cooler in position.

The governor linkage

This tractor component needs constant attention. If the linkage becomes dirty, it will stick; the engine will then be difficult to start, or it will run roughly.

Use a small brush and a nonflammable solvent to clean the linkage.

Be careful not to disturb any linkage settings that involve screws and springs.

Removing the mower deck

Unless other procedures are specified by your owner's manual, follow these steps to remove the mower deck in order to make other adjustments to the tractor.

1. Turn the ignition off.

2. Remove the spark plug wire from the spark plug.

3. Set the mower deck in its lowest position.

4. Turn the front wheels as far left as possible. If the deck on your tractor comes off the opposite way, turn the wheels as far right as possible.

5. Under the main frame (see drawing) disconnect the safety deck wire from the unit assembly.

6. Remove the cutter from the pull pin on the front of the deck. Remove the pin.

7. Move the deck forward and to the right (or left) to disengage the rear deck guide from its bracket.

8. Give the belt guides some slack at the engine pulley and remove the deck drive belt from the engine pulley. You now should be able to pull the deck from under the tractor frame.

Leveling the mower deck

Properly adjusted, the decks on most rider mowers should be no more than 1/8 inch lower at the front of the deck than at the rear of the deck. To check and adjust this cutting benchmark:

1. Inflate the tires to equal pressure.

2. On a level spot, such as a concrete walk or driveway, measure the height of the blade at the front and at the back. If the measurements are the same, or if the back is no more than 1/8 inch higher than the front,

the deck is properly leveled.

3. If adjustments are needed, shift the cutting height adjustment lever to its lowest cut position.

4. Put a block of wood or a brick under the front of the deck to remove the weight from the hitch.

5. Remove the cotter pin from the clevis pin with pliers, then remove the clevis pin.

6. To raise the front of the deck, turn the lift cable clevis clockwise; to lower the deck, turn the cable clevis counterclockwise. About one and a half turns will either raise or lower the deck approximately 1/8 inch.

7. Replace the clevis and clevis pin, and remove the block. Check the front and rear measurements once again. If you are satisfied, replace the cotter pin. If the deck needs more adjustment, repeat the procedures.

Making belt and chain adjustments

Both rubber V-belts and chains stretch. You can adjust them, but only up to a point. Then the belts have to be replaced or links have to be taken out of chains.

As a rule, a V-belt should deflect only about 1/4 to 1/2 inch when you press it down at the center between two pulleys. If your equipment has an idler pulley, you may be able to loosen the bolt that holds this pulley and slide it in a slotted hole toward the belt to tighten the belt.

Chain drives use chains that are almost identical to bicycle chains. Instructions for removing a link to shorten the chain are given earlier in this chapter.

You may be able to tighten the belts on the mower deck assembly (see drawing opposite) by simply adjusting the deck slightly.

1. Put the mower clutch lever in the disengage slot.

Belt adjustment. Belts, belt guides, and pulleys on rider mowers are usually mounted behind metal or plastic housings that are bolted or slip-fitted to the frame of the machine. Remove this housing to service the parts underneath. Notice how the belt guide (the flattened C-shaped part) overlaps the width of the pulley. The guide is adjusted with a bolt; set it about 1/16 inch from the top of the belt.

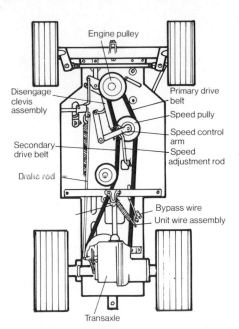

Engine pulley

Disengage clevis assembly

Primary drive belt

Speed pully

Speed control arm

Speed adjustment rod

Secondary drive belt

Brake rod

Bypass wire

Unit wire assembly

Transaxle

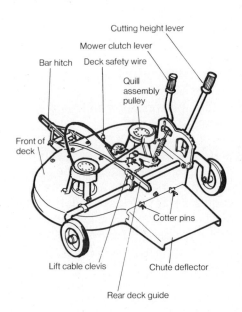

Cutting height lever

Mower clutch lever

Bar hitch

Deck safety wire

Quill assembly pulley

Front of deck

Cotter pins

Lift cable clevis

Chute deflector

Rear deck guide

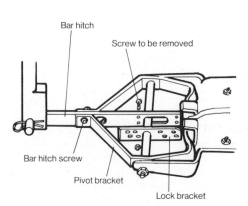

Bar hitch

Screw to be removed

Bar hitch screw

Pivot bracket

Lock bracket

(Left, top) **The under side of a rider mower.**

(Left, center) **A rider mower deck assembly.**

(Left, bottom) **Drive belt adjustment.** You may be able to tighten the mower drive belts by moving the mower deck toward the rear of the unit or loosen the belts by moving the deck forward. The belts may have to be adjusted by means of an idler pulley which is illustrated elsewhere in this chapter.

2. Remove the screw from the lock bracket in the bar hitch assembly (see drawing below, left).

3. Remove or loosen the lock nut on the bar hitch screw that secures the bar hitch to the pivot bracket.

4. To tighten the belt, slide the mower deck toward the rear of the unit. You will see the pivot bracket move when you do this. To loosen the belt, slide the deck toward the front of the unit. When the belt is properly tensioned, tighten the lock nut on the bar hitch screw.

5. Start the engine and move the throttle to "run." Throw in the mower clutch lever and let the blades spin at full speed. Disengage the clutch. The quill assembly pulleys should stop within seconds. If not, the belts are too tight; loosen them just a tad.

Note: additional information on belt and chain drives is in Chapter 5, page 85.

Making brake and speed adjustments

Some tractors have a brake and clutch unit controlled by just one pedal. On other models the unit may be equipped with an adjustable brake mounted on the transaxle. This part must be adjusted so the brake doesn't take hold before the belts disengage. You should make any belt adjustments before you make the brake, clutch, or speed adjustments.

Some units have a threaded rod running from the pedal to the brake drum near the axle. The adjustment procedure is shown here.

Sometimes turning the bolt doesn't work. If the adjustment is still faulty, the brake will grab or hold

when power is being transmitted; that is, the mower will move while you have your foot jammed on the brake. You'll also find that this will cause difficulty when you shift from one speed range or from one direction to another.

To adjust this brake/speed synchronization, follow this procedure:

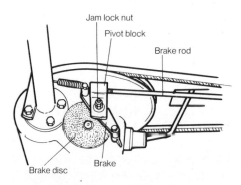

Jam lock nut

Pivot block

Brake rod

Brake disc

Brake

1. Brake adjustment. For brake and speed synchronization, first loosen the locknut and turn the adjustment bolt on the threaded rod until the brake pads clear the brake disc or the brake band almost touches the axle. When the pads or band are set, tighten the jam lock nut. You may have to hold the lock nut with a wrench so the adjustment stays. Then press the brake pedal to check the synchronization of the brake and the speed.

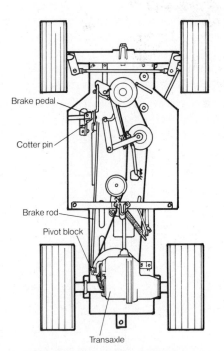

Brake pedal

Cotter pin

Brake rod

Pivot block

Transaxle

2. If turning the adjustment bolt does not synchronize brake and speed, remove the cotter pin at the brake rod and brake pedal and turn the rod a couple of turns counterclockwise into the pivot block. Follow the instructions in the text.

1. Put the shift lever in neutral. Move the speed lever to disengage.

2. Step down on the brake pedal as far as it will move and set the parking brake. You should not be able to push the unit without sliding the tires. If the wheels slide, the unit is in synchronization.

3. If the wheels turn, remove the cotter pin (if the nut has one) holding the brake rod to the brake pedal.

4. Turn the brake rod one or two full turns counterclockwise into the pivot block or bracket at the axle end of the rod.

5. Replace the rod on the brake pedal and replace the cotter pin.

6. Try the action again. If it doesn't work, you'll have to repeat the process until you get the right adjustment. You may have to turn the rod clockwise.

Adjusting the speed control lever

If the mower moves when the speed lever is in a latched or locked position the lever needs adjustment. First remove the mower deck (see above). Start the engine and put the speed control lever in a latched position (see drawing). Stop the engine and remove the spark plug wire. Then follow these steps:

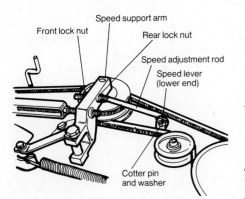

Speed control lever adjustment. Loosen a lock nut on the rear of the speed adjustment rod and turn it as described in the text.

1. Turn the front lock nut on the front end of the variable speed adjustment rod two complete turns counterclockwise.

2. Tighten the rear lock nut two complete turns clockwise. Replace the deck.

3. Put the shift lever in neutral, reconnect the spark plug wire, and start the engine.

4. Put the shift in forward gear. The mower should not move until the lever is moved out of the latched position. If the mower does move when the shift is in gear and the speed lever is moved about 2 inches forward, you will have to disassemble the mower deck again and make another adjustment.

Start the engine again and put the speed control lever in a latched position. Stop the engine and remove the spark plug wire. Then follow these steps.

1. Loosen the rear lock nut on the speed adjustment rod. Give it two complete turns counterclockwise. Tighten the front lock nut two complete turns clockwise.

2. Put the shift in neutral, reconnect the spark plug wire, and start the engine.

3. Shift into a forward gear. Move the speed lever forward. The mower should start moving when the speed lever is moved forward about 2 inches.

4. Stop the engine, remove the spark plug wire, and replace the mower deck. Hook up the spark plug wire and operate the equipment as usual.

Adjusting speed lever tension

If the speed lever tension is not enough to hold the lever in position, it should be adjusted.

1. Start the engine. With the speed lever pulled back in a latched position, shift into neutral.

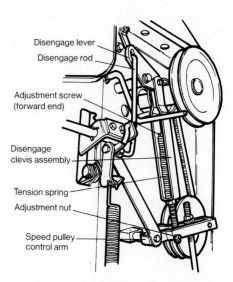

Speed lever tension adjustment. The disengage clevis should be adjusted when the speed lever doesn't return far enough to stop the unit. Make the adjustment when the speed lever is *disengaged* but not latched. Hold the adjustment screw at the forward end of the tension spring and tighten the adjustment nut so it is tight against the speed pulley support arm.

2. Turn the engine off and remove the spark plug wire.

3. Use a wrench to tighten the friction adjustment nut inside the console on the right side behind the engine. (It may be located differently on your equipment, but it will be near this position.) Give the adjustment nut one complete turn clockwise.

4. Replace the spark plug wire and start the engine. Shift the gears to neutral. Then push the throttle to the run position and the speed lever to the fast position.

5. Let the engine run a few minutes to see if the speed lever stays in place. If not, you will have to repeat the above procedures, turning the adjustment nut one more complete turn.

If the speed lever doesn't return far enough to stop the unit, make the adjustment shown in the illustration. Patience is the byword of this adjustment. You may have to tighten and/or loosen the nut a couple of times to get the tension right.

Adjusting the steering gear

Turn the steering wheel. If it seems to be loose or if the gears seem to slip, you may be able to adjust the sector gear to stop the slippage.

1. Start the engine and shift the gears into neutral. Move the speed lever to the fast setting. Don't put on the brake.

2. Stop the engine and remove the spark plug wire from the spark plug.

3. Loosen the sector gear mounting screw. It's under the main frame (see drawing). Turn the screw about a half turn counterclockwise. You will need a socket wrench with an extension for this job.

4. Turn the adjusting bolt so that the gear goes forward or backward as needed. When the bolt is in the forward position—toward the engine—the gear is tight. When the bolt is in the rear position—away from the engine—the gear is loose.

5. Tighten the bolt. Replace the spark plug wire.

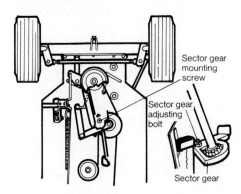

Steering gear adjustment. Loosen the sector gear mounting screw under the main frame and turn it as decribed in the text.

Replacing the drive belt

There is an easy way to replace rubber V-belts. Follow these steps to remove the old belt:

1. Remove the mower deck.

2. Remove the cotter pin and washer from the speed adjustment rod. Unhook the rod from the lower end of the lever.

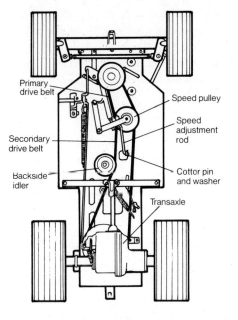

3. Move the rear idler pulley from the belt and roll the belt off the underside of the pulley. Then remove the belt from the speed pulley. The belt can be twisted sideways so it can be removed over the top of the speed pulley.

Why not just cut the belt? Because you have to loosen the pulleys in order to replace the belt. By removing the belt as detailed, you make the adjustments as you go so the new belt goes over the pulleys easier.

Replace the primary belt before the secondary belt. Here's how to do this:

1. Loosen the left belt guide on the upper engine pulley and pull it away from the pulley, then remove the secondary drive belt.

2. Remove the belt from the speed pulley by moving it over the top of the pulley. You may have to push the pulley toward the front of the unit and twist the belt sideways.

3. Remove the belt from the upper engine pulley.

4. Install the new belts in the reverse order of the removal procedures.

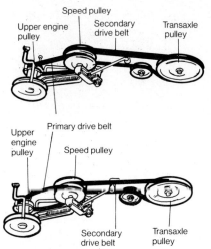

Belt adjustment. Secondary and primary belts go around pulleys. The position shown here is "fast." The replacement procedure is described in the text.

5. After the new belts are on, adjust the belt guides about 1/16 inch from the belts. You may have to adjust the speed adjustment rod slightly after the new belts are on. This is explained above.

Lawn tractor troubleshooting

You can apply the maintenance and repair information given above to the problems and probable causes listed here.

The engine won't start

■ Is the fuel line shut-off valve turned on?

■ Have you gone through the starting procedure, that is, switch on, fuel on, gears properly set, and so forth?

■ Is the battery dead?

■ Are all interlock switches and wiring operating properly?

■ Are the starter connections clean and tight?

■ Are throttle and choke in the fast or run position?

■ Are ignition wires, such as the

spark plug wire, properly connected?

■ Are lockout switches properly set?

■ Run through the solutions for engine problems in Chapter 5, beginning on page 76.

The engine turns over, but won't start

■ Are all interlock switches and lockouts on go?
Check starting procedure.

■ Is all wiring properly connected?
Check wiring system for tight connections, especially the recoil starter.

■ Is the tank filled with *clean* fuel?

■ Is fuel line shut-off valve open?

■ Are the throttle and choke in the run or fast position?

■ Are the gears properly set?

■ Run through the solutions for engine problems in Chapter 5, beginning on page 76.

The grass is cut poorly

■ Is the blade properly sharpened? (see pages 61-62.)

■ Is the blade tight on its mounting?

■ Is the underside of the mower deck clean and free from debris?

■ Is the mower deck properly set? (see page 68.)

■ Is the deck housing damaged?
This is a problem for a professional.

■ Are the bearings in the deck or cutting assembly badly worn?
You may be able to check this by wobbling the blades with your

hands. If they're loose, they must be replaced—a job for a professional.

The mower doesn't cut between blades

■ Are the blades worn or dull? (see pages 61-62.)

■ Are you mowing in high, wet grass?
This is a prime cause of this problem; postpone your mowing.

■ Are you running the engine at full throttle?
If yes, slow down.

■ Is the belt tension slack? (see pages 68-69.)

■ Is the pulley assembly out of line? (see page 71.)

■ Is the mower deck damaged in any way?
If the deck is damaged, it must be taken to a professional for repair.

The clippings won't discharge

■ Is the underside of the deck clean?

■ Is the grass very wet?

■ Are the blades correctly mounted?

The blade drive belt slips

■ Is the grass very high and wet?

■ Is the belt worn?

■ Is the belt properly tensioned? (see pages 68-69.)

The belt drive wears out quickly

■ Are the belt guides properly set? (see page 68.)

■ Is debris blocking belt travel?

■ Are the pulleys damaged in any way?

■ Is the deck properly leveled? (see page 68.)

■ Is the belt brake clearing the belt when the mower is engaged? (see page 69.)

The belt comes off frequently

■ Is the belt properly tensioned? (see pages 68-69.)

■ Are all belt guides properly set? (see page 68.)

■ Is the deck properly leveled? (see page 68.)

■ Are the pulleys bent or misaligned?

■ Is the inner surface of the engine drive pulley bent or rough?
If so, replace the pulley.

■ Is the blade throw-out assembly worn?
Have a professional replace it if it is.

The blades won't engage

■ Is the belt loose or broken?

■ Is the spring on the deck engagement assembly damaged? (see page 70.)

■ Is debris blocking idler travel?

The blades won't disengage

■ Is belt tension correct? (see pages 68-69.)

■ Is the spring on the deck engagement assembly worn or broken? (see page 70.)

■ Is there enough slack?
If you have just replaced the belts, you may have installed the wrong size.

■ Is there debris around the engagement idler?

Vibration

■ Are the blades loose or out of balance?

■ Are the belts badly worn?

■ Is there debris under the mower deck?

■ Are the engine mounts loose or damaged?

■ Is the engine drive pulley defective?
If the inner surface is worn, rough, or split, replace the pulley.

The deck or deck wheel strikes the rear wheel or tire

■ Is the deck drive belt adjustment too tight? Loosen it (see pages 68-69).

■ Have the belts stretched?

■ Is the belt worn?

■ Has the pivot tube been damaged?
If this is the problem, go to a professional for repair.

The unit drive belt squeals when braking

■ Are the brake and clutch synchronized? (see page 69.)

■ Do the drive belts need adjustment? (see pages 68-69.)

■ Is debris clogging the speed or clutching idler mechanism?

■ Do the brakes need adjustment? This is a job for a professional.

The unit drive belt comes off frequently

■ Is the belt tension correct? (see pages 68-69.)

■ Are the belt guides working properly?

■ Are the pulleys split or damaged?

■ Is the clutching idler pulley out of alignment?

The unit won't shift properly

■ Are you shifting correctly?
On many models, the mower has to come to a complete stop before the gears may be shifted.

■ Is the brake and clutch synchronization working properly?

The steering slips or is loose

■ Are the steering sector gear and pinion loose? (see page 71.)

■ Is the center pivot bolt on the front axle loose?

■ Are the ball joints worn?
If this is the case, take the tractor to a professional for repair.

The mower scalps the lawn

■ Is there a bent blade?

■ Has the mower height been properly adjusted? (see page 68.)

■ Are you mowing over ridges and humps? If you are, change your mowing pattern to eliminate this.

The unit won't pick up grass properly

■ Is the mower deck set too low? (see page 68.)

■ Is the discharge chute blocked?

■ Are the pulleys split or damaged?

■ Is there a buildup of grass clippings in the collector fan housing?

■ Are the belts properly tensioned? (see pages 68-69.)

■ Is the grass extremely wet? Water can add enough weight to the grass leaves to make pickup difficult. Wait for the grass to dry before cutting it.

5 Small Gasoline Engine Maintenance

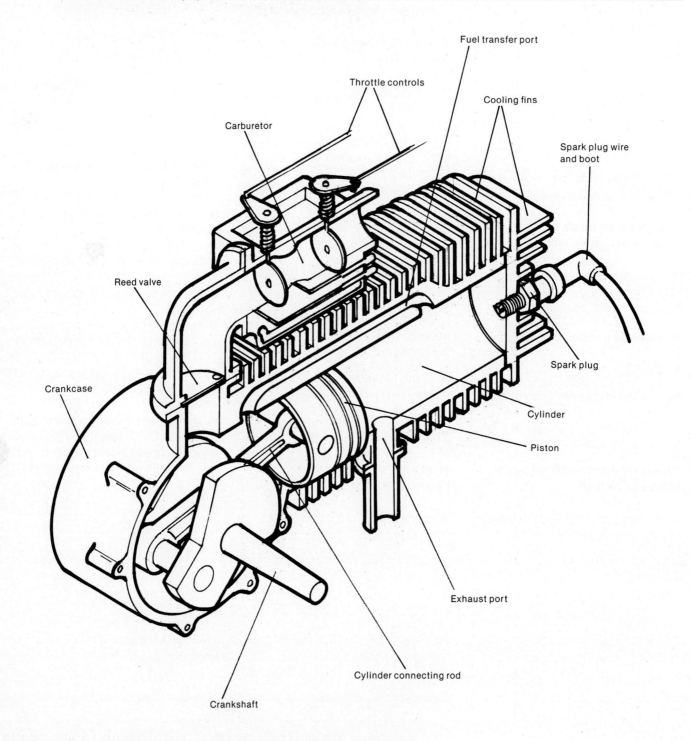

Throttle controls

Fuel transfer port

Cooling fins

Carburetor

Spark plug wire and boot

Reed valve

Spark plug

Crankcase

Cylinder

Piston

Exhaust port

Cylinder connecting rod

Crankshaft

Anatomy of a two-cycle engine. Fuel enters the cylinder through the reed valve; at the top of the piston stroke the reed valve shuts. The spark plug then fires the fuel, which pushes the piston downward, driving the crankshaft. When the piston reaches the bottom of the stroke, the exhaust port is uncovered and the exhaust gas is forced out. Electricity generated by magnets on the flywheel flows from the coil through the breaker points to fire the spark plug.

Rotary and reel lawnmowers, lawn edgers, snow blowers, and multipurpose garden tillers are among the most popular and useful walk-behind power machines. For the most part, this equipment is powered by two- and four-cycle, or four-stroke, gasoline engines that may appear complicated but are relatively simple mechanically. Maintenance and repair problems are very similar for both types of engines, so the procedures listed here are the same for both unless otherwise noted. Although the starter mechanism (rope or electric) and engine covering may look different, the engines themselves will be identical or almost identical regardless of the brand name. In short, if you see one, you've seen them all, with a few minor exceptions sometimes so subtle that only a professional can tell the difference.

Engines are usually labeled with the manufacturer's name. A metal tag will include the serial, model, and specification numbers; all of these are important when you buy replacement parts. See page 155 for a list of small engine manufacturers; you may need one of these names to order replacement parts.

Engine differences

The basic difference between a four-cycle and a two-cycle engine is this: oil is added to the *crankcase* of a four-cycle engine, but oil is added to the *gasoline* of a two-cycle engine. If your engine has a separate port for oil you can be sure it's a four-cycle engine.

A two-cycle engine is lightweight and furnishes more power, by size, than the four-cycle, and it is air-cooled. Simply stated, the two-cycle engine has one power stroke that drives the crankshaft for every two strokes the piston makes as it moves up and down in the cylinder. There are no separate exhaust or intake strokes. Exhaust gas in the cylinder is released when the piston completes the power stroke. Two ports in the cylinder let the exhaust escape. These ports operate similarly to the valves in a four-cycle engine.

The fuel for a two-cycle engine is pumped by the piston, which pulls the fuel and air mixture through the crankcase and up into the cylinder. A magnetic ignition fires the spark plug (there are no points or condenser). The magnets for the ignition are mounted on the rim of the flywheel.

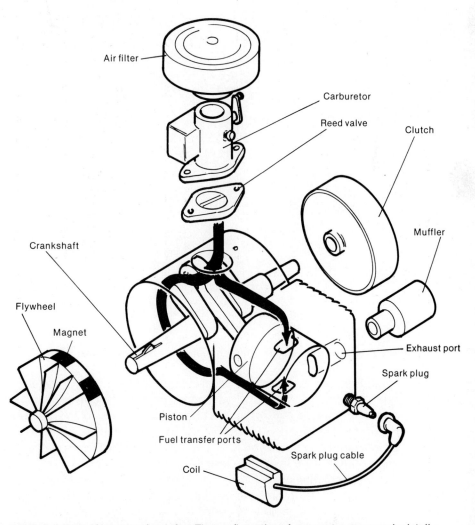

Air filter

Carburetor

Reed valve

Clutch

Muffler

Crankshaft

Flywheel

Magnet

Exhaust port

Spark plug

Piston

Fuel transfer ports

Spark plug cable

Coil

Additional parts of a two-cycle engine. The configuration of your motor may vary in details.

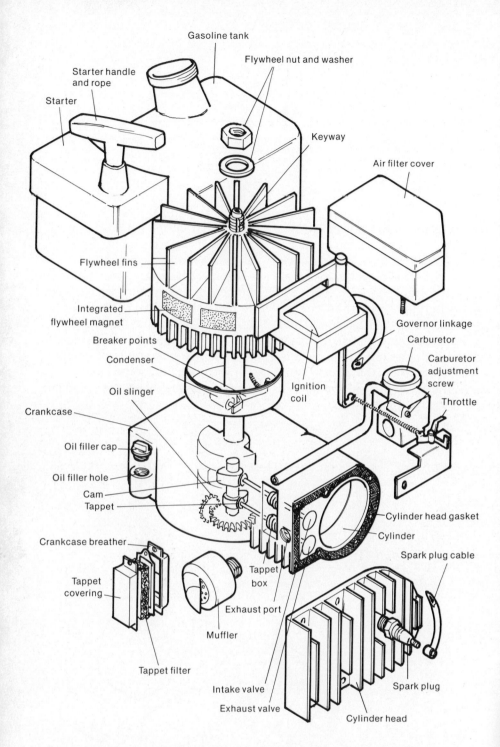

- Starter handle and rope
- Starter
- Gasoline tank
- Flywheel nut and washer
- Keyway
- Air filter cover
- Flywheel fins
- Integrated flywheel magnet
- Breaker points
- Condenser
- Oil slinger
- Crankcase
- Oil filler cap
- Oil filler hole
- Cam
- Tappet
- Crankcase breather
- Tappet covering
- Tappet filter
- Ignition coil
- Governor linkage
- Carburetor
- Carburetor adjustment screw
- Throttle
- Cylinder head gasket
- Cylinder
- Spark plug cable
- Tappet box
- Exhaust port
- Muffler
- Intake valve
- Exhaust valve
- Spark plug
- Cylinder head

Anatomy of a four-cycle gasoline engine. This is a common parts configuration.

The spark plug fires the fuel mixture in the cylinder.

A four-cycle engine is the type found in an automobile. But don't let this mechanical similarity scare you. The four-cycle engine on a lawnmower is simple mechanically. As is the two-cycle, the four-cycle engine is also air-cooled, not water-cooled. It has one cylinder, as does the two-cycle engine, not four, six, or eight cylinders as there are in a car. The number "four" refers to the strokes the piston makes in the cylinder.

The workings of a four-cycle engine follow this sequence: a carburetor mixes gasoline and air. This vapor mixture flows from the carburetor to the cylinder. The spark plug ignites the vapor within the cylinder.

The resulting explosion drives the piston down inside the cylinder. The piston, in turn, drives a crankshaft which turns the blade or tiller. The four strokes in succession are: intake (down), compression (up), power (down), and exhaust (up).

Engine problems and solutions

Dirt is the Number One problem with both two- and four-cycle engines. The reason is obvious: the engine works almost at ground level where spinning blades or tillers generate a whirlwind of dust that chokes engine air filters, fuel filters and lines, spark plugs, controls, and other component parts. The solution is to follow the regular cleaning maintenance, shown in detail in this chapter. This will virtually guarantee you trouble-free engine operation. In fact, a cared-for engine will outlast the rest of the equipment.

This is the cleaning maintenance routine:

1. After using the equipment let the engine cool. Then clean and hose down the housing, blades, and wheels and dry them with a soft cloth. Wipe the engine housing clean.

2. Keep air filters clean. Many filters can be washed with regular household detergent and water. Some fil-

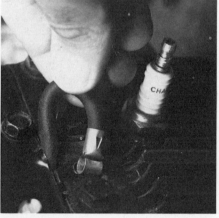

Safety first. Before you make *any* adjustment or repair to *any* power lawn equipment, disconnect the spark plug wire from the spark plug. It's a two-second job that can prevent serious injury.

ters have to be replaced at the start of every working season. If the equipment is used in extremely dusty or dirty conditions, clean or replace the filter after about twenty-five hours of use, or about every month if you mow an average-sized yard (one-third acre).

3. Keep the oil in four-cycle engines clean by changing it at the start of every season and once a month during the season. Check the oil level in the crankcase each time before the engine is started and put into service.

4. Regularly check the thin gasket that is sandwiched between the air filter and the top of the carburetor. A damaged gasket permits dirt and dust to be sucked into the engine parts.

5. If the engine has a fuel filter, change it at the start of every season and check it weekly for dirt deposits. Cleaning with fresh gasoline should restore the filter; if not, replace it.

6. Clean and lubricate controls and wheels at the start of every season and every two weeks during the season. No. 10 motor oil or a multipurpose lubricant and cleaner, such as WD-40, will do a good lubricating job.

For simplicity in troubleshooting and repair, divide the engine into two parts: electrical and mechanical.

For example, if the engine will not start, is difficult to start, or runs and then stops, look for trouble *first* in electrical components, such as the spark plug, points, condensor, and plug wires.

If the electrical parts seem to be operating, then look for the trouble in the mechanical parts: the controls, carburetor, governor, blades, filters, gaskets, and the crankcase.

Generally, the electrical parts are the big troublemakers. Something as simple as a loose wire can shut down the entire engine. Follow a systematic approach to the problem instead of jumping back and forth from electrical to mechanical. You'll find that checklist mechanics will start the engine faster than jump guessing. The key is patience, not especially skill.

Troubleshooting four-cycle gasoline engines

You won't find any panacea in the manufacturer's instructions or any book, including this one, for small engines that won't start and run properly. Some symptoms are so obscure that it takes a professional to spot the problem. But in general, malfunctioning four-cycle engines show symptoms that are easy to identify. By thoroughly checking the problem in an orderly fashion, as detailed below, you usually will be able to find the solution and save a trip to the repair shop.

The engine won't start

The trouble usually can be isolated into two categories: improper control settings and malfunctioning ignition parts.

Tools, materials, and supplies: screwdriver, wrench, pliers, spark plug, fuel cap, ignition wire, fuel.

■ Are the controls on the handle proper set on "start"?

■ Does the engine have fresh fuel in the fuel tank?

■ Is the tank more than half full of fuel?

■ Is the spark plug wire attached firmly to the spark plug?

Trace the sheathed control cable from the handle of the equipment to the throttle on the engine. The throttle should be fully opened when the control handle setting is on "start." As you move the control lever from "start" to "fast" to "stop," the cable should be clamped so that it operates the throttle properly. The cable can be slipping in the clamp just enough to cause the throttle to malfunction. You might not even see this slight movement.

Move the throttle to its open, or "start," position with your fingers. Push the throttle forward, toward the front of the engine. You may have to move the control lever with your other hand to ease the throttle open.

If the throttle cable is slipping in its clamp, adjust it as shown in the illustrations.

If the engine now starts, let it run for several minutes, then pull the control lever back to "stop." If the engine slows but does not stop, loosen the cable clamp with the

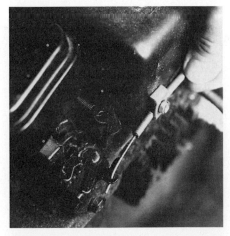

Cable control adjustment. Loosen the screw holding the cable clamp on the housing. Then push the cable forward toward the engine until the throttle stops. The throttle is now fully open. Set the handle control lever on "fast" or "start" and tighten the cable clamp.

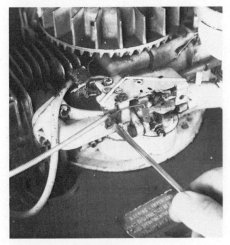

Another cable mounting. On some engines the throttle wire from the handle control is located on a special bracket, as shown here. To adjust it, loosen the clamp, push the throttle forward, set the control on "fast" or "start," and tighten the cable clamp.

screwdriver and pull the cable just a fraction of an inch toward the control lever until the engine stops. Then tighten the clamp. Start the engine once again and go through the control settings. The engine now should start, run slowly, run fast, and stop according to the labels on the control handle console.

■ Is the spark plug grounding device properly set? (see illustration.)

Some engines have a flap of metal that is pressed down over the end of the spark plug to stop the engine. If your engine has this feature, make sure the device is off.

■ Did you prime the engine, if the

Spark plug grounding device. This flap of metal attached to the engine housing—must be snapped off the tip of the spark plug before the engine will start on some models.

Priming devices. On some engines a primer must be pushed four to six times when the engine is cold in order to fill the carburetor with fuel. When the engine is hot, do *not* use the primer when restarting; this may flood the carburetor and prevent starting.

engine has a priming device? (see illustration.)

You need to push it quickly four or five times when the engine is cold to fill the carburetor. If the engine is hot, do not press the primer. You may flood the carburetor. Instead, pull the starter cord several times with the control lever in the "stop" position. This will help clear excess fuel from the fuel system. Then put the control lever on "start" and start the engine normally.

■ Is the grasscatcher properly engaged?

Some lawnmowers have a safety locking device on the catcher where it attaches to the mower housing. This device prevents the engine from starting until the lock is fully engaged or disengaged. If the grass-catcher is not being used, make sure the chute from the blade to the catcher is in position and locked.

■ Is the fuel cap properly vented?

Remove the fuel cap and check the cardboard insert under the top of the cap. Sometimes the space between this liner and the top of the cap becomes clogged with debris, shutting off the air supply to the fuel tank. Check the holes in the cap to make sure that they are open. If you have any doubt that the cap may be causing trouble, remove the cap completely and try to start the engine. If the engine runs, the cap is the problem. Either repair the cap or replace it. *Do not* run the engine without a cap on the fuel tank, and do not use a substitute plug such as a corncob or a piece of cloth.

■ Is the air filter clean and the gasket between the filter and carburetor in good repair? (see illustrations.)

■ Is the spark plug tight in its port?

■ Is the spark plug wire properly attached?

The tip on the end of the spark plug wire can become loose and corroded through use. Crimp this loop with pliers; remove corrosion with steel wool or sandpaper.

Air filter maintenance. Typical air filter is fastened to the top of the carburetor with a long machine screw. To remove the housing, back out this screw counterclockwise. Wash the filter with household detergent and water.

Air filter mounting gasket. A thin, rubberlike gasket is sandwiched between the bottom of the air filter and the top of the carburetor rim. Check this gasket and replace it if damaged.

Paper filter replacement. A replaceable, paper filter has a metal casing around the filter element to protect it. Usually, the entire cartridge has to be replaced. Remove it by pressing the spring clip together with pliers.

Oil bath filter. An oil bath air filter sits in a cup of engine oil. To clean it, remove the machine bolt holding on the lid and pull the housing apart. The filter element may be cleaned in household detergent and water. After cleaning, coat the element lightly with engine oil and replace it. Also clean out the cup and add clean oil. Replace any worn gaskets.

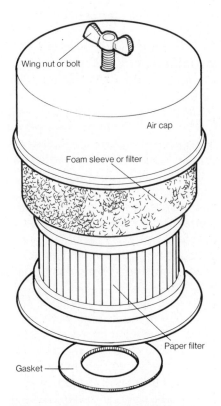

Anatomy of a foam or paper air filter. If the parts include a foam filter, wash this component in household detergent and water. Tap the paper filter lightly on a hard surface to remove debris, but do not wash or lubricate it. Replace all worn, broken, and cracked gaskets.

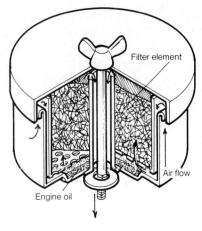

Anatomy of an oil bath filter.

■ Is the spark plug malfunctioning?
You can remove and clean the plug, but I recommend that you install a new plug at the start of every season. The cost of the new plug is not prohibitive, and you can usually be sure that the plug is not faulty.

Once in a great while, a new plug will turn out to be faulty. If you install a new plug and the engine won't fire even though all else seems to be in working order, try another new plug.

■ Are there breaks in the spark plug wire insulation?
Check this by crimping the wire between your fingers and looking for damage. If you spot trouble, replace

Spark plug wrenches. These have a hex shape on both ends to remove and tighten most small engine spark plugs. Use these inexpensive wrenches, instead of an adjustable wrench, which can damage the plug and plug port.

the wire. You may have to replace the entire coil since the wire probably is permanently attached. You can do this yourself; see below. A pro may be able to replace just the wire. Remove and take the coil and wire assembly to the shop and get a cost estimate.

■ Is the cutting blade loose?
Remove the spark plug wire, turn

Anatomy of a small engine coil.

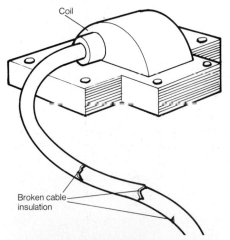

1. Coil replacement. Remove the metal housing from the top of the engine by turning out several bolts counterclockwise. One bolt fastens the air vane and coil; directly opposite, a similar bolt holds the coil.

2. The bolt holes are slotted so that the coil may be adjusted against the magnet on the flywheel to make the spacing .014 inches.

1. Electronic ignition. Solid-state systems use an electronic module located next to the flywheel, like a regular coil. To replace or adjust the module, remove the bolts holding the engine housing. Then remove the clamp that holds the ignition wire to the engine, as shown here.

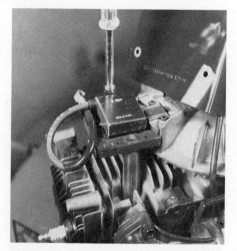

2. The electronic module is held by two bolts; turn them counterclockwise to loosen or remove them.

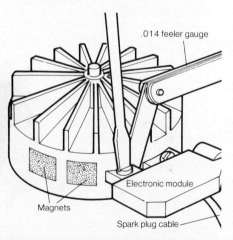

.014 feeler gauge

Electronic module

Magnets

Spark plug cable

3. Use a feeler gauge to set the spacing between the magnets and the module at .014 inch. If the magnets fail, replace the flywheel or have a professional make repairs.

the equipment over so the oil cap on the engine faces upward, and check the blade. Try to wobble the blade back and forth and up and down. If the blade is loose, tighten the blade bolts with a wrench. If the blade is loose, but the bolts can't be tightened, have a professional make the necessary repair.

Caution: do not, under any circumstances, operate the equipment until the blade is properly tightened and secure on its mounting.

The engine stops suddenly

Sometimes when the equipment is running perfectly the engine will stop and you won't be able to get it started again. If the engine has enough fuel, this problem can most likely be traced to two parts:

a dead condenser

a broken flywheel key

The key will break if the equipment blade strikes a hard object. It can happen without you even feeling the blade hit. The flywheel key is an engine timing device. Without it, the engine won't run at all.

Tools, materials, and supplies: wrenches or socket wrench assortment, screwdriver, flywheel puller, hammer, feeler gauge or matchbook cover, condensor, breaker points, flywheel key (usually in a tune-up package), new blade and bolt assembly.

■ Has the condenser under the flywheel stopped working?

It can fail at any time without warning. Even brand new condensers go bad, so don't be deluded into thinking that the problem may be elsewhere even if the engine has a new, or fairly new, ignition system. Instructions for installing a condenser are illustrated on page 89.

You can also check the flywheel key at the same time you check the condenser. A flywheel key is a rectangular piece of soft metal that fits into a slot along the top and side of the crankshaft. The metal is soft on purpose: when the blade hits a hard object, the key breaks and releases

the torque on the crankshaft. This prevents damage to the crankshaft, piston, valves, gears, and other working parts of the engine.

Replacement of the key is very easy: just remove the old key and install a new one. You may also have to replace the blade if it has been damaged or bent. These procedures are illustrated on pages 90 and 61.

■ How's the oil?

When you remove the oil refill cap, the oil port may appear to be full, but the engine may still need oil. Add more oil through a funnel until the oil seeps out of the port.

Start the engine. If the engine sounds noisy, the chances are the low- or no-oil problem has damaged the engine. It may need to be overhauled or replaced.

■ Are the fuel lines and fuel filters clean?

■ Has a vapor lock in the fuel system caused the engine to stop suddenly?

Let the engine become cool to the touch. Then try to start the engine. If the engine still won't fire, look for trouble in the carburetor. It may be dirty. If so, detach the spark plug wire from the plug, pour gasoline into the carburetor, and activate the starter once or twice. This permits the clean gas to rinse out the system. Let the equipment sit an hour or so, then start the engine normally.

■ Are the muffler and exhaust pipe blocked with grass and debris?

A plugged exhaust system can stop the engine and damage it. So can a rusted, corroded muffler.

If the muffler is still in one piece, you may be able to remove it with a pipe wrench by turning the entire muffler counterclockwise. Or the muffler may be mounted with bolts, which also turn out counterclockwise. If the muffler breaks off in the threaded exhaust port, you can use a tapered metal ream driven by a hand brace to remove the rusted metal. The metal is soft, but be careful with the ream so it doesn't dam-

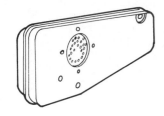
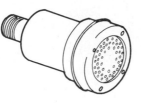

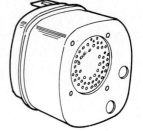

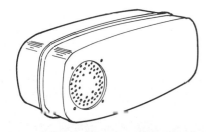

1. Muffler replacement. Universal muffler replacement kits, made to fit all models, are available; the more complicated ones shown above must be purchased at a lawnmower parts outlet. You will need the model number when buying a new muffler.

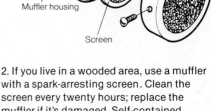

2. If you live in a wooded area, use a muffler with a spark-arresting screen. Clean the screen every twenty hours; replace the muffler if it's damaged. Self-contained mufflers, commonly found on four-cycle engines, simply screws into the engine housing at the exhaust opening.

age the threads in the exhaust port.

■ Is the spark plug wire snugly attached to the spark plug?

■ Is the linkage between the handle controls, throttle, and governor working properly?

The engine has no power and runs unevenly

These symptoms are usually caused by problems in the ignition or in the carburetor idle adjustment.

Tools, materials, and supplies: standard slot screwdriver, spark plug gap gauge, pliers, lubricating oil, spark plug, tune-up kit, steel wool.

■ Is the spark plug wire properly hooked to the spark plug?

Pull off the wire, reset or tighten the little loop of metal with pliers by crimping it, and clean the metal loop with steel wool or sandpaper. A rat-tail (round) metal file makes an excellent tool to ream the corrosion out of the loop.

At this checkpoint, make sure the throttle controls are free and working properly, not stuck on any of the various settings. Then make sure the air filter is clean.

Remove the spark plug and check the gap and the base of the plug for dirt. As a rule, spark plug gaps should be set at .025 inch (.75mm).

Your owner's manual will specify the proper gap; but if you don't have the manual, use the .025 setting. And if you don't have a gap gauge, you can substitute a matchbook cover; its thickness is approximately .025 inch. But for accuracy buy a feeler, or gap, gauge; the cost is nominal.

1. Throttle linkage maintenance. Remove grass clippings and other debris with a screwdriver or a soft brush.

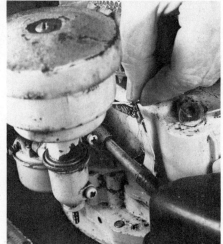

2. Worn and broken throttle and choke springs should be replaced. Repairs will be unsatisfactory.

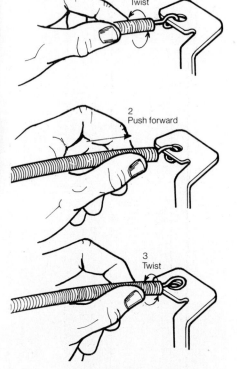

1. Removing control lever springs. First twist the spring toward the engine. When the end of the loop can be pushed under the control, push the spring forward, as in drawings 1 and 2. Continue twisting the spring toward the engine and the loop will snap out of the hole.

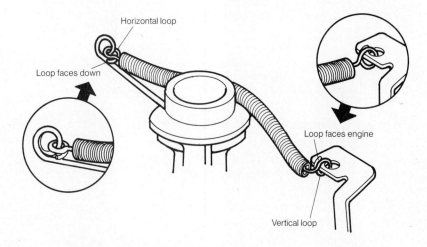

3. This is the correct position of springs on many standard four-cycle engines. Do not use pliers to install the springs.

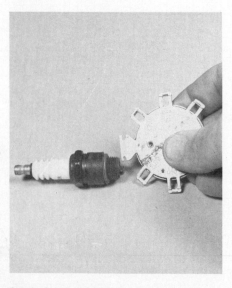

Spark plug gapping. Use a gapping tool to make spark plug gap adjustments.

■ Does the needle valve need adjustment?

It controls the flow of fuel into the carburetor (see illustrations). If this valve is bent or, more likely, incorrectly set, it causes loss of power and uneven engine running.

Examine the needle as shown in the illustration. If it looks bent or worn, replace the valve. Do not attempt to straighten it. If the needle is not bent or worn, replace the valve, turning it until it stops. Then open the valve one and a half turns counterclockwise. Start the engine and turn the valve clockwise until you hear the engine start to lose speed. This means that the carburetor is now set on a lean fuel mixture. Now slowly open the valve counterclockwise, just a tad past the point of the engine's smoothest operation. At this point, the engine should begin to run rough again. Finally, turn the needle back clockwise to a point between the last setting and the smoothest operation. This is the perfect setting.

Instructions for adjusting another type of carburetor are given in the accompanying captions.

■ Have you flooded the engine?

Running equipment extensively on hills and slopes can cause flooding. Flooding can also occur when you crank the engine with the spark plug wire disconnected and when the gas mixture is too rich, that is, when the needle valve is opened too far in the carburetor.

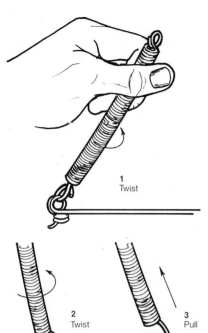

1
Twist

2
Twist

3
Pull

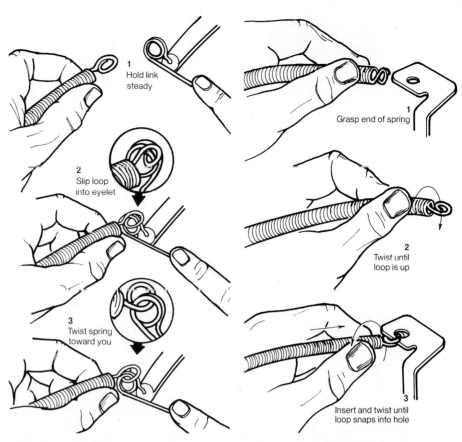

1
Hold link
steady

2
Slip loop
into eyelet

3
Twist spring
toward you

1
Grasp end of spring

2
Twist until
loop is up

3
Insert and twist until
loop snaps into hole

2. Remove eyelet springs by twisting the spring counterclockwise, as shown in drawings 1 and 2, and then pulling the spring up and off the eyelet.

1. Installing an eyelet spring. Steady the link with one hand (1); then slip the end of the loop on the spring into the link eyelet (2). Finally, twist the spring toward yourself. You'll have to practice this a couple of times until you get the knack.

2. To attach a spring to a control lever, turn the spring about three-quarters of a turn toward the engine (1). At this point, the loop of the spring should be pointing up. Insert the end of the loop into the lever hole. Twist the spring toward yourself. The end of the loop will snap into the control lever hole.

Needle valve check. Before adjusting idle and mixture valves, back out the needle counterclockwise with a screwdriver and examine it. Be sure the valve is in top condition—do not use valves with a worn or bent tip. A tension spring is usually threaded on the needle shaft; be sure to put it back in place.

Suction lift carburetor (right). The mixture screw regulates power. There is also an idle speed screw that keeps the engine running without skipping or stopping. Adjust the fuel mixture by turning the mixture screw as described opposite.

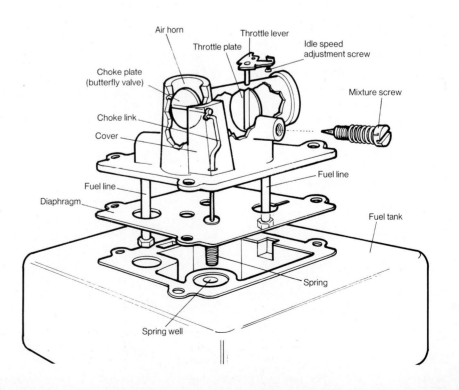

Air horn

Throttle lever

Throttle plate

Idle speed adjustment screw

Choke plate (butterfly valve)

Mixture screw

Choke link

Cover

Fuel line

Fuel line

Diaphragm

Fuel tank

Spring

Spring well

Mixture screw adjustment. On most suction lift carburetors the mixture screw is behind a bracket in front of and just above the cylinder head. There is a hole in the bracket through which a standard slot screwdriver is inserted. You'll have to get eye-level with the hole in order to see the screw. This view with the bracket removed shows how the adjustment is made.

Set the throttle control in the "stop" position. Pull the starter rope or crank the engine at least six times. The closed throttle produces a high vacuum and opens the choke. In turn, the vacuum cleans excess fuel from the engine. Start the engine.

If the engine continues to flood, set the needle valve as detailed above. If this doesn't work, there is another alternative, but you must be very careful when doing it: there is danger of the gasoline igniting in the carburetor.

Remove the air filter from the carburetor with a screwdriver. Insert the screwdriver into the carburetor barrel past the butterfly valve. The screwdriver keeps the valve open. Keeping your face and hands *away* from the carburetor, crank the engine. Repeat the cranking process several times. The engine should start. When it starts, remove the screwdriver and replace the air filter.

If this doesn't work, remove the air filter and insert the air filter bolt back into the carburetor through the opening in the butterfly valve. Turn down this bolt so it is approximately the depth it would be if the air filter were installed. Insert the screw-

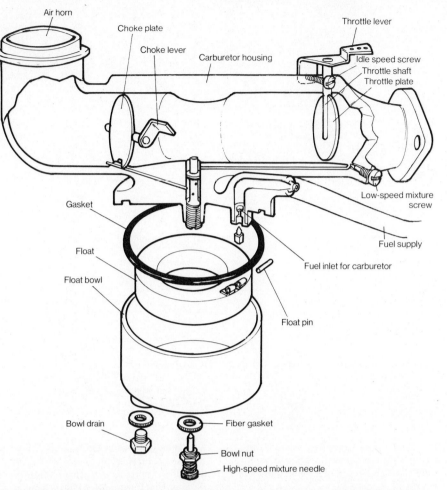

1. Anatomy of a float carburetor. This component, used on many brand-name lawnmowers and lawn equipment, seldom needs adjustment. If you trace the running problem to the carburetor, however, check your owner's manual for adjustment instructions or follow these steps: first turn all needle valves to the "closed" position. All needles turn clockwise to close. Open the valves one full turn. Now turn out the idle speed screw (top, above) until it is beyond the throttle lever. Then turn it back into the housing one full turn. Start the engine. (Instructions continue in the next caption.)

2. When the engine is warm, turn each of the needles about a quarter turn clockwise—first the low-speed needle, and then the idle speed needle. You will hear the engine start running smoothly. If not, turn one or another of the needles another quarter turn clockwise. This is a trial-and-error adjustment; you have to fiddle with the needles until the proper setting is achieved.

Bowl drain maintenance. Push up on the bowl drain screw to drain the sediment from the bottom of the bowl (index finger in this photograph). Do this every few weeks when the equipment is in operation. If the drainage matter feels oily or gummy disassemble and clean the carburetor. You can buy a parts kit for this at dealer outlets.

Idle speed adjustment. On many suction lift carburetors this part is located next to the air horn (left), as shown here. You turn a screw to adjust it. The governor of this type of carburetor operates by means of an air vane (the white flag near the coil here). As the engine speed increases, the fins on the flywheel create an air flow that moves the vane and closes the throttle. As speed is decreased, so is the air flow, and the throttle opens.

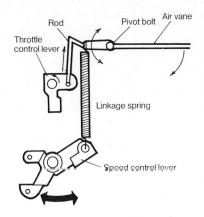

Anatomy of the air vane system. For the engine to run properly, the spring from the speed control lever to the air vane *must* be in good repair and attached properly to the linkage.

driver into the carburetor barrel and crank the engine. The engine now should fire. Replace the filter.

When the engine is running, adjust the needle valve (described above) so that the engine runs properly.

Check these other possible causes:

old gasoline

water in the fuel

faulty flywheel key

bad compression

faulty ignition points

The engine is hard to start, and there is kickback from the starter

These common problems are usually caused by belts or chains that are not disengaged when the engine is cranked.

Tools, materials, and supplies: standard slot and Phillips-head screwdrivers, adjustable or socket wrenches, lubricating oil, new belts.

■ Are the belts loose (in belt-driven equipment)?

The belt should deflect approximately ½ inch between pulleys. The belts can usually be adjusted at the drive, or power, pulley or sometimes at the opposite pulley. Loosen the adjustment bolt or screw, pull the belt to its ½-inch deflection point, and retighten the bolt or screw. If the belt can't be tightened properly, replace it. Belts stretch through normal use, and adjustment might not be possible.

■ Is the chain clean?

If the equipment has a chain drive, a dirty chain may be causing a drag on the engine. The solution is simple: clean the chain with gasoline and then apply lubricating oil.

■ Is all add-on equipment disengaged before you start the engine?

■ Is there trouble in the starting mechanism?

Vibration

If vibration is excessive, look for an out-of-balance blade. The blade may be twisted or badly nicked; it may have poor lift. Special details on blade sharpening are on page 62.

Tools, materials, and supplies: adjustable or socket wrenches, screwdriver, lubricating oil.

■ Is the blade tight?

Tighten the blade mounting bolt or bolts. They turn counterclockwise.

■ Are the engine mounting bolts tight?

These bolts hold the engine to the equipment deck. You may have to hold the bottom of the bolts with a wrench *under* the deck while you tighten the bolts on the *top* of the deck. These bolts turn clockwise for tightening.

■ Is the deck damaged?

If the deck is broken, cracked, or rusted badly, it may have caused the engine to drop out of alignment and, therefore, vibrate. If the deck is damaged, it must be repaired or replaced. Repairs usually involve welding, a job for a professional. If the deck must be replaced, you should get estimates; a new mower may be cheaper.

■ Improper carburetor adjustment. (See details above.) A rough-running engine can cause vibration.

■ A bent crankshaft. Take the crankshaft problem to a pro.

The engine is noisy

The trouble is almost always a muffler that's rusted out, badly bent, or missing completely. A new muffler will remedy the problem.

Tools, materials, and supplies: adjustable or socket wrenches, pipe wrench, metal reamer, hand brace, penetrating lubricant, new muffler.

■ **Is the exhaust system clogged?**
If you notice the equipment suddenly running quietly, check the muffler or exhaust system for clogging; remove matted grass clippings, dirt, and general debris.

■ **Has the muffler deteriorated?**
A deteriorated muffler must be replaced. Some mufflers screw in; others are held by two bolts to the muffler opening on the engine. Some are located above the equipment deck; some are located below the deck.

To remove an old muffler of the screw-in type, first lubricate the hub of the muffler with penetrating oil and let it sit for thirty minutes or so. You may have to tip the equipment on its side or top to do this. Then, try to remove the muffler with a pipe wrench; it turns counterclockwise. If it breaks off, try to remove the base with the pipe wrench if there is enough of a nub left to grasp with the wrench. If not, ream out the base with a metal reamer in a hand brace. The muffler metal is fairly soft, but go easy with the reamer so you don't damage the female threads in the engine block. Just a couple of turns with the reamer are usually enough to remove the metal. Then screw in the new muffler.

To remove bolt-held mufflers, use an adjustable wrench or socket set outfit. Give the bolts the penetrating oil treatment described above.

Turn out the bolts counterclockwise. If the bolts break off in the engine block, you may be able to remove them with a screw ejector device. However, broken bolt removal can be a troublesome job requiring special equipment too expensive to buy for a one-shot project, so go to a pro. Prices for bolt removal usually run under $5. After the muffler and bolts are off the engine, simply install the new muffler.

If the noise is not in the exhaust system but in the engine itself, check the oil level *immediately*.

The engine smokes

The good news is that this symptom may not be bad news, such as a broken piston ring, broken piston, or a damaged cylinder.

Tools, materials, and supplies: screwdriver and lubricating oil.

■ **Is the carburetor adjusted properly?**
Start the engine and set the throttle control at idle; then set it at full speed. If you notice black smoke coming out of the exhaust, the fuel mixture is probably too rich.

If you can't make the adjustment as described on page 82, have a pro make the adjustment with a tachometer. The cost is not prohibitive.

■ **Is the smoke blue and does it smell of burned oil?**
If so, the trouble is probably with the piston or in the cylinder. Blue smoke also is accompanied by excessive internal engine noise; the engine will make a dull knocking sound. Take the equipment to a professional and get an estimate before ordering repairs.

The engine overheats

This problem probably is a minor one, but don't ignore it. Prolonged overheating can cause serious damage.

Tools, materials, and supplies: screwdriver, adjustable or socket wrenches, putty knife, engine oil, stiff brush.

■ **How's the oil level?**
Stop the engine and check the oil level immediately.

■ **Is there dirt impacted around cooling fins?**
Keep these fins clean at all times. Use a putty knife and stiff brush to remove the debris.

■ **Are all coverings, shrouds, and blower housings in position?**

If not, air can't properly circulate around the cooling fins.

■ **Is the carburetor adjusted properly?**

■ **Is the muffler obstructed with dirt or debris?**

■ **Is the engine overloaded?**
You may be running it too fast for too long. Or the engine may be burdened by too much add-on equipment. Stop the engine, let it cool, and disengage the extra equipment. Then test the engine without the equipment. If it runs cooler, you've solved the problem.

■ **Is there a buildup of carbon inside the cylinder head?**
This is easier to correct than you might think. Remove the throttle controls with a socket wrench (if necessary), and back out the bolts holding the cylinder head in place.

Remove the cylinder head, labeling the bolts and holes as you go (see illustrations) so that you can replace them in order.
Check the gasket under the cylinder head for damage. If it is worn, replace it with a new one.

Remove the carbon from the back of the cylinder head and the top of the cylinder and valves with a putty knife or steel brush as shown in the illustrations.

Reassemble the parts, reversing the sequence you followed to disassemble them. The proper sequences are shown in the diagrams opposite. Turn the bolts clockwise until they are snug, but don't overtighten the bolts. When the bolts are snug, tighten each one in sequence again so that you turn each one approximately the same number of times. After assembly, give the engine a compression test (see page 93).

Most small engines do not need to have the cylinder head bolts tightened with a torque wrench to measure pressure pounds, but it would be a good idea for you to check with a pro or a dealer if you are in doubt. They will give you the proper torque values for your engine model.

1. Cylinder head maintenance. To remove the cylinder head to correct carbon buildup problems, first remove the air filter and the bracket that holds the throttle assembly. Then turn out the cylinder head bolts counterclockwise. Label bolts and holes in order of removal so that reassembly will be correct and efficient.

2. Take the cylinder head off. You may have to insert the tip of a screwdriver between the cylinder head and engine block to pry off the head. Go easy so you don't damage the gasket. Another method is to tap the edge of the head with a rubber hammer.

3. Examine the valves for burning and pitting. You can pop them out of their seats by moving the engine crankshaft; turn the cutting blade or tiller tines slowly. If the valves are in bad shape, they should be replaced. These valves and cylinder head are carbon-covered, but in good condition.

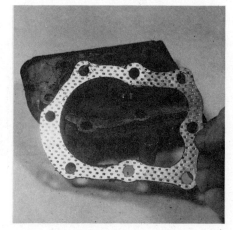

4. Scrape the carbon from the piston and valve surfaces. Be careful you don't dig into or scratch the metal. Use an engine cleaner solvent to help remove the deposits. If you notice lots of oil escaping around the piston, it could mean that the piston rings are badly worn.

5. Clean the carbon from the cylinder head with a putty knife. Since the head is dish-shaped, be extra careful not to dig into the metal. Finish the job with a wire brush, carbon solvent, and steel wool.

6. The cylinder head gasket—usually metal-clad—does not need to be replaced with a new one if it is in good condition. However, since you have gone through the work of removing the cylinder head, it's a good idea to start reassembly with a new gasket. They are inexpensive.

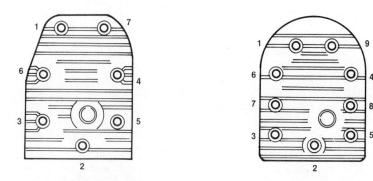

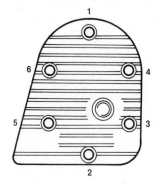

7. Replace the cylinder head and gasket and tighten the bolts in sequence. Three standard sequences are shown here. Don't overtighten or you'll crack the cylinder head or strip the bolt threads.

Other possible causes of overheating include improper tappet clearance or tappets that are too loose. Consult a professional if you think the tappets are causing your problem. Another possibility is improper timing, and this too is a job for a pro.

Maintenance: do it annually without fail

Engine manufacturers and professional small engine mechanics are sticklers about regular maintenance. You should be, too. Maintenance is vital; you should check the oil, service the air cleaner, change oil, etc., according to the specifications listed in your owner's manual. If you can't find the manual, here's a general checklist to follow:

oil check: every five running hours

clean air filter every twenty-five hours

adjust plug gap every 100 hours

clean combustion (cylinder head) chamber every 100 to 300 hours

replace rings every 500 to 1000 hours

overhaul engine every 1000 hours

General maintenance—changing the oil and fuel and cleaning the air filter and equipment housing—should be done at the start of every season in which you'll be using the equipment. It's a smart idea to repeat this maintenance routine about half way through the season and at the end of the season.

How to tune a four-cycle engine

It takes about an hour to replace the condensor, points, spark plug, and oil on a four-cycle engine, even if you've never attempted this job before. There is very little skill involved; the replacement parts are inexpensive and readily available. The tune-up parts are sold in kits; you need only know what brand the engine is; it will appear in the list on the kits, which sell for about $5. Reg-

1. Annual maintenance. At the start or end of the equipment use season, take time to tighten all bolts and screws on the equipment, including engine mounting bolts, bolts on mufflers, carburetors, cylinder heads, and so forth.

3. Assemble the cleaned filter in the housing and put several drops of light or engine oil on the filter through the bottom breathing holes of the housing.

5. When you open the oil port, the engine may appear to be full of oil, but don't be deluded. Try turning the blades or tines to shift the crankshaft and make room for more oil. Use a funnel to prevent messy spills that attract dirt.

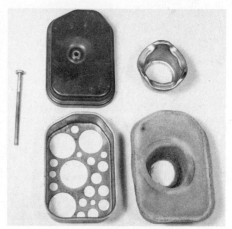

2. Service the air filter, either by washing it with regular household detergent and clean water or by replacing the filter entirely. A standard four-cycle engine filter is shown here. The metal clamshell housing, held together by one bolt, holds the rubberlike filter. The round metal component fits inside the filter. Replace a worn or damaged filter.

4. Keep the engine oil level full at all times. Most oil ports are capped with a two-pronged stopper that can be loosened counterclockwise. Change the oil frequently. The oil drain plug is usually under the deck at the bottom of the engine.

6. Lubricate all wheels, control levers, cables, and chain drives. While you're working, use a putty knife and stiff-bristled brush to clean away grass debris from under the deck, around the engine's cooling fins, and at grass chutes.

ular tools that you probably own already can be used; one exception is a flywheel puller. This piece of equipment sells for about $2 to $5, and it can be used until the manufacturers change the engine design.

Of course, if the engine is running smoothly, there is no need for a tune-up. Don't fix it if it works. But this rule does not apply to the regular maintenance procedure described in this chapter.

As a general rule, the engine should be tuned after about 100 hours of operation. Consider it preventive maintenance. Usually the condensor goes bad during this period, so it must be replaced as part of the tune-up; and the points and plug gap must be checked even though the engine is humming along.

As you operate the equipment during the season, get into the habit of cleaning the air filter after every ten to twelve hours of operation. The cleanliness of the air going through the carburetor into the engine will extend the life of the engine more than any other factor, including frequent oil changes. Small engines must inhale more than 10,000 gallons of air for each gallon of fuel burned.

When you do tune-ups or any general repairs, set the equipment on a sturdy table about the height of a cardtable. This will save a lot of bending and stooping. Have plenty of overhead light. You'll need to block the wheels. Try a short length of 2 × 4 across the front and rear wheels. This procedure is better than servicing the engine out on the lawn where nuts and bolts can easily be lost in the turf grass.

Compression and valve checks

If engines don't operate at the compression level they were designed to, the fuel doesn't burn efficiently and you don't get the performance you've paid for. Four-cycle engines have poppet valves that affect the engine's compression. A loose spark plug, worn or broken piston rings, or a

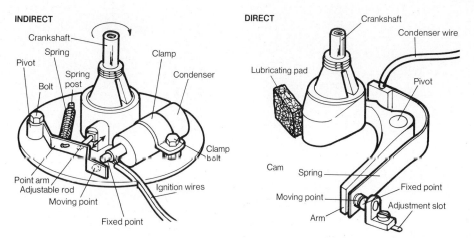

INDIRECT — Crankshaft, Spring, Pivot, Bolt, Spring post, Clamp, Condenser, Clamp bolt, Point arm, Adjustable rod, Moving point, Ignition wires, Fixed point

DIRECT — Crankshaft, Condenser wire, Lubricating pad, Pivot, Cam, Spring, Fixed point, Moving point, Adjustment slot, Arm

Basic ignition systems. Two types of points-and-condenser ignition systems are shown here. Both are mounted under the engine flywheel. Most Briggs & Stratton engines use indirect points; most Tecumseh engines use direct points.

1. Flywheel removal. The first job in a tune-up is to remove the engine cover and the flywheel. Turn out the bolts that hold the cover on. Also remove throttle controls (usually are clamped to the housing) from the handle. You don't have to remove control springs. If the engine cover is integrated with a pull starter, remove the starter completely.

2. Remove the wire screen that covers the flywheel. It's a good idea to store parts in marked envelopes so you can identify them for correct reassembly.

3. This type of clutch assembly can be removed by holding the cutting blade with one hand and turning the clutch *gently* with the wrench. The metal is very soft, so be careful. If the clutch won't budge, try placing one end of a wooden block against a screw ear and tapping the other end lightly with a hammer. If the engine doesn't have this clutch arrangement, you will find a nut and washer holding on the flywheel. Hold or block the blade to loosen the nut counterclockwise with a socket wrench.

4. With the clutch off, the flywheel key is visible at the bottom of the key slot in the crankshaft. If this key is bent, and the engine won't run, remove the flywheel and replace the key. Then reassemble the engine and try to start it. You may not need new points and a condenser. *(continued on page 90.)*

5. A flywheel puller is necessary to remove the flywheel. To use the block puller shown here run the threaded bolts into the matching holes on top of the flywheel. Turn the nuts under the block of metal tight against the block. Then turn the nuts on top of the block of metal down and tight against the block. Now turn the head of each bolt an equal number of turns. The wedging action of the puller against the top of the crankshaft pulls the flywheel up and off the crankshaft. As soon as you hear a pop, the flywheel is loose and may be lifted off the crankshaft.

6. The face of this flywheel puller fits over the top of the crankshaft. Strike the puller with a hammer, as shown, to pop the flywheel off. *Do not* strike the top of the crankshaft with a hammer; you will damage the shaft.

7. The flywheel key fits into a slot along the side of the crankshaft. There is also a slot in the flywheel hole to accept the key. The key is an essential part of the ignition timing; if it's broken, even slightly bent, you may not be able to start the engine.

1. Indirect points replacement. The ignition system is under the flywheel. It is covered with a metal lid held by machine screws. The system shown here is the indirect point assembly. You'll need an adjustable or socket wrench to draw and drive the solid head screws.

2. Remove the condenser clamp and the condenser first. Do not disassemble the points at this time, since you can use this part as a reference later. Two small wires are threaded into a hole at the top of the condenser. A tension spring holds the wires in position. Depress the spring and release the two wires; the condenser is now free.

3. Remove this rod from the ignition housing. Although it seldom needs to be replaced, check it for wear. Clean it and re-install it. (In direct ignition systems, a similar rod is located on a V-shaped arm on the points.) The rods are not included in tune-up kits; buy them at repair shops.

4. Remove the moving point. When you take out the slotless screw the spring and the point lift off. Then, install the new condenser, but leave the clamp loose.

5. Install the new moving point, attaching the spring to the arm of the point and the spring post. Move the condenser forward so it touches the tip of the moving point. Then turn the crankshaft, as shown here, until the moving point opens to its widest gap. You'll have to try this a couple of times; the trick is to stop turning the crankshaft just before the point snaps closed.

6. With the moving point set at the widest gap, insert an .025 inch feeler gauge between the condenser and the moving point. Check your owner's manual to see if the gap for your system is different. With the feeler gauge in position, move the condenser forward until its point and the point on the moving point both just touch the gauge. Then tighten the clamp condenser. If you don't have a feeler gauge use a matchbook cover, which is about .025 in. thick. Reassemble the parts and start the engine.

1. Direct points replacement. To replace a direct point ignition system, first remove the engine covering and the flywheel, as shown above for the indirect system. The puller you tap with a hammer works best on this type of engine equipment. Use a screwdriver to flip open the spring clip that holds the metal lid over the ignition parts, as shown here.

2. Looking down on the direct system, the condenser is at the left; the points are in the housing, center. The coil is at the top *(continued on page 92)*.

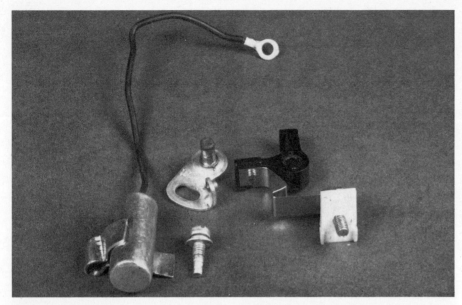

3. The tune-up kit for direct systems includes a new condenser (top), points (center), the point pivot, and a screw for the point pivot. Change just one component at a time to avoid reassembly problems. Before you install this system, *gently* burnish the surfaces of the points with fine sandpaper or a metal file to remove any foreign matter that may have collected on the points.

4. To begin installing a direct ignition system, remove the wires on the old movable point (white). They are secured with a nut that turns counterclockwise. Then pry out the movable point with the tip of a screwdriver. The whole assembly lifts straight out. You don't have to code the wires; they can go on the point screw in any order.

5. Remove the old fixed point by backing out its holding screw counterclockwise. Then install the new fixed point, as shown, and insert the new movable point in the housing. When both are assembled, move the fixed point so its tip just touches the tip of the moving point. Leave the screw snug but not tight so you can move the point later to set the gap.

6. Remove the old condenser by taking out the machine screw that secures it. Install the new condenser and then reconnect all wires to the moving point terminal and secure them with the nut. At this time also check the rod that touches the crankshaft for wear and replace any damaged wires and terminals.

7. Thread the flywheel nut back onto the crankshaft. Then turn the crankshaft with a wrench. When the moving point is fully opened, and just before it snaps closed, insert a .025 inch feeler gauge (or matchbook cover) between the points. Move the fixed point with the slotted hole toward the moving point until both barely touch the feeler. Then tighten the screw on the fixed point. Reassemble the engine and start it.

cracked cylinder head can cause poor compression. If the engine is hard to start, puffs out lots of blue-colored smoke, and runs roughly, even after it has been properly tuned and the parts are functioning properly, suspect bad compression.

Tools, materials, and supplies: socket set, spark plug wrench, open-end wrench set, feeler gauge, ruler, standard slot screwdriver, needle-nose pliers, oilstone valve replacement kit (including new valves, springs, spring caps, and retainers), lubricating oil, grease, wiping cloth.

1. Make sure the little metal washer at the base of the spark plug is in place. Tighten the spark plug in its port. Do not overtighten. Start the engine. If it still runs rough, make the following checks in sequence.

2. Remove the spark plug cable and hook it on its keeper. Then slowly pull the starter cord. If the flywheel turns exceptionally easily as you pull the cord and you feel no drag,

poor compression may be the problem. The flywheel should offer some resistance when turned.

3. Remove the spark plug wire and the spark plug from its port. Place a finger or thumb flat over the port and make the rough-and-ready compression test shown in the photograph.

4. Take the engine to a pro and have him test the compression with a compression gauge. You can buy a compression gauge and do this job yourself, but the cost may be prohibitive unless you intend to run compression tests on a regular basis. A pro may check compression free or for a nominal price.

5. Remove the cylinder head (page 87) and the tappet cover (shown on this page) and check the poppet valves.

You can readily see if the valves at the cylinder head are worn or encrusted with carbon. Test the

springs inside the tappet box to see if they are worn or broken. The illustrations show the procedure to follow. If the valves are defective, replace them. In the long run, new valves are less expensive and easier to work with than repaired valves. You also have the satisfaction of operating with new parts.

Different model engines have different valve clearances. You may find these measurements in your owner's manual. If not, check with a dealer for the specifications.

If, during your checks, you find the piston rings are damaged or the cylinder head is cracked or broken, have a professional make the repairs. But get an estimate first; a new short block may be less expensive than repairs.

The tales spark plugs can tell
Spark plugs offer a good starting point for engine troubleshooting analysis. Many times you can quickly spot the problem just by removing the spark plug and looking at the tip

Compression test procedure. Remove the spark plug wire and the spark plug. You may also have to remove the engine's head covering. Place the flat of your thumb or finger over the spark plug port and turn the flywheel. You should feel suction—the more, the higher the compression. If the suction is light, suspect valve or piston trouble.

1. Valve appearance check. Remove the cover on the tappet box. Turn out the bolts that hold it, as shown here. Then remove the cylinder head to expose the tops of the valves (see page 87).

2. The springs, stems, retainers, and caps of the valves are visible when the tappet cover is removed. If you find weak springs, burned valve margins, heads, or faces, replace the damaged parts with new ones.

Anatomy of a valve assembly

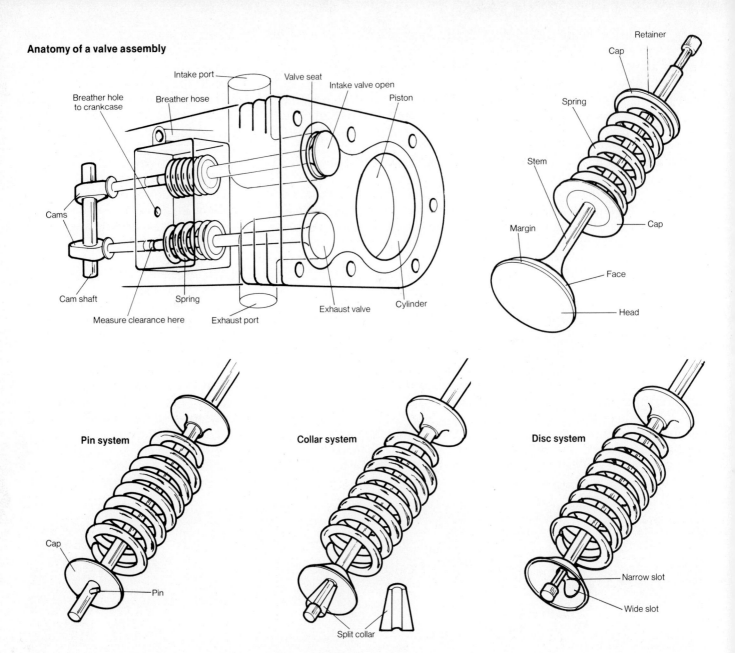

Intake port

Breather hose

Breather hole to crankcase

Valve seat

Intake valve open

Piston

Cams

Cam shaft

Measure clearance here

Spring

Exhaust port

Exhaust valve

Cylinder

Retainer

Cap

Spring

Stem

Margin

Cap

Face

Head

Pin system

Cap

Pin

Collar system

Split collar

Disc system

Narrow slot

Wide slot

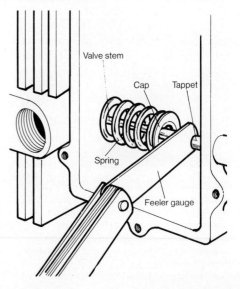

Valve clearance check. Turn the crankshaft by hand so both valves close. Measure the gaps with a feeler gauge that matches the specifications for the engine. If a gap is too wide, replace the valve. If the gap is too narrow, remove the valve (see following illustrations) and take some metal off the tip of the valve stem by rubbing it on an oilstone. Keep the tip square.

Valve stem

Cap

Tappet

Spring

Feeler gauge

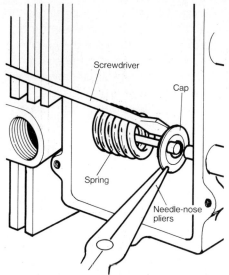

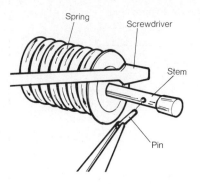

1 Valve removal procedure. Compress the valve spring with a screwdriver. Then pull off the retainer cap with pliers. The slotted disc retainer is shown here. Once the spring is loose, the valve may be removed by pulling it out of the engine at the cylinder head.

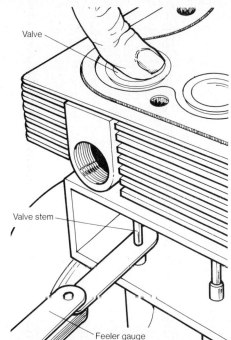

1. Valve installation. Insert the new valves into the engine through the top of the cylinder head. Do not install the springs or caps at this point. Push the valves tight and turn the crankshaft slowly until the valves are closed. Then, with one hand, hold the valve heads tightly against the valve seat and check the clearance with a feeler gauge. If the valves sit too tight, remove them and grind the tips lightly with an oilstone. Go easy; just a couple of swipes across the abrasive is enough. Reinsert the valves and check them again. Repeat the grinding if needed.

2B. To replace a pin, compress the spring, using a screwdriver to force the cap upward. The spring is strong; you may need a helper to hold it compressed while you insert the pin with pliers.

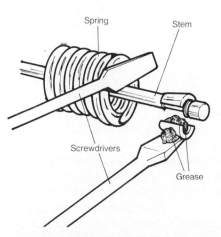

2C. To replace a split collar, compress the spring and push the collar halves onto the stem. Stick them in place with a daub of heavy grease. Once they're in place, release the spring to put tension on the collar.

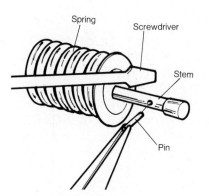

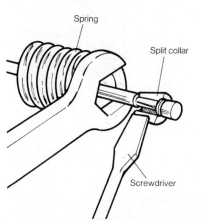

2. The spring retainer cap may be held by pins or a split collar. To remove both, turn the crankshaft until the valves open fully. Then compress the springs and pull out the pins or the split collar. You may have to twist the valves after they are open to align the pins or collars.

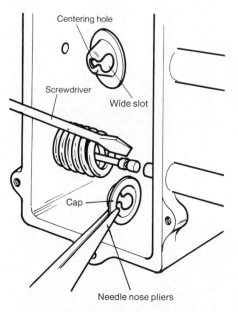

2A. When the clearance is properly set, install the springs. To replace the disc retainer, shown here, insert the stem through the wide slot and then pull the disc so the stem snaps into the narrow slot.

(the ground electrode) of the plug. With the clues it provides, you can make the right engine adjustments.

Tools, materials, and supplies: spark plug wrench, stiff-bristled toothbrush, feeler gauge, sandpaper, steel wool, new spark plug, clean wiping cloths. *For adjustments:* standard slot screwdriver, household detergent, lubricating oil.

You should change the spark plug in any small engine at least once a year. The best time is at the start of the operating season, for example, in the spring for lawnmowers. You should replace the plug if any of the problems listed below are found. Otherwise, don't replace the plug if the engine is operating normally. In this case you can clean the plug with a stiff-bristled toothbrush during mid-season maintenance.

Anatomy of a spark plug

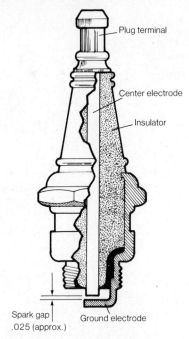

Plug terminal

Center electrode

Insulator

Spark gap
.025 (approx.)

Ground electrode

All replacement spark plugs *must* be intended for use in the type of engine you own. *Do not* use automobile spark plugs in small engines. Since the base of automobile plugs is longer than that of small engine plugs, the top of the piston will hit the bottom of the auto plug and cause costly damage. Always buy replacement plugs made specifically for your engine model.

The gap specifications for plugs varies from engine to engine. The proper gap spacing is given in your owner's manual. If you can't find the manual, a .025 gap is standard (see page 82 for details).

Reading the tip deposits

Deposits on the tip of the plug, that is, on the ground electrode, can tell you what is causing the engine to malfunction.

■ Light, brown powder

This deposite indicates that the engine is functioning normally. If there is no encrusted deposit, remove the powder with a stiff brush.

■ An oily plug

Greasy, black deposits, sometimes encrusted with hard carbon, are caused by worn-out piston rings

which let oil seep past the piston and out of the top of the cylinder onto the bottom of the spark plug. New rings will have to be installed to solve this problem. This is a job for a professional, but be sure to get an estimate first.

If your engine is two-cycle and the plug is in this condition, you may be mixing too much oil with the fuel. Reduce the amount of oil in the mixture.

Other causes include a clogged air filter and an engine that is running too fast at idle.

Clean the filter with household detergent and water, dry it, and oil it lightly. The oil attracts and holds the dust. Install a new filter if it is replaceable.

To set the idle speed, adjust the idle valve clockwise or counterclockwise (see page 82 for details).

■ Heavy, black carbon

This deposit is usually crusty, not oily or powdery, and very black. The coating is caused by a clogged air filter (see pages 78-79), a partly closed choke, high-octane gasoline, or a mistimed engine (take the saw to a pro).

■ Yellow deposits

These result from a too-lean fuel mixture, high-octane gasoline, or a

Heavy, black carbon or oil deposits.

clogged muffler and exhaust ports. Buy a gasoline with a lower octane rating. Adjust the needle valves on the carburetor counterclockwise (see page 82) to make the fuel and air mixture richer. For muffler problems, see page 81.

■ Pits in ground or center electrodes

You may have to remove the carbon in order to see wear and pitting. In some cases, the tip of the plug will look off-white and burned. The trouble is generally caused by an air and fuel mixture that is too lean. Turn the needle valves on the carburetor counterclockwise about a quarter of a turn.

Incorrect timing can also cause burning (take the saw to a pro); look for debris clogging the cooling fins. Also check to make sure the spark plug is properly threaded in the plug port in the engine.

■ Insulator cracks

Usually, the damage is caused by something striking the outside of the plug. Excessive heat from the engine might cause the porcelain insulator to crack and even break. Check the cooling fins to make sure they are clean. Replace the spark plug. A cracked insulator cannot be repaired.

■ Bad cable connection

This doesn't affect the look of the tip of the plug, but it can cause hard starting and poor running. Press the metal tip of the cable with pliers to make a more closed position; clean off any corrosion with sandpaper or steel wool. If you notice any cracks or breaks in the spark plug cable running from the coil, the cable (or coil) should be replaced.

Two-cycle engine problems

Two-cycle and four-cycle engines share many of the same problems and solutions. In some situations, however, a two-cycle engine demands special treatment; these matters are discussed here. You may also find the sections on four-cycle engine problems in this chapter and the rider mower troubleshooting section in Chapter 4 helpful.

A two-cycle engine parts identification chart appears at the beginning of this chapter.

The subjects covered here include: general maintenance, fuel, the air filter, the carburetor, the ignition system, and storage procedures. The exhaust system is not discussed here since it is identical to the four-cycle system explained earlier in the chapter. A comprehensive troubleshooting routine concludes this section.

General maintenance

Dirt is the worst enemy of almost any machine. In a two-cycle engine, dirt can foul the air filter, carburetor, fuel, ignition system, blade, wheels, and throttle controls. By systematically cleaning only the air filter, for example, you can prevent lots of grief with no-starts, rough idle, loss of engine power, and other problems.

Before you start the mower, make a habit of cleaning the grass pulp from under the deck, checking the air filter, and making sure the throttle linkage is free and clear from debris. After each use, let the mower engine cool. Then wipe the metal parts with a lightly oiled cloth. Tighten all the bolts and screws that you can see. Make sure all sprockets, open gears, wheels, and other lubrication points are oiled. And, every month or so, pull out the spark plug to check for carbon and make sure the exhaust system is clean and free of carbon.

If your lawn is fertilized, it's a good idea to hose under the deck after you use the mower. Wait until the engine has cooled. The water rinse removes any particles of fertilizer, which are a prime cause of deck rust-out.

The fuel system

Two-cycle engines require gasoline mixed with oil, and this is where many owners of two-cycle lawnmowers have trouble. They use an incorrect mixture or the wrong type of oil and gasoline.

If there is not enough oil in the mixture, the engine will begin to run hot. The piston and cylinder, starved for lubrication, will wear against each other, causing serious damage.

If there is too much oil in the mixture, gum and carbon accumulate in parts of the engine. This also leads to engine problems and failure.

The fuel used for two-cycle engines must be absolutely clean and fresh *regular* grade gasoline

unless the lawnmower manufacturer specifies otherwise.

The oil you mix with the fuel should be a two-cycle engine oil recommended by the manufacturer. *Do not* use regular automobile oil; it contains additives that will absolutely ruin the engine with just one tankful of gas and oil.

Do not just fill the gas tank on the engine about half full of fuel and then add the oil. Instead, measure and mix the two-cycle oil and fuel together in a separate gas container. Then shake the container *vigorously* to mix both components.

If you do not know what the fuel and oil ratio is for your lawnmower, phone a retailer that sells the brand or ask a professional repair person for the formula. See page 115, for more information on fuel and oil mixing.

Fuel tanks in two-cycle engines usually have a fuel filter inside the tank. When this filter becomes clogged, the engine will be hard to start or won't start at all. Inspect this filter at least three times during the mowing season. You can pull it from the tank with a hook fashioned from a hanger (see page 108). If you are mowing under very dusty or dirty conditions, inspect the filter at least once a month during the mowing season.

Clean the filter with gasoline or compressed air. The best procedure is simply to replace the filter; the cost is not prohibitive.

Fuel tanks can become dirty and encrusted with a varnish or a gummy coating from oil and fuel. If the mower has been in storage for a time, remove the fuel tank from the engine and flush it out with clean gasoline.

Check fuel lines often. A kinked line can cause engine trouble. Also, the lines may be subject to wear, especially at connections. Replacing and removing the lines usually involves no more than releasing a spring clip or nut. You can buy fuel lines at lawnmower repair shops and dealers.

Fuel caps need frequent attention They are vented so that air is pulled

into the tank to prevent a vacuum. Keep the air vent open; a pin or small wire usually fits the air passage.

As the fuel goes from the tank to the crankcase, it passes through the carburetor. This system has three basic parts: the choke plate, or valve; the throttle plate, or valve; and the reed valve.

All three valves accumulate dirt; all three are subject to some wear. The valves should be kept clean by scrubbing them with gasoline and an old toothbrush. The reed valve is behind the carburetor; you have to remove the carburetor and reed valve housing to get at this valve. If the valve looks worn, it can be quickly replaced with a new one. The standard gap specification is .01 inch (see drawing and photographs). As you clean, be sure that you don't disturb the settings of any needle adjustments on or around the carburetor assembly.

The air filter

This part is easy to find: it is usually held in a plastic or metal box in front of the carburetor. Remove the spring that holds the box lid or flip the lid off with the tip of a screwdriver.

The air filter is probably washable. Rap the filter against a hard surface, a workbench top, for example, to remove all the dirt you can. Then wash the filter under the kitchen faucet with regular household detergent and rinse it in clean water. Lightly oil the filter before replacing it. The oil attracts and holds dust and debris.

If the filter is paper or a replaceable type, knock out as much dirt as possible and reinstall the filter. If the filter is really dirty, and a shake-out doesn't clean it appreciably, replace the filter. Start each mowing season with a new filter if the filter is the paper cartridge type.

Carburetor adjustments

Every time you clean or replace the air filter make a habit of running a lightly oiled cloth around the carburetor housing. Remove the chunks of oil and grease that you find there. Use a toothbrush to remove debris that the cloth can't reach. Close the

1. Carburetor inspection. *(left, top)* With the air filter insert removed on this two-cycle engine you can see directly into the carburetor area. The fuel lines are positioned directly in back of the air filter housing. Remove the filter housing to get at the carburetor.

2. *(left, below)* Here the carburetor is dismounted. Move the choke lever (bottom) and you can see the butterfly valve move. If the valve is broken, bent, or won't turn, you may not be able to replace it. However, you probably can replace the whole assembly, which is screwed or bolted to the housing.

3. *(below)* The reed valve can be seen after the choke assembly is removed. The reed valve feeds the fuel and oil mixture from the carburetor into the cylinder. Many different designs are used, but they all have to be cleaned or replaced occasionally.

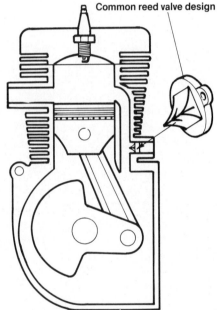

Common reed valve design

choke before you start work.

Many two-cycle engines have carburetors that permit three basic adjustments: the throttle, the low-speed mixture, and the high-speed mixture. These adjustments may be marked:

I for idle or throttle

T for idle or throttle

L for low speed

H for high speed

Although preset at the factory, these screws may have to be adjusted from time to time, but avoid doing this for as long as you can. When you must make the adjustments, turn the screws or needles in *very* small increments. Never force the adjustments and never turn the needles down tight into the threaded holes. The needles are very delicate; too much pressure can damage them. Once damaged, the needles must be replaced. There is more

information on needle adjustment elsewhere in this chapter and on page 110.

Here is a standard procedure for making the adjustments. If you have an owner's manual or similar literature, use it for the specifications. If not, these instructions should work:

1. Remove and clean the air filter.

2. Remove any grease and dirt around the adjustment needles. Use a toothbrush and a clean, lightly oiled cloth.

3. Locate the needle adjustment screws on your motor. The I or T needle is usually a bit larger than the L and H needles. If you can't identify it, follow the linkage from the throttle lever to the throttle shaft. The needle adjustment will be at this spot. The screws usually are spring loaded; that is, there is a coil spring under the head of each adjustment screw.

4. Turn all the screws clockwise with a screwdriver until they are seated. Do not force the screws and do not press down on the screws after they are seated.

5. Turn each screw *except* the T screw counterclockwise one turn.

If you live at an elevation more than 5000 feet above sea level (Denver, for example), turn the screws counterclockwise three quarters of a turn.

6. Turn the T screw counterclockwise until you feel pressure on the screw. Then turn it clockwise one full turn.

7. Set the mower in the "start" mode, or close the choke.

8. Start the engine.

9. Set the mower in the "run" mode or push the choke to its "off" mode.

10. Let the engine warm up. If the engine will not run, try turning the T adjustment needle clockwise about a quarter turn. The engine will run rough at this point.

11. Turn the L screw either clockwise or counterclockwise until you hear the engine run smoothly. You will have to fiddle with this several times until the engine runs smoothly, but don't loose patience. And don't make several turns with the screwdriver. Make tiny movements.

As you make the adjustments, the engine sound may indicate that the fast idle is too fast. If so, try turning the T adjustment screw about a quarter turn counterclockwise. This will decrease the fast idle speed back to normal.

12. Set the engine in the "fast" mode.

13. If the engine sounds rough or is hesitant moving from idle to fast speed, turn the H needle counterclockwise until the engine smooths out.

14. Move the speed control back to idle. Wait one minute. Move the speed control back to fast speed. If the engine takes the speed progression smoothly, turn the H needle counterclockwise about a sixth of a turn. Just back it off very slightly.

15. If you can't get either a low or a high speed setting that is satisfactory, there could be other problems.

First make sure that the spark plug is clean and properly gapped. Then check all electrical connections. They should be clean and tight. Is the fuel cap vent open? Is the fuel clean, fresh, and properly mixed?

Should all of these checks be okay and you can't make the adjustment, take the mower to a professional. The trouble could be in the crankcase or carburetor. Or the ignition system could be grounding out between the flywheel and the spark plug.

The ignition system

Most two-cycle engines now have a solid-state or electronic ignition system that does away with the old breaker points and condenser arrangement.

There are no repairs that you can make to a solid-state ignition; it works or it doesn't work. But you can replace the assembly, as illustrated in this chapter. To check the system, hold the spark plug wire about 1/8

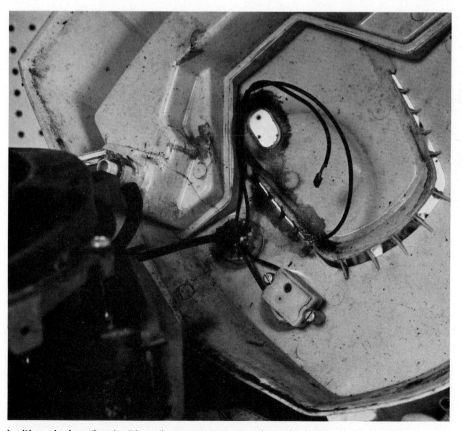

Ignition wire location. Ignition wires on some two-cycle engines are mounted on the underside of the plastic or metal engine cover. The terminals probably will be spade connections; just pull them straight apart.

inch from an engine part, such as a cylinder head bolt. Have a helper gently pull the starter cord a couple of times. If you see a spark jump from the end of the spark plug wire to the bolt, the system is working. If no spark is present, the primary system may be malfunctioning, but don't touch it until you make sure all ignition wires are clean and tightly connected to terminals.

Many ignition systems use spade connections, that is, flat metal terminals that slip into a matching receptacle. These connections can break or become unhooked or corroded, which can cause problems. If, after cleaning and adjusting, the spark plug wire still won't spark, the system must be replaced or repaired by a pro.

If the ignition system has points and a condenser, you will find these parts either under the flywheel, directly fastened to the flywheel under the rim of it, or near the flywheel in a small metal box. The latter arrangement is known as an external system.

If the parts are under the flywheel, you will have to remove the flywheel; the method is described in this chapter. If the parts are on the flywheel, loosen the screws that hold two seals into the flywheel. Then pry out the seals. This will expose the points and condenser. If an external system is used, just remove the cover from the box to expose the parts.

Changing the points and condensor is almost identical to changing the same parts on a four-cycle engine (detailed above). However, the points and condenser replacement parts should be made specifically for your model; they may not be readily available at hardware and home center outlets. In that case, phone mower dealers or repair shops that sell parts for your specific lawnmower.

The standard breaker point gap on many two-cycle engines is .02 inch. Your engine may have different specifications. Consult the owner's manual, ask a retailer, ask a pro, or buy a repair and maintenance manual for your mower. It is sold by the manufacturer or a dealer retailing mower parts.

If cleaning and tightening wire connections, changing the solid-state system, or changing the points and condenser, or resetting the points don't correct the no-spark problem, you may have a cracked flywheel. Take the mower to a professional. A flywheel crack can be so fine that you can't see it. Special equipment is needed for detection. Therefore, any other repair procedures that you would do would be a waste of time and, perhaps, money. Another ignition problem for a pro to fix is incorrect timing.

Spark plugs on two-cycle engines are serviced the very same way as their four-cycle counterparts. However, the electrode generally will appear darker in a two-cycle engine since the oil is mixed with the fuel and comes in contact with the plug.

Change the spark plug in a two-cycle lawnmower engine at the start of each mowing season, even if the plug is functioning properly. The cost of a new plug is nominal, and you eliminate possible ignition trouble right at the outset.

The standard spark plug gap for two-cycle engines is .025 inch. There are exceptions, so check your owner's manual for the manufacturer's recommendations.

Engine troubles can often be traced by examining the electrode end of a spark plug. Here is a list of tell-tale signs:

■ Electrode is gray or dark brown but not oily or flaky.
   This is the normal condition.

■ Electrode is oily and black.
   There is too much oil in the fuel and oil mixture, or you're using the wrong type of oil.

■ Electrode has black graphite deposits on it.
   The engine is operating on too rich of a fuel and oil mixture, or the engine's choke may be sticking open.

■ Electrode has a sooty deposit.
   Look for a dirty muffler and exhaust system.

■ Electrode is a white or tannish color.
   Adjust the carburetor to a richer setting. Also look for an air leak.

■ Electrode is burned.
   The engine is running too hot. First make sure the cooling fins are clean and the ports that supply fresh air to the engine are not clogged with debris. Then check the exhaust system for carbon buildup. The wrong spark plug and a broken or cracked flywheel also can cause this problem.

■ Electrode has a yellowish deposit.
   Using the wrong oil in fuel mixture is usually the trouble. Or you may have dumped the wrong kind of fuel additives in the tank. In this case, take the mower to a pro for inspection; the engine may have to be replaced.

Storing a two-cycle engine

Two-cycle lawnmower engines need special storage attention; a more complete discussion of this subject is in Chapter 6, page 116. Even though you intend to use the mower in several days, you should put it away with a full fuel tank. Clean the blade, housing, engine, and wheels either with water from a garden hose or with a cloth. Go over the metal surfaces with a lightly oiled cloth.

If you store the mower for longer than sixty days, drain the fuel tank, start the engine and let it burn all the fuel in the lines, and then remove the spark plug. Pour about 2 tablespoons of two-cycle engine oil into the spark plug port and pull the starter rope several times to work the oil into the cylinder and onto the piston. Replace the spark plug in its port.

Clean the machine thoroughly and oil any moving parts such as a chain drive and the wheels.

It's a good idea to put the mower deck, engine, and other parts into a large plastic garbage bag and tie the bag at the handle assembly. The bag will protect the mower from dirt and debris during storage.

Troubleshooting two-cycle mowers

Finding the solution to a mechanical problem starts by identifying and eliminating the simplest and sometimes most obvious causes and then working down a checklist of more complicated possibilities. This is how this troubleshooting checklist is organized: from the simple to the complicated. Some of the complicated solutions are explained in this and other chapters. Those that are best left to a professional repair person are so noted.

So, pick a problem and let the chart listings lead you to a solution.

The engine won't start or is difficult to start

■ Is the switch on?

■ Is there fuel in the tank?

■ Are you using a proper fuel and oil mixture? (see pages 97 and 115.)

■ Is the engine primed (if it has primer)?

■ Is the spark plug wire connected?

■ Is the fuel cap vent open? (see page 78.)

■ Is the engine properly choked?

■ Are the control settings on the handle set to "start" or "run"?

■ Is the clutch in position?

■ Is the grass catcher properly installed?

■ Is the air filter clean? (see pages 78-79.)

■ Is the fuel filter clean? (see page 108.)

■ Is the fuel shut-off valve open?

■ Is the engine flooded?
If so, remove the spark plug, pull the starter rope a couple of times, and replace the spark plug.

■ Is the spark plug getting a spark? (see page 99.)

■ Are the ignition wires clean and tightly connected?

■ Is the fuel line open and not kinked?

■ Is the carburetor properly adjusted? (see pages 97 and 110.)

■ Is the throttle and choke linkage clean and working smoothly?

If, after checking the above, you still have problems, other possible causes include:

dirty fuel (replace it.)

malfunctioning breaker points (see pages 89-92.)

a broken flywheel key (see pages 89-90.)

The following problems must be repaired by a professional:

a clogged fuel pump

a damaged diaphragm in the fuel pump

improper timing

a damaged or improperly set magneto coil

poor compression

The engine won't crank

■ Is the blade blocked?

■ Is the starter unit jammed?

■ Is there dirt around the flywheel?

■ Is the flywheel key broken? (see pages 89-90.)

Take the engine to a professional for repair of these problems:

broken piston rings

a broken or damaged connecting rod

The engine runs unevenly

■ Is the carburetor adjusted properly? (see pages 97 and 110.)

■ Is the fuel and oil mixture correct? (see pages 97 and 115.)

■ Is the fuel line dirty, blocked or kinked? (clean or straighten it.)

■ Is the spark plug dirty or fouled? (see pages 95-96.)

■ Are the points correctly gapped? (see pages 89-92.)

■ Are the points burned or pitted? (see pages 89-92.)

■ Is the reed valve stuck or clogged? (see page 98.)

These problems require professional help:

incorrect timing

leaky seals or gaskets

The engine runs, but lacks power

■ Is there enough of the fuel and oil mixture?

■ Is the fuel and oil mixture correct? (see pages 97 and 115.)

■ Is the vent in the fuel cap clogged? (see page 78.)

■ Is the air filter clean? (see pages 78-79).

■ Is the fuel filter clean? (see page 108.)

■ Are the spark plugs dirty or badly gapped? (see pages 82, 95-96.)

■ Is there carbon at the exhaust port? (clean it.)

■ Does the carburetor need adjustment? (see pages 97 and 110.)

- Is the choke set properly?

- Is the throttle set properly?

- Did you check for a worn, bent, or stuck reed valve?

- Did you check the ignition wiring?
  Loose connections in the ignition wiring will cause cut-out only when the machine is being used.

These possibilities must be repaired by a professional:

leakage around the gaskets

damaged piston rings

damaged connecting rod

The engine runs, then stalls

- Is the high-speed (H) needle properly set?
  Turn it counterclockwise for a richer fuel mixture.

- Is there enough of the fuel and oil mixture in the tank?

- Is the air filter clean? (see pages 78-79.)

- Is the fuel filter clean? (see page 108.)

- Is the choke setting correct?

- Is the fuel and oil mixture correct? (see pages 97 and 115.)

- Is the throttle sticking? (see pages 77-78.)

- Are the spark plugs functioning correctly? (see pages 95-96.)

- Are the points gapped properly? (see pages 89-92.)

- Are the ignition wires loose?

Vibration

- Is the lawnmower blade in balance?

- Is the blade set tightly on the shaft?

- Is the blade the correct one for your model?

- Are the engine mounting bolts loose?

- Is the flywheel key damaged? (see pages 89-90.)

Other possible causes to be repaired by a pro include:

damaged bearings

damaged crankshaft or rod

The engine overheats

- Are the cooling fins and ports clogged?

- Is the air filter clean? (see pages 78-79.)

- Is the engine overloaded?
  You can place too much stress on a self-propelled unit, and you can overload with too many accessories.

- Is the fuel and oil mixture correct? (see pages 97 and 115.)

- Are there carbon deposits at the exhaust port? (remove the muffler and clean the port.)

- Are the spark plugs malfunctioning? (see pages 95-96.)

- Are the points properly gapped? (see pages 89-92.)

- Is the carburetor clean? (see page 85.)

- Is the high-speed carburetor setting correct?
  Chances are the setting is too lean; turn the H needle a quarter of a turn counterclockwise.

- Are the bolts holding the carburetor tight?

- Is the flywheel bolt loose?

The following need a professional's attention:

wrong timing

a carbon-blocked cylinder

The engine smokes

- Is the choke setting correct?

- Is the fuel and oil mixture correct? (see pages 97 and 115.)

- Is the high-speed carburetor setting correct?
  Chances are the setting is too rich; turn the H needle a quarter of a turn clockwise.

- Is the exhaust port blocked with carbon? (remove the muffler and clean the port.)

If the piston rings are damaged, go to a professional for help.

Care and repair of pull starters

Rope-pull recoil spring starters are usually standard equipment on all walk-behind lawnmowers and other small machines. Rider mowers have a battery-operated starter; these are discussed in Chapter 4.

The big problem with rope-pull starters is that the rope breaks if it is pulled or jerked too hard. If the rope is difficult to pull, the trouble most likely is in the engine or under the mower deck, not in the starter.

Recoil spring starters are under tension and, therefore, dangerous when the unit is disassembled. Wear safety goggles and gloves when replacing a spring or a starter rope. Here are the procedures:

1. Disconnect the spark plug wire from the spark plug.

2. Remove the housing in which the starter is located. It is bolted to the engine housing and the bolts turn counterclockwise for removal.

3. With a screwdriver, bend back

1. Recoil starter repair. To replace a recoil starter rope or spring, remove the starter housing from the mower and pry up the metal tabs that hold the recoil assembly in the housing.

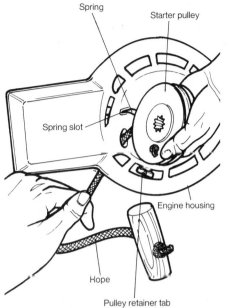

2. Thread the rope through the opening in the housing, seat it in the hub of the pulley, and wind the rope around the starter pulley.

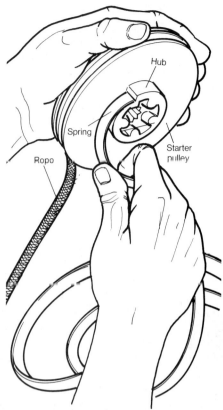

3. Attach the spring to the pulley hub in the notch provided. The spring is wound the direction opposite that of the rope.

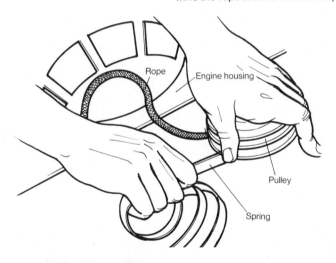

4. Lay the starter pulley on a flat, sturdy surface and coil the spring around the pulley. You may need a helper to handle the rope while you wind the spring. Then follow the concluding instructions in the text.

Starter gear maintenance. Some rope pull starters have a gear assembly that moves in toward the engine along a spiral-grooved shaft when the rope is pulled. Keep this gear and shaft clean. Any debris on either part can prevent the gears from properly meshing.

the small metal tabs that hold the starter pulley in position. Remove the handle from the starter rope. A knot or a pin through a knot usually holds it in place.

4. As you lift the pulley out of the housing, the spring will uncoil. Be very careful at this point; the spring can snap out like a whip.

5. Pull out the start rope.

6. If you are installing a new rope, thread the rope down through the hole in the housing. Install the handle at this time, if the handle isn't already mounted on the rope.

7. Tie a knot in the other end of the rope and slide the rope in the notch or hole in the pulley for the rope.

8. If you are replacing the old spring or rewinding it, slip the notched end of the spring into the slot in the base of the pulley. Coil the spring around the hub in the same direction it protrudes from the hub. Then wind the spring around the hub. Have patience; it may take several trys before you get it right.

9. Put the hub of the pulley on a flat surface to wind the spring, after you start the spring around the hub.

10. When the spring is fully wound, wind the rope around the pulley in the direction *opposite* to the spring. Have a helper wind the rope while you hold the spring.

11. Hook the spring into a notch in the housing; the notch is located around an engine cooling vent. Pull the rope taut with the handle.

12. Reinstall the pulley assembly into the housing and bend over the metal tabs that hold it in place. Then let the pulley release itself very slowly. This lets the spring reseat itself. You can now bolt the housing back on the engine.

If your mower has a spring wind-up starter (you wind a crank to load the spring and then flip a lever to start), take it to a pro for repair.

What type of oil and when?

Contrary to popular belief, detergent oil should be used in four-cycle engines since it keeps the engine cleaner and helps deter gum and varnish deposits on the working parts.

In the summer months, use SAE 30 oil. If this is not available, use SAE 10W-30 or SAE 10W-40.

In winter months at temperatures under 40 degrees F, use SAE 5W-20 or SAE 5W-30. If this is not available, use SAE 10W or SAE 10W-30.

If the temperature is below 0 degrees F, use SAE 10W or SAE 10W-30 diluted 10 percent with kerosene.

It is extremely important that you change oil in the crankcase after *every* twenty-five hours of engine operation. If you are working in extremely dusty or dirty conditions, change the oil more frequently.

Quick fix: ignition

Remove the spark plug with a wrench. Have a helper hold the tip of the spark plug cable about 1/8 inch from a cylinder head bolt. You crank the engine. Look for a spark across the 1/8-inch gap. If the spark jumps the gap, the ignition system is working. Therefore, the no-start or hard-start trouble may be the spark plug. Install a new spark plug.

If you don't see a spark across the 1/8-inch gap, the trouble may be:

condenser failure (see pages 89-92.)

a shorted ground wire (if so equipped)

shorted stop switch (if so equipped)

a broken flywheel key (see 89-90.)

dirty, burned, or incorrectly gapped breaker points (see pages 89-92.)

a bad interlock system (between the engine and grasscatcher)

worn bearings (have a pro replace them.)

Quick fix: carburetion

When the engine won't start or operates unevenly, faulty carburetion may be the trouble. First be sure the fuel tank is at least half full of clean, fresh gasoline. Then make sure all fuel switches and valves are in an open position.

Next remove the spark plug. If the tip of the plug is wet with fuel, the trouble may be:

overchoking

a too-rich fuel mixture (see pages 97 and 110.)

water in the fuel (replace it.)

a stuck inlet valve on flow-jet carburetors (take the tool to a pro.)

If the spark plug tip is dry, the trouble may be:

a leaking carburetor gasket

a dirty carburetor screen or valve

a stuck inlet valve on flow-jet carburetors (take the tool to a pro.)

a bad fuel pump on Pulsa-Jet carburetors (take the tool to a pro.)

Check to see if fuel is getting to the combustion chamber this way:

1. Remove the spark plug.

2. Pour a small amount of gasoline into the chamber through the spark plug hole. Then replace the plug.

3. Crank the engine. If the engine fires, then quits, look for trouble as noted under "dry plug" above.

Quick fix: compression

A simple way to check engine compression is to spin the flywheel in reverse rotation (counterclockwise). But disconnect the spark plug wire first.

If compression is good, the flywheel should snap back quickly as you spin it. However, if the compression seems to be bad, look for these problems:

a loose spark plug

a bad cylinder head gasket

loose bolts on the cylinder head

bad valves or valve seats (see pages 93-95.)

not enough tappet clearance (see pages 93-95.)

These are problems for a pro:

a warped cylinder head or valve stem

worn cylinder bore or worn rings

a broken connecting rod

6 Chain Saw Maintenance

Chain saws require dedicated prework care and maintenance. This regimen may take more of your time and effort than what you spend actually cutting wood. But any professional repair person will tell you that it's lack of care and maintenance that causes rust, dull chains, clogged air filters, chain saw breakdowns and poor performance.

Heed all warranties

If you own a new saw that is still under a warranty, and most of them are covered for several months to a year, know what the warranty covers before you attempt any repairs or pay for any repairs.

Repairing the tool yourself, or even having an unauthorized professional repair it, could void the warranty. The retailer from whom you bought the saw can tell you where the saw must be taken or sent for repair, or look on the warranty certificate. After the warranty expires, check to see if you would save mailing, handling, and transportation costs by repairing the saw yourself or by taking it to a pro in your community.

How a chain saw works

Most chain saws have two-cycle gasoline engines. More information on this subject appears in Chapter 5.

Chain saws develop from about 6000 to 11,000 rpm when the throttle is fully opened. This force whisks the chain around the bar at a terrific speed. The chain moves forward on

top of the bar, that is, from the engine toward the tip of the chain bar; on the bottom side of the chain bar the chain moves back toward the engine.

The bottom side of the chain bar is the working, or cutting, edge of the chain. When the chain is chewing through a piece of wood, it tends to pull the saw away from you. You have the best control over the saw when cutting with the bottom edge of the chain.

If you use the top of the chain to cut (which you *should not*) the saw is forced toward you, and your control over the saw is not positive. At the tip of the saw, where the chain is moving downward, the reaction of the saw in the wood is to jerk upward or kick back. You can completely lose control of the saw if you cut with the tip.

Some saw manufacturers place a nose guard over the chain bar at the tip to prevent the saw from accidently striking an object on the tip and kicking back. The guard may be removed for pocket or plunge cuts in wood. But for regular cutting work, the guard should be left in position.

How to cut with a chain saw

The proper cutting procedure for using a chain saw is this:

1. With the engine running, place the bottom of the chain nearest the engine against the wood. Let the weight of the saw make the initial cut.

2. As the saw cuts, lower the front of the chain bar, that is, push it downward. The saw should pivot at the base of the engine where the chain bar and the engine meet.

3. As the cutting continues, lower the back of the saw, letting the rear end of the chain do the cutting.

4. Drop the nose of the saw once again.

What you are doing basically is rocking the saw as the chain bites through the wood. Most inexperienced owners do just the opposite: they try to cut with the front end of the chain by applying lots of pressure to the saw handles in an

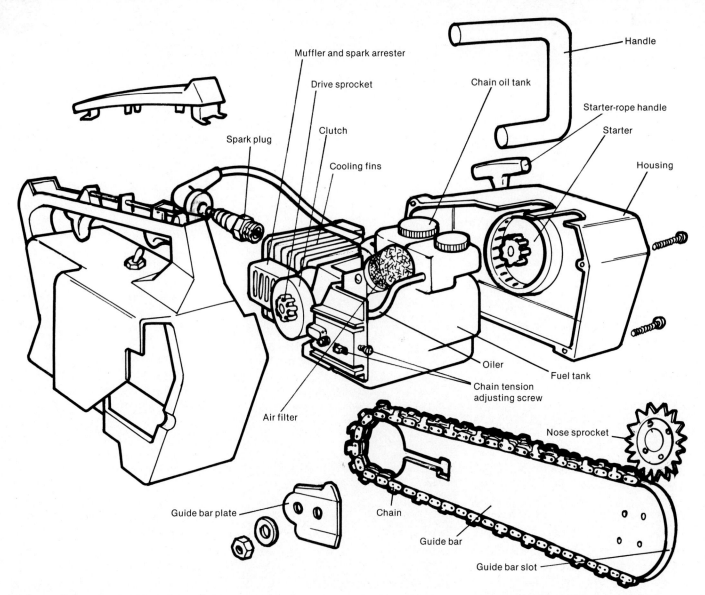

Muffler and spark arrester

Drive sprocket

Clutch

Cooling fins

Spark plug

Handle

Chain oil tank

Starter-rope handle

Starter

Housing

Air filter

Oiler

Fuel tank

Chain tension adjusting screw

Nose sprocket

Guide bar plate

Chain

Guide bar

Guide bar slot

Anatomy of a chain saw. This exploded diagram locates the parts that need maintenance and repair, as described in the text. Your chain saw may vary slightly in configuration. The housing may be removed by backing out screws or bolts found in or near the saw handle.

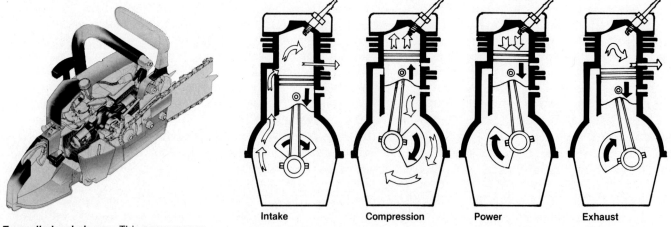

Intake

Compression

Power

Exhaust

Two-cylinder chain saw. This newcomer on the market is made by Echo Inc. Maintenance is similar to standard one-cylinder, two-cycle engines. The lever handle at front is a chain brake; it's found on many chain saws.

Two-cycle engine stages. Two-cycle engines burn fuel mixed with oil. In the intake mode, the piston moves down and fuel is sucked into the combustion chamber. In the compression mode, the piston moves up and the fuel is sucked into the crankcase. At the top of the stroke, the spark plug fires the fuel mixture, driving the piston downward and turning the crankshaft. As the piston descends the burned fuel gases are blown out through the exhaust port.

1. Air filter maintenance. Remove and clean the air filter frequently. Sawdust can block air to the carburetor, as shown here, causing saw malfunction.

2. If the filter is matted after cleaning, raise the fibers with a wire brush. Stroke the surface very lightly, just enough to raise the nap slightly. Then reinstall the filter.

attempt to push the saw down through the work. This can break the chain quickly, overheat the chain, overload the engine, and cause other troubles. Let the saw do the work; you steer.

General maintenance

Wipe the engine and chain bar clean after each use. A small amount of light oil or WD-40 on the cloth will help. When it's clean, lightly oil the chain, moving it around the bar with a gloved hand.

After the saw has been used for 8 to 10 hours, remove the air filter and clean it. If you have access to compressed air, use a hose to blow out the dirt. Otherwise, wash the filter in a mixture of the fuel the saw uses. Do

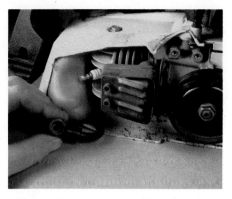

1. Spark plug maintenance. Continually check the condition of the spark plug wire and the plug boot for damage. To reach the plug, remove the engine housing, which is usually on the left side of the engine.

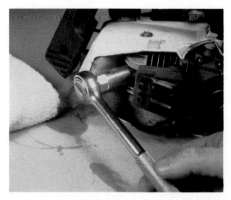

2. *Always* use a spark plug socket wrench to remove the spark plug. The spark plug turns out counterclockwise.

3. Use a spark plug made for chain saws, not for lawnmowers or other engines. The difference in size is usually noticeable (at left is a lawnmower plug), but not always.

this outdoors, and dry the filter outdoors, too.

Never operate the saw without the air filter. If you do, the engine may be damaged by sawdust particles sucked through the filter opening into the engine.

Keep the cooling fins and air inlet openings of the starter cover and the cylinder clean. Use an ice cream

Muffler maintenance. Carbon buildup is normal at the muffler and exhaust port of the engine. Keep these parts clean as described in the text.

stick or a soft-bristle brush to remove all sawdust, grass, and debris. A dirty engine may become overheated.

After 30 or 40 hours of operation, remove, clean, and inspect the muffler and spark arrester, if the muffler has one. Remove the housing that covers the muffler first (see photos, this chapter). The muffler and spark arrester are screwed to the engine housing. You may need an Allen or hex wrench to turn out the fasteners. Scrape carbon deposits away with a putty knife and shine the metal with a wire brush. If the deposits are bad, try removing them with a strong solvent (mineral spirits, for example). WD-40 sometimes removes or helps remove deposits.

While the muffler is off the engine, take a close look at the exhaust port. If you find carbon deposits here, very slowly pull the starter rope until the piston inside the cylinder covers the entire exhaust port. You'll see the piston moving into place as you pull the rope.

Then, with an ice cream stick or a small wooden scraper made out of a paint paddle, remove the carbon from in and around the exhaust port. *Do not* use a metal tool for this job; any metal can damage the piston if the tool gouges it.

Use compressed air, if you have it, to remove the debris. If not, turn the engine over so the exhaust faces downward and wipe with a soft cloth or brush away the debris.

Check spark plugs at least twice during the cutting season and change them when the electrodes

1. Fuel filter maintenance. The fuel filter usually is located inside the fuel tank. To remove it for changing or inspection, fashion a fishhook from a length of clotheshanger wire, as shown here. Just bend the end of the wire over with pliers so you can snag the filter.

2. Pull the filter out of the tank and check it for dirt. It can usually be removed from the fuel line by depressing a clamp with pliers. Clean the filter with fuel. Or better yet, replace it with an inexpensive new filter. Be sure you secure the fuel line after the filter is removed for cleaning or replacement. Fasten a C clamp or Vise Grip pliers *lightly* to the line.

1. Starter rope adjustment. A limp starter handle indicates that the starter rope has stretched. Shorten the rope, as explained in this chapter. Take the saw to a professional repair person if the recoil spring malfunctions. The spring, which is under heavy tension, is potentially dangerous.

2. The handle, after shortening the rope, is now in the proper position. When you crank the engine, use a short and gentle pull. If the engine is difficult to crank, look for problems in the engine first, not in the starter assembly. Troubleshooting the problem is explained in this chapter and in Chapter 5.

Oiler adjustment

If your saw has an automatic oiler, it will have been adjusted at the factory to average cutting conditions. You can adjust the oil flow, however, for heavy or long projects: turn the adjustment screw clockwise to reduce the oil flow; turn the screw counterclockwise to increase the flow.

As a rule of thumb, the screw should not be turned any more than

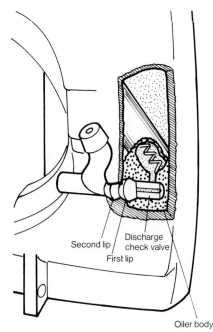

Second lip

Discharge check valve

First lip

Oiler body

Chain saw oiler. Most oilers look like the one shown here. If the hole in the oiler becomes clogged, clean it with a piece of fine wire, not a stick or toothpick.

one quarter of a turn each time. Make this adjustment and then check the oil flow on the chain.

Manual oilers have oil passages that are usually kept clean by pressing on the manual oil button. If more oil is needed on the chain than the automatic oiler is supplying, it's better to use the manual oiler than to adjust the automatic oiler.

Chain bar maintenance

Chain bars should be turned over after each day's use to promote even wear on the bar. Make sure the bar groove in which the chain runs stays clean. You can buy an inexpensive cleaning tool for this job. After the

become worn or clogged with carbon. It is difficult to recommend a specific time to change a plug, but it's a good idea to begin each cutting year with a new one—the cost isn't prohibitive. Always remove the plug with a spark plug socket wrench. Don't use any other tool; you may damage the engine. Be sure to push the ignition switch to the "off" position before changing a plug.

To refurbish a used plug, burnish the electrode with medium-grit sandpaper sandwiched between the gap.

The plug gap should be set at .025 inches or .635 mm. Bend the side electrode only. This is a standard setting; if you have an owner's manual, follow the manufacturer's recommendations for gaps.

Check the fuel tank cap or the vent in the cap each time you refuel. Make sure this vent is open; otherwise, pressure or vacuum will build up in the tank, upsetting fuel flow. Use a wire or a pin to clean the vent; do not use a wooden probe. Wood can break and block the vent.

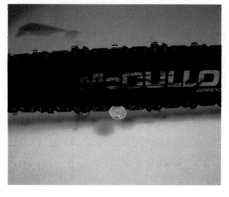

Regular maintenance. After each use, always clean the saw, the chain, and the bar. After cleaning, wipe all surfaces with a lightly oiled cloth to leave a thin oil coating. If the saw is fuel-powered, fill the fuel tank and set the saw level on a shelf or table. It's also a smart idea to tighten all housing bolts after each use, since saw vibration loosens screws and bolts quickly.

groove has been cleaned, sight down the bar in good light. The bottom of the groove should be square and the sides should not be worn. If they are, buy a new bar; a worn bar will cause the chain to twist slightly in the groove and break.

After sawing, check the oil openings at the base of the bar. If they're filled with sawdust, open them with the tip of a depth gauge tang or any tool that will go into the passages. Always check these openings by pressing the manual oiler; if they're open, the oil will squirt out freely.

Correct chain tension requires constant maintenance. Check it before you use the saw, *without fail.* The chain should be fairly snug on the bar, but loose enough so that you can slide it around the bar with a gloved hand. Chains actually stretch

1. Chain tension adjustment. On most saws turn a screw at the front of the housing to adjust tension. On other models, you loosen or remove a bolt near the clutch and sprocket. To change the sprocket, you have to either hold the flywheel nut on the opposite side of the engine with a wrench or block the piston with a special tool. Your owner's manual or saw service center will tell you what tool you need.

2. When you are tensioning the chain, pull out at the end of the chain bar, as shown. When the tension is correct, secure the chain and bar bolts, which lock the bar and chain to the saw. After adjusting the chain, reoil it before you start working again by pressing the manual oiler.

Gauging chain tension. If you can slip a dime between the bottom of the chain and the chain bar and the dime sticks, the tension is about right. You should also be able to turn the chain easily with your gloved hand around the chain bar. The chain should fit firmly in the bar channel or groove

and become loose on the bar due to normal wear. When you no longer can take up the slack by adjusting the tension, you can remove one link from the chain to shorten it and thereby tighten it on the bar.

If you are installing a new chain, soak the chain in oil overnight before mounting it on the bar. After it has been mounted on the bar, run the engine for about 10 minutes without cutting any material. During this period, push the manual oil button every thirty seconds or so. Give the chain plenty of oil. After ten minutes, check the chain tension and adjust it if necessary. Then, as you use the saw for cutting, keep the chain well lubricated and check the tension frequently.

Chain maintenance. Soak new chain in SAE 10 motor oil and store used chain in SAE 10 motor oil. You can use bar and chain oil for this, but regular motor oil is less expensive. When you service the chain and bar, turn the bar over when reconnecting it to spread the wear.

3. Clean around the clutch and sprocket area when you re-tighten the chain on the chain bar. A toothbrush makes an ideal cleaning tool. The tank for chain oiler is shown capped near the top at the front of the saw.

Sprocket replacement. Inspect the nose sprocket of the chain bar frequently for wear on the tips of the teeth. You may be able to replace the socket by removing the rivets that hold it. But it is better to install a new bar; the cost is not prohibitive.

Chain saw engine troubleshooting

Chain saws are no exception to the rule that a piece of mechanical equipment can wear out, break down, and generally cause trouble. In this section, I've made a list of problems with your chain saw that you probably can solve. However, if —after going down the troubleshooting checklist and performing the procedures mentioned—you can't correct the problem, take the saw to a professional who has the expertise and equipment needed. Make sure that you get a bottom-line price before the pro does any work on your equipment. Repairs could cost more than the saw is worth.

Since any mechanical problem can have many causes, you have to eliminate them one by one to solve the problem. The following troubleshooting guide for a chain saw engine is a series of questions. Answer them one at a time; each answer eliminates one possible cause of your problem. Some of the questions call for obvious action; the obvious solution is not spelled out. When the required steps are complicated, however, I've explained everything in detail.

If the engine won't start . . .

Answer these questions:

■ Does the engine have fuel?

■ Is the fuel properly mixed to the correct gasoline and oil ratio? (see page 115).

■ Is the fuel fresh?

■ Is the switch fully pushed to the "on" position?

■ Is the switch causing a ground?
Disconnect the switch wire and tape it with plastic electrician's tape. Then try to start the engine. If the engine starts, the problem is in the switch. Buy a replacement switch and wire it in just like the old one. The switch comes as a self-

contained component. Don't attempt to repair a part of the component.

■ Are all visible wires tightly connected to terminals?

■ Are the terminals clean and free of corrosion?
If not, disconnect the wires, polish the terminals with steel wool, and reconnect the wires. Use steel wool for shining and removing corrosion.

■ Is the spark plug clean and properly set?
You can tell whether or not the spark plug is receiving power by disconnecting the spark plug and grounding it to a handle screw. (Do not ground the plug near the spark plug port; keep it away from fuel.) Pull the starter rope and crank the engine. You will see a spark. If not, check the spark plug wire insulation to make sure that it is not damaged. The usual wear spot is where the wire goes through the fan housing.

■ Is the air filter clean? (see page 107.)

■ Is the choke sticking open?
Follow the linkage from the throttle to the carburetor. Clean it if it's fouled. However, a stuck or damaged butterfly valve (choke plate) may be causing this problem. Repair of this is a job for a professional.

■ Is the carburetor properly adjusted?
First, check the air filter, the spark plug, and the throttle linkage. If these are in proper order, then check the carburetor adjustment screws. If they have been turned, this could be the problem. These screws are set at the factory and *seldom* need to be turned. However, if you suspect they have been, read the instructions on page 110 or in your owner's manual.

■ Are the fuel lines kinked?
Check the lines and look closely for a broken, cut, or worn fuel line. You can replace the flexible line.

Carburetor adjustment. Idle and speed adjustments are preset at the factory and should not be moved. However, if the saw is running rough, adjustments can be made with a screwdriver. The text explains the correct turning sequence. Before making any adjustments, make sure that the air filter and exhaust and muffler are clean and free from any carbon buildup.

■ Is the engine getting fuel?
First, pull the starter rope a couple of times. Then, with a spark plug wrench, remove the spark plug and check the electrodes. If you see fuel and water on the plug, the engine is receiving fuel, but the fuel is not pure enough to ignite. If you are not getting fuel, pour about a teaspoon of fuel mixture into the cylinder. Then replace the spark plug and crank the engine. If it starts and then stops quickly, the problem is a blocked line between the tank and the engine.

■ Is the fuel filter working?
Check the condition of the filter, which is inside the fuel tank. You can fish it out with a piece of bent wire (see page 108). Flush the filter with fresh gas or replace it if it appears damaged.
If the engine still won't start, take the saw outside and drain the gas tank into a tub. Then disconnect the fuel line from the tank to the carburetor and clean or replace it. Reconnect the line, fill the tank with fuel mixture, and crank the engine.

■ Is the pulse passage to the crankcase plugged?
You can clean it with wire after you have removed the carburetor to

Resetting carburetor adjustment screws

If you can't find your owner's manual, here is the standard adjustment procedure for carburetor adjustment screws. It should work. If it doesn't, take the saw to a professional for repair.

1. Turn both the low- and high-speed fuel needles on top of the saw three quarters of a turn open (counterclockwise) from the present setting. Try to start the engine. If the engine doesn't start, open the needles another quarter turn. Then turn the choke lever to its closed position and crank the engine.

2. If the engine doesn't start at this point, close the needles one and a half turns, close the choke, and crank the engine.

3. When the engine starts, let it run for several minutes.

4. Adjust the low-speed fuel needle until the acceleration sounds clean and smooth. Then adjust the idle speed screw so it goes to the fastest engine speed before the clutch engages. The engine must idle without the chain moving. Keep your hands away from the chain and bar while making these adjustments.

5. The high-speed adjustment must be made while the saw is under a load; do not adjust it by sound. Test the engine while making a cut. If the mixture is too rich, the engine will stall. If the mixture is too lean, the saw will lack power. Adjust the high-speed needle in the cut.

6. After the two adjustments have been made, try the idle and acceleration procedure again. You may have to adjust the idle and the speed needles just a tad.

You may be able to make only one more adjustment to solve the problem. Make sure the fuel inlet control lever is on the flat surface of the carburetor body. It can be adjusted to .015 inch above the body, but no more. This is a general setting; check the owner's manual for your model or have a pro make the setting if you are in doubt.

get at these holes, which are directly under the carburetor.

These problems are for a professional with special equipment to solve: dirty inlet valves, damaged diaphragms or gaskets, and a wrong kind of gasket on the crankcase (this last is very unlikely).

■ Are the breaker points and condenser malfunctioning?

Not all saws have these parts. If your saw does and they are malfunctioning, the engine won't start. I recommend that you install a new set of points and a condenser (see Chapter 5, page 89, for this technique) rather than tinker with the old ones. The standard gap setting on the points is .018 inch.

Other ignition troubles could be a damaged coil or weak flywheel magnets. These are problems for a professional. If the ignition is electronic, chances are that the ignition module is faulty. Consult a pro, who will test the module and replace it if necessary.

■ Is there carbon buildup in the exhaust port and muffler?

The right way to remove carbon is discussed on page 107.

Other possible problems include: crankshaft seals, a broken flywheel or a broken flywheel key (see Chapter 5, page 89), air leaks in the engine, bad rings, broken connecting rod, broken piston, and broken crankshaft. All of these are jobs for a professional.

If the engine doesn't run smoothly . . .

If the engine starts but doesn't run properly, check these faults.

■ Rough idle

Look for a dirty filter, the usual cause if the engine idles roughly. If the filter is clean, the low-speed mixture screw may need adjustment (see opposite). Check all the seals and tighten the bolts around the seals to stop any air leaks.

Other possibilities include a damaged air valve, a very dirty carbu-

retor, and a leak in the fuel line. These three problems are jobs for a professional.

■ Engine starts and then stops
  These are the possible causes.

dirty air filter (see page 107.)
water in the fuel mixture (replace fuel.)
plugged fuel tank vent (clean it.)
air leaks (tighten engine bolts.)
dirty fuel filter (see page 108.)
clogged fuel line (clean it.)
incorrect fuel and oil mixture (replace fuel.)

A damaged diaphragm or a dirty inlet valve may also be the cause of this problem. Take the saw to a professional for repair.

■ Engine runs after switch is off
  The causes, in order, are below.

dirty spark plug (see page 108.)
malfunctioning switch (see page 110.)
corroded terminals (see page 110.)

■ No power

A too-rich fuel mixture is usually the problem and you can tell by the exhaust: it blows lots of black smoke. Try adjusting the carburetor settings, following the owner's manual or the general settings described on page 110.

Other problems you can correct include:
dirty air filter (see page 107.)
plugged fuel tank vent (clean it.)
plugged fuel line (clean it.)
bad spark plug (replace it.)
worn or dirty chain or bar groove (see pages 109, 112-113.)
broken nose sprocket on bar (see page 114.)
the chain brake is on
exhaust and muffler carbon buildup (see page 107.)
air leaks (tighten body bolts.)

Worn or broken piston rings, cylinder, crankshaft, or connecting rod must be repaired by a professional.

■ Engine floods

The choke probably is closed. Open it and crank the engine. Trace the linkage to make sure the choke is closing. Sometimes the linkage becomes so dirty that the choke lever doesn't work properly. A little WD-40 on a toothbrush will clean it.

If this doesn't solve the problem, check these:

plugged fuel tank vent (clean it.)
clogged fuel filter (see page 108.)

A professional will have to deal with a damaged diaphragm, a blocked or damaged inlet valve, damaged adjustment needles, and an incorrect inlet lever setting.

■ **Engine won't run at full speed**
Look for dirty air and fuel filters first (see pages 107 and 108.) Then look for a choke or throttle that is blocked by grease. Then check these points:

bad spark plug
wrong gap at breaker points (see Chapter 5, page 89.)
carbon buildup on the exhaust and muffler (see page 107.)

You'll have to take the saw to a professional for repair if the diaphragm is damaged, if the inlet valve is dirty, if the needle adjustment is incorrect, if the timing is off, or if engine parts (piston, cylinder, crankshaft, rod) are broken or worn.

■ **Engine overheats**
There are two things to check first: the fuel mixture may be incorrect (see page 115) or there may be severe carbon buildup around the exhaust and muffler (see page 107.) The cooling fans on the engine may be dirty and the cooling vents in the saw housing may be plugged. After these possibilities are cleared up, check these:

high-speed setting too lean (see page 110.)
dirty spark plug
A professional will have to correct these matters: incorrect timing, damaged diaphragms, bent adjustment needles, and worn inlet valves.

■ **Saw runs fast**
This seldom happens, but if it does, look for a slipping sprocket at the engine. You may be able to

tighten it by removing the housing. Use a socket or adjustable wrench, blocking the edge of the sprocket with a piece of wood so you can tighten the nut holding the sprocket. If this doesn't solve the problem, take the saw to a professional.

■ **Saw runs slowly**
This is almost always caused by dirt. Check the chain and chain bar for debris that may be blocking the chain bar groove.

The other causes include: a worn chain bar, a worn chain, and a broken nose sprocket on the chain bar. These may be corrected by replacing the chain or chain bar.

■ **Saw cuts poorly**
The saw may need sharpening (see illustrations and instructions on pages 113-114.) It is possible that the chain, the bar, or both, may need to be replaced.

If these don't correct the problem you're using the wrong cutting procedure. Work from the bottom of the chain, don't twist the saw, and don't use too much downward pressure.

■ **Saw sticks in the wood**
Try increasing the rpm. If this doesn't help you're probably using too much downward pressure or you're not oiling the chain enough as you're making the cut.

There may be too much sap residue on the chain and chain bar. Clean them both with kerosene.

■ **Saw bucks**
Always cut with the bottom edge of the saw and avoid touching the work with the tip or the top of the saw. Keep a firm and even downward pressure on the saw, rocking it slightly up and down from the base of the chain and chain bar to the tip of the chain and chain bar.

There may also not be enough oil on the chain.

■ **Chain breaks frequently**
The chain bar may be worn; replace it. Or the chain bar may be bent; replace it. Don't try to straighten it. Other possibilities are:

twisting the saw in the cut
using too much pressure downward on the saw
If the chain bar is out of alignment, take the saw to a professional.

■ **Chain won't track**
Check for the following problems. Solve them by replacing the damaged part (see pages 112-114).

worn chain bar
bent chain bar
bent or damaged groove in the chain bar
worn chain drive links

Chain and chain bar troubleshooting

Manufacturers use different chain designs; you'll find these three: chipper, chisel, and semi-chisel. Each of these designs is available in various types for different purposes. For example, the full-house is for cutting soft metal; skip, for cutting softwoods; and standard, for all-around cutting.

Your big problem will be worn chains (which you can sharpen—see opposite), broken chains (which you can repair if only a few parts are broken; if not, replace the chain), worn and dirty grooves in the chain bar, and malfunctioning sprockets on the tip of the chain bar. Fortunately,

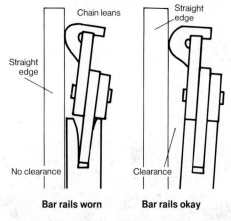

Bar rail inspection. Worn chain bar rails let the chain tilt so that the cut isn't true. Worse, the worn rails can cause the saw to overheat and bind. You can check for wear by placing a straightedge, such as the edge of a steel ruler, against the chain and the bar. If the rails are worn, replace the bar.

these problems are fairly easy to correct. In fact, since new replacement parts are not prohibitively expensive, time-consuming repairs may not even be necessary.

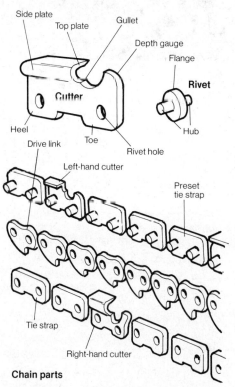

Chain parts

Anatomy of a saw chain. Refer to these standard component names when you buy a new chain or have a used chain serviced by a pro.

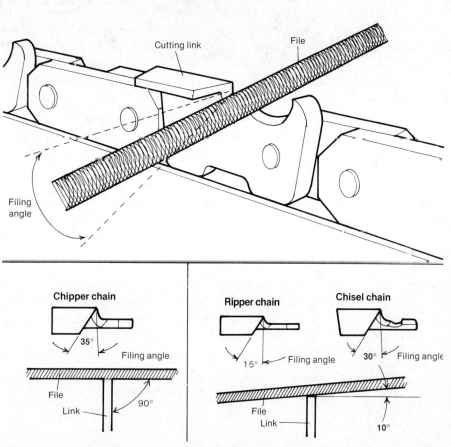

1. Sharpening cutting links. Use a file guide, set to the filing angle shown above for your type chain, to maintain the proper link shape. In addition, hold the file level for a chipper chain; tilt it 10° for the other two types. For example, if you have a ripper chain, set the file guide at 15° and tilt the file 10°. Work the file as described in the text. *(continued)*

Chain sharpening

You can buy four basic types of chain sharpening outfits: an electric hand grinder, an electric disc grinder, a hand file guide, and a fluted shaft. You furnish muscle power for the last two types.

The most popular of the four is probably the hand file guide, and I recommend it for its simplicity. The following illustrated instructions pertain to this type, although all types usually come with printed directions.

You will need two files for the job: a round file and a flat file. The round file must be round from tip to tang; do not use a tapered rattail or triangular cant file. Two sizes are standard: the 7/32-inch-diameter for 3/8-inch pitch chain, and the 5/32-inch-diameter for both 1/4- and 3/8-inch pitch chain. You may find the smaller file easier to work with. Since the files are not expensive, it is worth the investment

to buy both sizes. You need the flat file for removing the projecting parts of the depth gauges.

You also will need a depth gauge tool for filing; I recommend the Pitch-N-Gauge made by Granberg. The Oregon company also manufactures gauges and jigs. Check out all types in the store before you buy. One type may be easier for you to understand and use than another.

How to sharpen the chain

Below are the procedures for sharpening chain by hand; they apply to most chains.

1. You can sharpen the chain on the saw or remove the chain and put it in a vise made for the job. Some file guides have built-in vises. I recommend that you remove the chain from the bar if the sharpener guide

doesn't have a built-in vise. A vise holds the chain steadier for sharpening than the chain bar.

2. Select the proper diameter round file for sharpening. Your owner's manual should tell you the right diameter. If you can't find the manual, a retailer that sells chain will advise you if you take the chain to the store. You'll also need a file guide marked for a 10- to 35-degree top filing angle.

3. Hold the file firmly at the correct top filing angle. Then apply filing pressure against the face of the chain tooth. Push the file toward the outside of the tooth, as shown in the illustrations.

As you pull back the file for the next filing stroke, release the pressure. Cut on the forward stroke only.

4. Stroke the cutting edge with the round file four or five times and then check the sharpness of the tooth with your finger. If the tooth is sharp, move the file down into the gullet and draw the file across it. You don't want to sharpen the gullet; just clean it with the file.

5. Sharpen the teeth completely on one side of the chain before you start to sharpen the teeth on the other side. You can mark the starting point with a tab of masking tape.

To keep the chain in balance, give each tooth the same number of file strokes when removing metal. You may find that some of the teeth take more sharpening strokes than others. These teeth have become hardened by heat generated by the chain going through material, and they will probably have a blue tinge. Use the number of strokes it takes to sharpen a hardened tooth as your standard for all the teeth.

6. After sharpening the teeth you must lower the depth gauges to match the teeth height. To do this, put the depth gauge tool over two cutter teeth, with the gauge on the first cutter projecting up through the slot in the tool.

7. Use a flat file to remove any part of the depth gauge that projects above the tool.

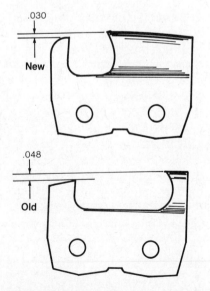

2. After you file the cutters, lower the depth gauges slightly, as indicated in this drawing.

As a rule of thumb, the depth gauge should be about .025 to .04 inch below the top of the cutter of the chain. This holds for a fairly new chain with a 1/4- to 1/2-inch pitch. For specific measurements, consult your owner's manual or check with a chain retailer.

8. When the depth gauges have been filed, round off their leading edges with the file, keeping the same profile as on the original depth gauge.

9. Work back over the cutting edges after the depth gauges have been filed. Just touch them up with the file; one light stroke is usually enough.

10. Clean the chain by soaking it in a pan of kerosene. If you have sharpened the chain on the saw, clean chain bar grooves, sprocket, and bar so that all metal filings are removed.

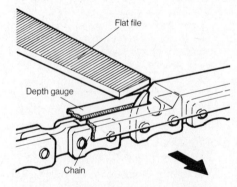

3. Use a depth gauge tool as a guide and a flat, smooth metal file; keep the file square on the work and stroke the file forward only. After the depth gauges have been lowered, lightly round their forward corners. See illustration of the cutter for the right shape.

Repairing saw chain

A chain saw chain is put together like a bicycle chain; links in the chain may be removed or replaced.

For this you need an anvil and a punch. The anvil has grooves that accept chain of various sizes. The anvil also has different-sized holes to accept the punch. The illustrations below show how to proceed.

When the chain and chain bar produce smoke. This common chain bar problem is almost always caused by a lack of oil on the chain. Make sure that there is plenty of oil in the chain oil reservoir.

The chain and bar also can smoke in cold weather. Try thinning the oil just a tad with kerosene or diesel fuel. Warning: don't thin it too much. The chain and bar will continue to smoke, and you will damage the saw.

Smoke may also be caused by:

dirt in the bar chain groove
plugged oil outlet opening (see page 108.)

If the seals in the oil pump are defective, take the saw to a pro.

Replacing worn chain sprockets

When you buy a new chain for the saw, you also should buy a new sprocket for the chain. If you check the sprocket at any time and see that it is worn, replace it. The cost is not prohibitive. To replace the sprocket:

1. Remove the spark plug wire.

2. Remove the spark plug.

3. Remove the bar, chain, and starter housing.

4. Place a 1/2-inch socket wrench on the flywheel nut; then turn off the clutch nut clockwise with a second wrench. The wrench on the flywheel nut helps prevent the assembly from turning while you remove the clutch nut.

5. Remove the dust plate and clutch (see page 109).

6. Take off the sprocket, drum, and sprocket bearing by pulling them off the spindle. Lubricate the bearing with nonfibrous chassis grease. Install the new parts in the reverse order.

7. Tighten the clutch nut; it turns counterclockwise. Don't turn it too tight or you'll loosen the flywheel nut. Replace other parts in reverse order.

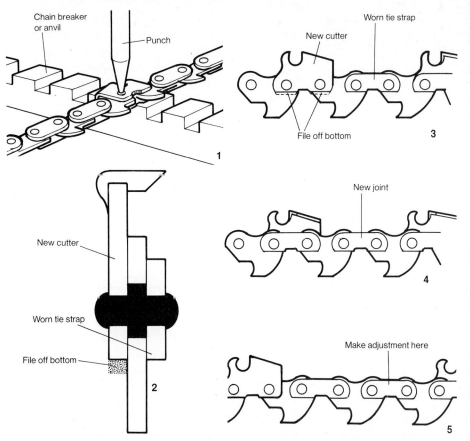

Chain link replacement. You can remove and replace broken or worn out links by punching out the rivet with a chain breaker, or anvil, and punch (1). On a worn chain, the tie straps and cutters will be a different size from the new parts. Any new part must be filed to match the old ones (2 and 3). Otherwise, the new part will ride lower, causing trouble. To shorten or lengthen the chain, remove the tie strap between a right- and a left-hand cutter. You may have to rejoin the chain loop between two left- or two right-hand cutters (4). If the chain sequence has *two* tie straps and a drive link between two cutters, the new parts can be added or old parts removed at this point (5).

Care and repair of pull starters

Gasoline-powered chain saws almost always have pull-rope, or recoil, starters similar to those on lawn-mower engines. The starters have very strong spring assemblies that sometimes pop out violently from their housings during disassembly. Therefore, I recommend that you take your saw to a pro for starter service. There are, however, minor adjustments that you can make.

If you break the starter rope often, you probably are pulling too har and long on the rope; ease up a little. Rope breaking may also be the symptom of a hard-to-start engine (see page 110).

Replacing the starter rope. The starter rope can be easily replaced on many models. Here's how to do it.

1. Buy a starter rope that fits the pulley assembly.

2. Remove the housing that covers the starter rope assembly. It is held by screws, usually through the handles, that turn counterclockwise with a Phillips-head screwdriver.

3. Attach the handle to one end of the new starter rope and slip the other end into the notch in the outside diameter of the starter drum assembly. You'll see the notch as you move the drum.

4. Rotate the starter drum about two turns clockwise. Make sure the end of the rope is in the notch. Then let the rope wind up on the drum through spring pressure. When the rope is rewound, the handle will stand straight up in the cradle of the rope assembly.

5. Pull the starter rope out its entire length, and turn the drum clockwise. It will turn 1 or 2 inches. This indicates that the spring is not too tight. If the drum can't be turned, the spring has bottomed out. Repeat the winding procedure, Step 4, but turn the drum one turn less.

If the handle does not stand up in the cradle but flops over on one side, the rope is probably stretched. This can be fixed.

1. Remove the starter housing (see Step 2, above).

2. Pull up on the rope, moving the drum only slightly.

3. *Hold on to the rope* under the cut and cut the handle off the rope with a knife. The rope will slip out of the cradle if you don't hold it, and you will have to rethread it up through the cradle.

4. Thread the end of the rope through the hole in the handle and tie a knot in the rope so it can't slip back down through the hole.

Some handles have a recessed washer through which the rope is threaded. This helps prevent the rope from pulling out. Other systems use a recessed metal pin to which the rope is tied.

Other starter problems. Worn or broken pawls and a worn ratchet usually are to blame for a starter that slips. This is a repair job for a professional with special tools. If the starter doesn't rewind the cord, the spring has broken or become unwound. This, too, is a job for a pro.

If the starter seems to be jammed, remove the starter housing cover and look for sawdust, debris, or broken parts.

Chain saw fuel

Since chain saw engines are two-cycle, oil must be mixed with the gasoline. The type of oil and the correct mixture of gasoline and oil are important to the maintenance of the saw.

Use oil made specifically for chain saws—not for automobiles, outboard motors, snowmobiles, or any other engines that use a gas and oil mixture.

Unless the manufacturer specifies otherwise, the gasoline you use should be *fresh, regular, leaded gasoline.* Premium-grade or high-test gasoline usually burns too hot for chain saw engines. You must use gasoline that has been refined recently, not last year; old gasoline can get stale. Gasohol is not recommended because it attracts condensation of water, which is the chain saw's biggest enemy.

The ratio of oil to gasoline must be correct and exact. If you just pour a little oil into the tank and top it off with gasoline and then slosh the mixture around, you are asking for lots of trouble. Incorrect ratios can cause piston failure, quickly damaging the cylinder wall, crankshaft, bearings, rod, and other parts. If you use too much oil in the mixture, the parts become gummed, especially the spark plug, and the saw won't even run.

The table gives the quantities of gasoline and oil for making a 20:1 mixture, the standard ratio. Combine the gasoline and oil in a gasoline container with a flexible pouring spout and strainer. First pour in half of the gasoline and all of the oil, close the container tightly, and shake the container as hard as you can. Then add the rest of the gasoline and shake the container vigorously again.

GASOLINE AND OIL FOR THE STANDARD RATIO

Gasoline	20:1 Ratio SAE 40 Two-Cycle Oil	
½ gallon	3.2 oz.	95 ml (cc)
1 gallon	6.4 oz.	190 ml (cc)
5 gallons	32.0 oz.	950 ml (cc)
1 liter	1.7 oz.	50 ml (cc)
5 liters	8.5 oz.	250 ml (cc)
20 liters	34.0 oz.	1000 ml (cc)
1 imperial gallon	8.6 oz.	250 ml (cc)
2 imperial gallons	17.1 oz.	500 ml (cc)
5 imperial gallons	43.0 oz.	1250 ml (cc)

Some chain saw manufacturers distribute their own brand of oil, which should be used. Be sure to check the manufacturer's recommendations for gas and oil mixtures for your saw, although the standard mixture is probably acceptable.

For chain lubrication, use only chain-bar-sprocket oil; it has additives that reduce friction and wear. Some chain saw manufacturers sell oil under their label for this purpose. If you can't obtain this brand, use SAE 30 *nonadditive* motor oil for temperatures above 40 degrees F. For temperatures below 40 degrees F, use SAE 10 *nonadditive* motor oil.

Storing a chain saw

While usually not the case with lawnmowers and other equipment with gasoline engines, storing a chain saw can be a problem. For example, if the saw is not stored properly the carburetor diaphragm may dry out, and you'll have to replace it; fuel lines can become gummed with fuel deposits.

For short-term storage (a couple of weeks or so), fill the gas tank and place the saw on a level spot with the engine in the normal, up position. The reason for filling the tank is to prevent water condensation in the tank and fuel lines.

For long-term storage, you should keep the fuel tank full, and you should run the saw for five minutes every thirty days or so. If you can't follow this regimen, you have two other choices which are outlined below.

First, you can add a fuel stabilizer, which extends the life of the fuel by preventing it from breaking down and turning gummy. Fill the tank with fuel mixture, plus the stabilizer. Crank up the engine and run it a couple of minutes. Stop the engine by overchoking it.

Second, you can drain the fuel system completely; several chain saw manufacturers recommend this procedure.

Drain the tank in a tub, outside in a safe spot. Then crank the saw and run it at idle speed until the engine stops. With a spark plug wrench,

remove the plug and pour a tablespoon of chain saw motor oil into the spark plug port. Then pull the starter rope several times to work the oil into the engine. Replace the spark plug.

To store the chain and bar for a long period, remove the assembly from the saw and drop the chain into a can of No. 10 oil. Coat the bar liberally with oil and wrap it in plastic wrap, the kind you use for foodstuffs.

Store the engine in a plastic garbage bag; just put the saw inside and tie off the top.

Even if you follow these procedures to store the saw for a long period, you should reassemble it every six to nine months and start it for a brief period. This removes gum from the fuel lines, and, most important, keeps the carburetor diaphragms moist.

If the saw is difficult to start after long storage, try this:

1. Remove the air filter.

2. Pour a half-teaspoon of the proper fuel mixture into the carburetor air intake, under the air filter.

3. Pull the starter rope several times until the engine starts.

You may have to repeat the fuel injection technique several times until the engine runs properly. If you get too much fuel into the air intake and carburetor, you may flood the engine. As soon as the engine is functioning properly, stop it and replace the air filter.

Electric chain saw maintenance

Other than its motor, an electric chain saw is almost identical in working detail to a gasoline-powered saw. The motor powers a clutch and sprocket assembly that drives a chain around a chain bar. The saw has an oiler for the chain.

Electric saws are actually easier to maintain than their gasoline cousins, but you are limited as to reach by the power cord and as to capacity by length of chain and bar. Standard bar lengths are 8, 10, 12, and 14 inches.

The 14-inch model will handle fairly good-sized logs; the smaller models are ideal for trimming trees and removing brush.

Most electric saws have a manual oiler, oil level indicator, antikickback bar tip, trigger-lock control, cushioned handles, and double insulation to eliminate electrical shock. The chain guide bars are reversible, and some models have an automatic chain-sharpening device.

Electric chain saw problems

■ No power
First check for a blown fuse or a tripped circuit breaker at the main electrical service entrance to your home. The blown fuse or tripped breaker indicates that there is a power overload on the circuit. This can be caused by too much pressure on the saw while cutting (which causes the saw to bind in the material) or by the wrong size extension cord wire. Always use No. 12 or No. 14 wire in an extension cord.

The power cord disconnect at the saw or the power cord itself may be defective; replace them.

Burned-out brushes in the saw motor and a malfunctioning switch will cause this problem, and they must be repaired by a professional.

■ Motor overheats

The chances are you are biting off more wood than the saw can chew. Work slowly.

Check these possible causes:

wrong size extension cord (see above.)
blocked air vents to motor
dirty chain and chain bar
worn chain or bar (see page 112.)
worn or broken sprocket or clutch (see page 114.)

If the brushes are worn, take the saw to a pro for repair.

Other problems, common to both electric and gasoline chain saws, are discussed earlier in this chapter.

Working with chain saws

Safety must always be your first priority with chain saws. Actually, a chain saw is no more dangerous than a power circular saw, a lathe, or any woodworking tool with a moving blade. But there are special precautions you *must* take with a chain saw to prevent accidents from happening.

■ Work with someone else in the area, within shouting distance, who can get help in an emergency.

■ Always start the saw in an area that is clear of tools, fuel containers, wood, and debris.

■ To start the saw, put it on solid ground and stick your foot through the handle. Hang on to the front handle with one hand and pull the starting rope with the other hand. Keep yourself and all other people and objects away from the chain end of the saw—*always!*

■ Always wear safety goggles, leather gloves, ear plugs, and clothing that hugs the body. When working in the woods, wear a hardhat, absolutely without exception.

■ Do not smoke while working with the chain saw.

■ Always let the saw cool down before you refuel, and move to a safe place before you start refueling. Open the fuel cap slowly.

■ Don't start the saw again where you have refueled; move about 10 feet away

from this spot. If you have spilled fuel on the saw, let the fuel dry before you start the saw.

■ Always keep a firm grip on the saw while it's running. Remember that kickback is caused by: the saw striking tree limbs or other objects at the tip of the saw; the saw hitting metal, cement, or other hard materials; running the saw too slowly at the start or during the cut; a dull or loose chain; cutting above your shoulder height.

■ Don't set a hot saw down on any substance that will burn, such as dry grass.

■ Don't operate the saw while you are sitting in a tree or standing on a ladder. Fell the tree first, then cut it into the desired pieces.

■ Be careful when cutting small-diameter saplings and brush. Flexible growth can snag the chain, whipping the saw toward you or pulling you off balance.

■ Do not carry the saw around while it's running. Shut off the saw each time you move, without fail.

■ When possible, cut logs or other wood on a buck, never directly on the ground. The saw can hit the ground and kick back toward you.

■ When cutting logs on a slope, stay on the uphill side.

Where to write

If you need answers to specific questions about chain saws that are not covered in this chapter, write to one of the many chain saw manufacturers in the United States. Here is a list of their names and addresses. Address your questions to the "Consumer Information Director" of the company.

Homelite
Box 7047
144401 Carowinds Boulevard
Charlotte, NC 28217

McCulloch Corporation
5400 Alla Road
Los Angeles, CA 90066

Wen Products, Inc.
5810 Northwest Highway
Chicago, IL 60631
(electric chain saws)

Remington Chain Saws
Desa Industries
AMCA International Corp.
25000 S. Western Avenue
Park Forest, IL 60466

Dynamark Corp.
875 N. Michigan Avenue
Chicago, IL 60611

Oregon Saw Chain Division
Omark Industries, Inc.
9701 S.E. McLoughlin Boulevard
Portland, OR 97222

Sabre/Townsend Saw Chain Co.
P.O. Box 6396
Columbia, SC 29260

7 Repair and Care of Trimmers, Edgers, Snow Throwers, Tillers, and Other Power Tools

Tool manufacturers have added electric motors and gasoline engines to an amazing variety of lawn and garden equipment, from snow throwers and garden tillers to shovels, rakes, and hoes.

This chapter is devoted to the care and repair of those power tools that homeowners are likely to own today or those they may own in the future.

POWER TRIMMERS

The most common grass trimmers use an electric motor mounted vertically so that the motor shaft spins a spool of nylon line, or string. The line, whipped around at high speed, severs grass blades. More powerful trimmers have a lightweight two-cycle engine that spins either the line or a blade similar to the one on a portable circular saw. The blade model is for trimming brush, for edging and pruning, even for mowing and scalping grass, weeds, and other vegetation.

Economy-model electric trimmers sell for about $15 and are ideal for cutting an 8-inch swath of grass. They are best used, however, to trim grass from around tree trunks, porch steps and decks, outdoor lighting poles, and the like. The motor for the economy models is usually in the 2 amp range, which provides plenty of power for light-duty trimming jobs.

Mid-range electric trimmers include both the 3 amp lightweight and the 5 amp heavyweight. The motor is matched to the cut of the trimmer: the 3 amp motor for cutting

1. Maintaining trimmers. Dirt, debris, and compacted grass clippings clog the cooling slots of a trimmer motor and cause it to overheat. Clean out these slots each time you use the trimmer.

2. An old toothbrush makes an excellent tool for cleaning trimmers since the small bristles work into tight quarters.

10- to 14-inch swaths and the 5 amp motor for 16-inch string cuts and blade cuts. Larger units are powered by two-cycle gasoline engines. The smallest gasoline engine is 12 cc; the largest is 86 cc.

General maintenance

Electric trimmers need little maintenance. Inspect the connections on the power cord every time you use the trimmer. Look for frayed cord around the connections and breaks in the insulation. Check the condition of the receptacle into which you plug the extension cord. Although the nylon string is not sharp enough and the motor is not powerful enough to cut an extension cord, don't put the cord in the way of the trimming element.

Clean the line spool and the plastic spool housing after each use. If the motor is at the cutting end of the trimmer (which is usually the case with electric models), make sure the motor cooling vents are free from grass clippings and other debris. Clean these ports with an old toothbrush and a wooden scraper fashioned from a paint paddle. *Do not* wash the area with soap and water; if this mixture runs into the motor, it may cause a short circuit.

Hang the trimmer up on a hook when you store it; the plastic parts will crack or break easily if stepped on or roughly manhandled.

Electric trimmer troubles

The problems with electric trimmers fall into just two categories: the power cord and power supply, and the nylon line.

Regardless of the size of the motor, use an extension cord with No. 12 or No. 14 gauge wire. No. 16 or 18 wire is too small and does not supply enough power to the motor; running the motor on low voltage can ruin it. Worse, it can melt the insulation on the power cord, exposing bare power wires and causing electrical shock or fire.

To connect the trimmer to the power supply, always plug the cord into the trimmer *first*; then put the tool down and plug the cord into the

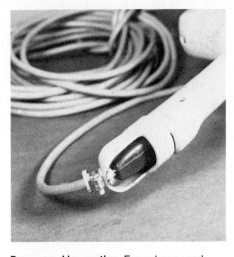

Power cord inspection. Frayed, exposed, bare, and cut power extension cords cause problems with electric motor-driven equipment. Examine connections frequently and replace any damaged cord with No. 12 or No. 14 gauge wire.

power outlet. This way, you avoid electrical shock when plugging the trimmer into a live circuit. Make sure all connections along the power line are tight. Don't leave the prongs on a plug partly exposed; firmly press the male end of the plug into the female socket.

The nylon or monofilament string or line—the cutting edge—comes in a roll that you thread around the spool on the end of the trimmer. The line also comes wound on a spool; you just replace the spool when the line runs out.

Using the wrong size line or the wrong type of spool causes problems. The spool may jam on its spindle, or the line will not unwind properly; both result in poor cutting. Buying the wrong product is easy because many of the spools look alike. Different lines look similar, too, although thickness and gauge can vary considerably.

When you purchase new spools or line, always take the model number of the trimmer to the store. Match the model number with the numbers on the package and do not accept substitutes. This sounds elementary, but you'd be surprised how many spool and line problems are caused by an owner trying to use the wrong size spool.

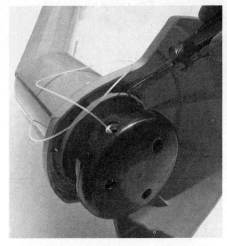

Trimmer line adjustment. Spool-fed trimmer line should be the right size and mounted on the right spool for your model. If the line sticks in the spool, suspect unraveled line within the spool. Caps for most spools simply turn off counterclockwise. Block the spool or shaft with a screwdriver, as shown here, in order to turn the cap.

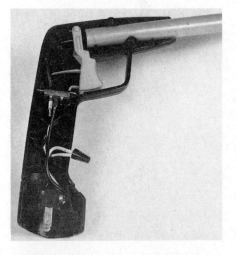

1. Trimmer switch replacement. A handle trigger switch controls a spring-loaded toggle switch on many trimmers. The white (negative) wire runs through the switch and is connected with a wire nut. The power (hot) wire is connected to the switch with a spade connection.

2. The molded plastic trigger pivots in the handle on a plastic pin. The toggle switch is activated by a plastic prong on the bottom of the trigger.

Switches and motors

The switch on an electric trimmer, which is usually operated by a trigger assembly, is mounted in the handle of the trimmer. The switch itself is a simple toggle type; squeezing the plastic trigger flips the switch inside the handle on and off.

If the trimmer won't run, first check the power by plugging in another appliance that you know works. If this appliance doesn't work, go back along the power cord, checking the connections right to the power outlet. Then check the fuse box or circuit breaker inside the house.

If the trimmer is receiving power, check the trigger. The handle of most trimmers is held together with self-tapping metal screws with a Phillips slot. Remove these screws counterclockwise and pull off half the handle. This will expose the trigger assembly and the switch. Look carefully at the trigger. It may have worked out of its mounting hole, or the plastic prong that activates the switch may be bent or broken. You may be able to buy a new trigger at a retail outlet that sells your model trimmer. However, chances are good that you will have to order this part from the manufacturer. Expect to wait six weeks.

If the trigger is working, check the prongs for the power cord and then check the switch. The prongs may be bent or twisted in the handle assembly; the switch may not be sliding along its track properly. Buy replacement parts from the manufacturer; it's doubtful that you will find them at a retailer, although a repair shop may stock them.

Replacing a switch unit is simple. Just disconnect the wires from the defective unit, remove it, put in the new unit, and rewire it like the old one (see illustrations in this chapter).

But before you go to the work of locating the parts, try to find out the price of a new switch assembly. If you own an economy-model trimmer, it sometimes is less expensive to buy a new trimmer than to replace parts.

Many trimmers use a universal electric motor (see photo), which has carbon brushes that press against a commutator. When these soft carbon brushes wear down, the motor sparks.

On more expensive trimmers, you may be able to open the motor housing and change the carbon brushes. The housing is made of two parts held together by self-tapping screws. Back out the screws counterclockwise; they usually accept a Phillips screwdriver. Some motor housings have an information label stuck across the joint where the housing parts fit together. If the label is stuck tight, use a razor blade or a utility knife to cut it so the housing can come apart.

The brushes are usually mounted at the top end of the motor. They are held in place either by a screw cap or by clips. If a screw cap is used, remove it counterclockwise with a

1. Edger motor repair. Remove the edger handle to make way for removal of the edger housing. Several screws hold the power head together; turn them out counterclockwise. The power wire runs down from a switch on the handle.

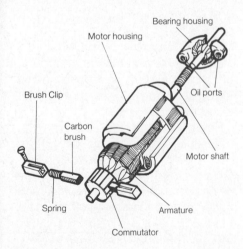

2. The insides of a universal electric motor look something like this. These brushes are spring-loaded and held by screw caps. To replace the brushes, remove the screw caps on either side of the motor housing.

3. The carbon brushes are held in small plastic clips that slide into a slot on each side of the commutator. The wires have been disconnected here. Very carefully pry out the brushes with the tip of a screwdriver.

4. The new rectangular carbon brushes will fit into the old clips, or the brushes and clips will be sold as one unit. Hold the tool so that the motor shaft is vertical, as shown here, to keep the commutator in position as you install the brushes and clips. Otherwise the springs will force the brushes into the motor housing, and you won't be able to put the commutator in place.

standard slot screwdriver. Under the cap is a coil spring, and under the spring are the brushes. You probably will have to turn the motor on its side to tap out the brushes.

Replace the parts in the same order they came out of the housing: brushes, spring, cap. Be sure to change both brushes while the motor is out of its housing. New brushes are easy to locate; most hardware and electrical stores that sell motors stock them. Take the old brushes with you to get exact replacements.

Clip-type brushes are usually made for specific motors, so you will have to buy replacements from the dealer, a pro shop, or the manufacturer.

The clips hold the brushes in place by pressing against a harness next to the commutator. First disconnect the wires going to the brushes. Pull the spade connections straight off; don't wobble them. Then lightly pry the brushes out of the harness with the tip of a screwdriver. Slip the new brushes into the harness with your fingers and connect the wires as shown in the illustration.

Other motor troubles include worn bearings, a bad armature, and a bent motor shaft. All of these are jobs for a professional repairman. Get a repair estimate before commissioning the repair. A new trimmer may be less expensive than making these repairs.

Sometimes the wire that runs from the handle to the motor becomes twisted and breaks. You may be able to replace it by disassembling the handle housing and the motor housing. Make sure that the replacement wire matches the original wire. The replacement job is a simple matter of disconnecting the old wire and connecting the new one.

Troubleshooting electric grass trimmers

This checklist covers problems, possible causes, and the best solutions for malfunctioning trimmers. For additional help, consult the section on edgers in this chapter.

The motor won't run

■ Is the trimmer getting power?
Check the power cord along its length; then check the fuse box or circuit breaker panel in your home. If you have an older home, look for more than one power panel or fuse box.
Check the trigger and the switch in the handle for damage. If this isn't the problem, disassemble the motor housing and look for a power break; there could be a short circuit or trouble with the commutator and armature. These repairs should be made by a professional.

The motor runs, but with no power

■ Is the string spool jammed?
Check for debris around the spool and the spool shaft, which is connected to the motor.

■ Are the carbon brushes bad? (see pages 120-121.)

■ Is the power cord the right size for the trimmer and for carrying power from the power source to the trimmer? (see page 119.)

Repair of these problems is a job for a professional:

damaged commutator

bad armature

damaged motor bearings

bent motor shaft

The string won't unwind properly

■ Are you using the correct size string or spool?

■ Is the string properly mounted on the spool?
Most trimmers cut from the left side, so the debris is thrown away from the operator.

■ Is the spool jammed?
Check the spool and the spool shaft for debris.

The spool jams

■ Are you using the correct size string or spool?

■ Is debris preventing rotation?

Other possibilities—professional repair jobs—are:

bent motor shaft

malfunctioning commutator or armature

The string unwinds too fast

■ Are you using the correct size string or spool?

■ Is the string wound tightly enough on the spool?

■ Are you tapping the automatic string feed too often?

Vibration

■ Is the spool properly connected to the motor shaft?

■ Are you using the correct size string or spool?

■ Is the handle assembly properly locked onto the shaft to the motor?

■ Is the debris guard properly locked to the motor housing?

Excessive noise

■ Is debris stuck around the spool?

These problems must be corrected by a pro:

worn bearings

bent motor shaft

malfunctioning motor components

Gasoline grass trimmers
Two-cycle gasoline engines power grass trimmers that go anywhere. The units are very similar to electric trimmers; they use monofilament line that cuts grass, or they employ a saw blade to cut grass, brush, and small trees.

Engine maintenance and repair
For all practical purposes, the engines function the same way as those found on chain saws. See Chapters 5 and 6 for engine care and repair. Don't overlook the information on four-cycle engines, since some of the repair procedures also apply to two-cycle engines.
Upkeep of a gasoline-powered trimmer is simple. Clean the spool after each use with household detergent and water applied with a brush. To remove heavy debris, make a wooden scraper from a paint paddle, or use a plastic scraper intended for removing ice and snow.
The air filter on the engine should be removed and cleaned after the trimmer has been operated for eight to ten hours, more frequently if you are working under dusty and dirty conditions, such as along a gravel or dirt road.
After each use, clean the cooling fins and air inlet openings around the housing; an ice cream stick makes a good tool for this.
Keep a sharp eye on the carrying harness and straps; keep them in good repair, with all clips and fasteners in working order. Inspect the trimmer or blade guard before each use;

tighten all visible nuts and bolts with a wrench.

Store the trimmer up and out of the way. The working parts of the engine are delicate; if the trimmer accidentally falls onto a hard surface, such as a concrete floor, engine parts may break or come apart.

The drive shaft

Gasoline-powered trimmers usually have a flexible shaft running from the engine to the string spool or the blade at the bottom of the trimmer.

This shaft should be lubricated with lithium grease or with a lubricant recommended by the manufacturer after every twenty hours of operation. The shaft on your trimmer may have oil ports or grease fittings for lubrication. However, you may have to remove the shaft housing to lubricate the flexible shaft.

To remove the shaft housing, back out the fastener that holds the shaft housing to the engine. Then pull out the shaft and lubricate it. When you reassemble the shaft and housing, make sure that the shaft is properly matched to the clutch housing. There are two flat sides on the shaft that match two flat sides on the clutch housing. Check for a correct match by turning the spool; the flexible shaft should also turn.

Cutting head troubleshooting

The string won't unwind

■ Are you using the correct size string or spool?

■ Is the line properly mounted on the spool?

■ Is the spool properly mounted on the flexible shaft?

■ Is the spool tight in the flexible shaft?

■ Is the spool jammed by debris?

The string cuts improperly

■ Are you using the correct size string or spool?

■ On a multiline spool, is the line trimmed evenly?
The lines must be the same length. Trim to adjust.

■ Is the spool properly mounted on the flexible shaft?

The spool won't turn

■ Is the spool blocked by debris?

■ Is the flexible shaft properly mounted in the clutch housing?

If the flexible shaft is broken, take the tool to a pro for repair.

Vibration

■ On a multiline tool, are you using only one spool?

■ Is the blade on the blade-type unit out of balance or improperly mounted?

■ Is the flexible shaft properly mounted in the clutch housing?

■ Is the spool properly mounted on the flexible shaft?

■ Are the bolts holding the line or blade guard properly tightened?

■ Are the handlebars tightly mounted in the correct position?

Electric edgers

The motor on an electric edger is mounted horizontally so that the motor shaft provides the power for the edger blades. Other than the motor configuration, the differences between an edger and a trimmer are few.

Like any tool powered by electricity, your reach with an edger is limited by the power cord. The power cord must be No. 12 or No. 14 gauge wire. The cord connections must be tight-fitting. When the edger won't run, follow the troubleshooting guide for trimmers (see above).

Blades for electric edgers vary from 6 to 8 inches in diameter. Blade cutting depth runs to about 2 inches; the depth may be preset or can be adjusted by moving the wheels or a lever on the handle.

Some edgers are convertible; that is, the motor can be turned so the

Edger blade removal. Two wrenches are needed to remove edger blades, both electric- and gasoline-powered. Use one to hold the motor and engine shaft and another to turn the nut holding the blade.

edger becomes a trimmer. The same cutting blade is used.

General maintenance

Edger blade maintenance can demand a lot of attention since the blade often strikes concrete driveways and walks and other hard surfacing materials. Some blades have a distinct cutting edge, and others have a square-shouldered cutting edge that bypasses a stationary cutting edge on the bottom of the edger housing (see photograph). To sharpen any type of blade, remove it from the edger. You may need two wrenches: one to hold the hub of the motor shaft still and another to turn the nut holding the blade to the motor shaft.

Use a smooth-cut or bastard flat file for sharpening. Put the blade in a vise and follow the existing angle (about 75 degrees) on the blade with the file. If the blade is square, just file straight across the edge, holding the file flat against the edge. You must take off the same amount of metal with each stroke or you'll put the blade out of balance, causing excessive vibration and damage to the motor.

Therefore, for sharpening jobs other than light touch-ups, have a professional do the work. But get an estimate first; it may be cheaper to buy a new blade than to have an old one sharpened.

For motor maintenance, repair, and troubleshooting of electric edgers, see the section on electric trimmers.

Gasoline edgers

Edgers powered with gasoline engines are available in several sizes. Blade diameters range from 6 to 10 inches for cuts up to 4 inches deep. Most of them are driven by 3½ hp, four-cycle engines. Most models have two wheels at the back and one wheel at the front to guide the edger along driveways and walks.

Power edgers must be kept clean and free of debris around the engine and cutter blade housing. Blades are removed for minor sharpening as described under electric edgers.

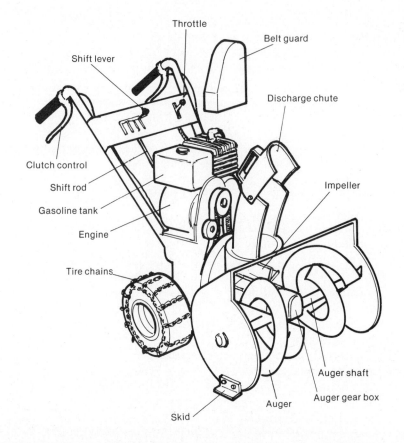

Parts locater for a snow thrower. Most throwers look like this one; your model may be slightly different, but most of the maintenance and repair procedures will be the same.

Muffler replacement. Mufflers have one thing in common: they rust out. In ice and snow conditions, metal rusts faster than usual. Replace the muffler when the metal becomes soft.

For gasoline engine maintenance and repair, and troubleshooting, refer to the section on four-cycle engines in Chapter 5.

SNOW THROWERS

The best time to care for and repair a snow thrower is in the spring, summer, and fall months when it isn't snowing. Snow throwers are in many ways related to garden tillers. The controls and engine configurations are similar; both use belt and chain drives.

Most snow thrower problems are caused by lack of maintenance. If the equipment is put away wet, rust forms on vital working parts. Wetness also strips lubrication from moving parts, further encouraging rust and corrosion. Therefore, after each time the unit is used in the snow, carefully wipe *all* wet surfaces dry with a cloth; then lubricate chains, bearings, gears, and shafts.

Snow throwers are usually powered by four-cycle gasoline engines. See Chapter 5 for engine maintenance, repairs, and troubleshooting.

The auger

The auger at the front of a snow thrower gathers snow into a housing where it is fed to an impeller that discharges it through a top chute.

Along the outside bottom edge of the auger housing are two adjustable skids. The skids must be set just high enough to clear uneven walks and driveways and graveled surfaces. If the machine is difficult to move forward, look for trouble here first. Skid height may be adjusted by moving bolts mounted in slotted holes.

Auger maintenance also should include lubrication of the gear box that connects the auger and the impeller. Unless otherwise specified by the manufacturer, use SAE 10W-40 motor oil for lubrication.

The belts

The drive belts on a snow thrower are similar to those on a rider tractor (see Chapter 4). They can be adjusted if the auger or impeller is sluggish, sticks, or fails to turn at all. Loose belts can prevent the snow from

1. Auger maintenance. Auger skids, mounted on the bottom of the auger housing, are adjustable so that you can raise the height of the auger housing to ride over uneven pavement. You may wear out several skids before the season is over, but never run the thrower with the auger housing scraping along the ground.

being discharged properly and, sometimes, can prevent the wheels from turning when the thrower has been shifted into gear.

By adjusting the idler pulley (see photograph) you may be able to tighten the belt enough to take up the slack. The pulley may be moved forward or backward by adjusting a bolt in a slotted hole. The belt should deflect about 1/4 inch when it is pressed down between the pulleys. All worn or cracked belts must be replaced with new ones; make a visual check of the belts at the start of the winter season. Instructions for changing belts are given in Chapter 4.

Keep the disc drive clean (see photo) and properly adjusted. You will have to remove the metal housing that covers the disc drive; bolts hold the covering in place. You may be able to adjust the drive if there is too much clearance between the

2. The auger gear case is in the center of the housing on the shaft. It should be kept full of oil. I recommend SAE 10W-40 oil, but check your owner's manual for the manufacturer's recommendation. To open the gear case, just remove the screw cap, as shown, by turning it counterclockwise with a wrench. Pour the oil into this opening.

Belt drive adjustment. To increase or decrease tension in the belt assembly on a snow thrower, shift into neutral, loosen the shaft bolt on the idler pulley (center) with a wrench, and slide it back and forth. Then put the shift in forward and check the tension on the belt.

Disc drive maintenance. The disc drive is a flat steel dish that turns a vertical wheel that has a rubber rim. Keep this assembly clean and free of oil and grease.

Snow thrower troubleshooting

Using the parts locater drawing and the photographs, you will be able to solve most snow thrower problems. For solutions to engine troubles, consult Chapter 5.

The wheels won't turn

■ Are the shift control rods and clutch cables adjusted properly?
They can be set with a screwdriver or a wrench (see page 126).

■ Is the belt or drive chain loose?
Adjust the idler pulley or remove a link or two from the chain (see pages 62-63 and 71). If the belts are badly worn, replace them.

■ Is the transmission oil level low?

■ Are the drive pins on the wheels broken?
The pins let the thrower freewheel, that is, release it so it can be pushed by hand.

Chain drive adjustment. The chain drive on a thrower can be tightened by moving the engine backward or by removing a link from the chain. Clean and lubricate the chain at the start of each winter season.

drive and speed discs. If not, have a pro make the needed adjustments or repairs. To check the disc clearance, put the shift lever in neutral. Then slip a thin piece of cardboard (shirt boards are best) between the speed and drive discs. If the clearance is properly adjusted, there should be no drag when the machine is in neutral.

Snow dischargers

This assembly includes the auger, impeller shaft, impeller, and dis-

charge chute. When the snow won't discharge, the problem most likely is a discharge chute blocked by ice and snow. If possible, move the snow thrower into a warm room and let the snow melt. Or try to remove the blockage with a screwdriver.

Discharge problems also can be caused by running the machine in a high, instead of a low, gear. Slipping belts, broken auger shear bolts, and not enough lubricant in the auger gear box are other possible causes.

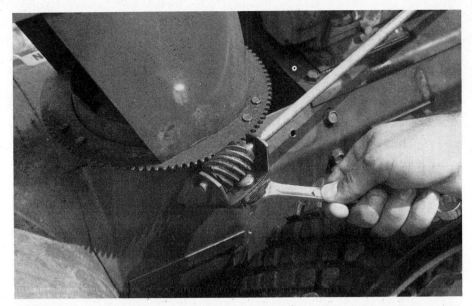

1. Control adjustment. Adjust the worm gear that turns the discharge chute so that the gears don't mesh too tightly. Keep the gears lubricated with a water-resistant grease. If the chute is difficult to turn during operation, look for snow and ice buildup on both gears.

The wheels slip

■ Do the tires need chains?

■ Are you running the machine too fast?
   Shift into a lower gear.

The auger turns too slowly

■ Are the drive belts loose? (see page 126.)

■ Is any snow or ice blocking the auger and impeller units?

■ Is the auger box low on lubricant? (see page 125.)

No snow discharge

■ Is the discharge chute blocked?

2. The choke is not always connected to the control console; you may find a push-primer mounted on the engine. Keep this assembly tight on its mountings. Replace the push-button spring if it becomes weak.

3. On snow throwers and tillers, controls from the handle console are usually rods that are screwed into connections at the other ends. Sometimes the rods have to be disconnected at the control console in order to make adjustments. If this is true on your equipment, remove the cotter pin that holds the rod to the control handle.

■ Are the drive belts properly tensioned? (see page 126.)

■ Are the auger shear bolts broken?

■ Are you working the unit too hard?
   Shift into a lower gear.

Vibration

■ Are any bolts loose?
   Tighten all visible bolts and screws.

■ Is the auger bent or broken?

■ Are the belts properly tensioned? (see page 126.)

GARDEN TILLERS
Tillers are first cousins to snow throwers. Instead of an auger, the tiller has a group of tines that plunge into the earth and break it up.

Most tillers are powered by four-cycle gasoline engines. Any engine problems you might have are discussed in Chapter 5. Other problems fall into just two categories: the belt drives and the tines.

Belt drives
The belt drive on a tiller varies from manufacturer to manufacturer. I've given a composite picture here, one that explains most tillers.

In the drive train, the pulley attached to the crankshaft turns counterclockwise. When the machine is shifted into forward gear, the forward idler puts tension on the belt that drives the jackshaft (the largest) pulley *counterclockwise*. When you put the unit into reverse gear, the reverse idler puts tension on the belt that turns the jackshaft pulley *clockwise*. To check the tension, put the tiller in gear. Push down on the belt about midway between pulleys. The belt should deflect only about ¼ to ½ inch.

The tension of these belts can usually be adjusted by loosening the bolt that holds the idler pulleys. The bolt hole is slotted so that the pulleys can be moved forward or backward. To

Clutch control adjustment. For continuous operation, most clutch controls have a spring-loaded locking device which lets you steer the thrower without continually gripping the clutch lever. When the spring weakens with age, remove it by unscrewing the fastener at the other end of the lock and install a new one.

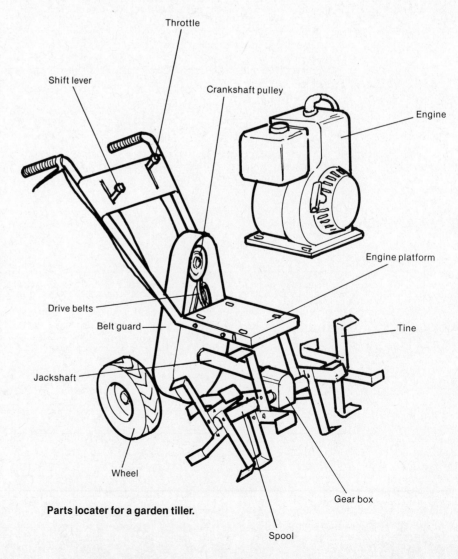

Parts locater for a garden tiller.

increase the tension, first put the tiller into neutral. Then loosen the bolt on the idler pulley so that it increases the tension of the belt. Tighten the bolt, put the transmission into forward gear, and test the belt for the 1/4- to 1/2-inch deflection.

Some of the pulleys are equipped with adjustable belt guides; the guide should be approximately 1/16 inch from the top of the belt.

The tines

Some tillers have self-sharpening tines (check your owner's manual). Others have to be sharpened. To do this, use a smooth, flat file and maintain the original angle on the cutting surface. The tines do not have to be balanced, as lawnmower blades do, after sharpening.

If the tines are bent, replace them. The tines are bolted to the spool; remove the bolts or cotter pins and slip the tines off the spool. The tines are usually in two configurations: some face left; others face right. When you remove the tines, be sure to mark them so that you can replace them properly.

Lubrication

Before each use, check the lubricant level in the transmission. Do not run the machine with the lubricant level low. Follow the manufacturer's recommendations for the proper type and level of lubricant. If you've lost the manual, the standard lubricant is SAE 90 gear lubricant or SAE 50 non-detergent motor oil. Fill the transmission to the top with lubricant.

Troubleshooting tillers

See Chapter 5 for information on engine troubleshooting. Transmission belt problems are also discussed in Chapter 4.

The belts squeal and smoke

■ Is the belt tension correct?
Deflection should be about 1/4 to 1/2 inch between pulleys. (see pages 128-129.)

Another tiller configuration. This tiller has rear-mounted tines with the drive belts positioned along one side of the machine. Although this design is different from that of the machine in the drawing (opposite), the parts work in a very similar way.

Belt adjustment. If the belt is properly tensioned, you will be able to depress the belt only about 1/4 inch between the pulleys. The small idler pulley (center) is mounted in a slotted bolt hole so the pulley can be moved to adjust the belt tension.

Tine replacement. To remove the tines, pull the cotter pins holding the tine spool to the shaft. The tines curve in opposite directions; mark them on removal so you can replace them on the shaft in the same position.

■ Are the belts the correct size?

■ Are the belts properly mounted?

■ Are the belt guides rubbing on the belts? (see page 68.)

■ Are the belts badly worn?

■ Are the pulleys out of alignment?

The clutch won't engage the gears

■ Is the belt tension correct? (see pages 128-129.)

■ Is the spring on the clutch rod loose?

Tighten the bolt that holds the spring to increase spring tension.

The drive slips out of gear

■ Are the belts too loose? (see pages 128-129.)

■ Is the linkage between the shift and the belts loose or worn?

Control rod adjustment. Turn the turnbuckle nut on the end of the threaded rod. You may have to release the controls at the console (see the section on snow throwers). Turn the nut clockwise to tighten or take up slack in the rod; turn counterclockwise to loosen the tension.

■ Is the spring on the clutch rod loose?

Tighten the bolt that holds the spring to increase spring tension.

LEAF BLOWERS

These electric- or gasoline-powered machines generate a wind volume of from 100 to 250 cubic feet of air per minute. This blast is used to blow dirt, debris, grass, and leaves into a corral where it may be picked up and bagged for removal or for use as compost. The wind for the blower (which may also be used to remove light snow) is generated by a fan or impeller driven by a gasoline engine or an electric motor. The fan or impeller blows the wind through a tube or hose.

The electric units operate on regular house power with an extension cord. The gasoline-driven units are usually powered by a two-cycle engine.

One common complaint about blowers is lack of wind power. This is usually caused by an undersized blower rather than mechanical failure. The solution: buy a blower big enough for the job.

The fan or impeller is mounted in a housing directly next to the power source. This assembly should be kept free of obstruction; on many models, you can open a screen cover to remove debris.

Blower repairs

If the blower is gasoline-powered, consult Chapters 5 and 6 for maintenance and repair procedures. If the blower is electric-powered, use the information under edgers and trimmers in this chapter. This section includes photographs that show how to change the switch and brushes on an electric motor.

Filter maintenance. Clean paper air filters with compressed air or by tapping them on a hard surface. If the filter looks extremely dirty, replace it. On the average, most tillers take two filter replacements each season.

2. Power line connections to the blower motor are mounted on a circuit card; the connections here are made with wire nuts. Unscrew the nuts to replace defective wiring.

Control maintenance. Keep tiller control linkage tight and well lubricated. Unless otherwise specified by the manufacturer, use SAE 30 oil.

3. Brushes in the electric blower motor are held with clips, as shown here, or are spring-loaded and capped with a screw, as shown in the drawing for the electric grass trimmer section of this chapter. If clips are used, pry out the brushes very gently with the tip of a screwdriver.

1. Blower electrical repairs. This electric leaf blower uses a simple toggle switch mounted in the handle of the blower housing. To replace it, separate the two halves of the housing by removing several screws; the switch is connected with spade terminals.

HEDGE CLIPPERS AND GRASS CUTTERS

Mechanically, these portable power tools are very much alike. The bypass-type blades are driven by gears turned by an electric motor. The difference is that the hedge clipper uses house power from an extension cord while the cutter may run on rechargeable batteries.

Hedge clippers

The prime maintenance requirement is keeping the movable blades clean and sharp. Wood and sap lodge in the necks of the blades and the moving spline, causing the tool to work sluggishly or cut poorly. The best way to clean the blades and spline is to scrub them outdoors with a toothbrush dipped in mineral spirits.

If the blades—especially the moving blade—are nicked, they must be replaced. To remove an old blade, first remove the screws that hold the parts of the housing together. Then use a wrench to remove the fasteners that hold the moving blade to the stationary blade (see photo). The fasteners turn counterclockwise. Fasten the replacement blade to the stationary blade with the new fasteners provided with the new blade. Don't reuse the old fasteners.

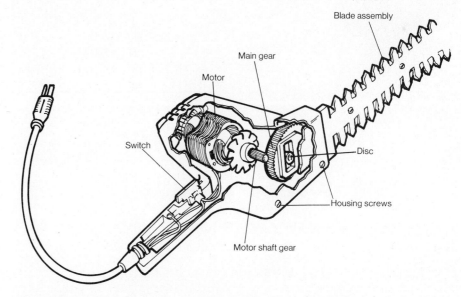

Clipper electrical repairs. Access to the switch and motor is through the housing, which splits apart when several screws are removed. You can replace the switch, the brushes in the motor, and the gears.

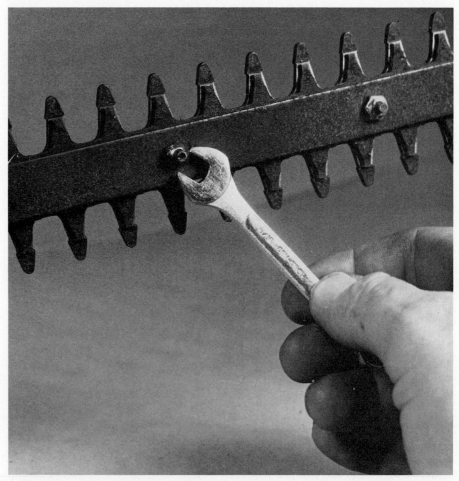

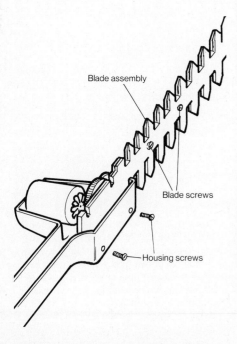

1. Replacing hedge clipper blades. Take out the housing screws at the base of the blade.

2. Fixed and moving blades are held together with a bolt and nut fastener. To install a new movable blade, remove the old one from the fixed blade, as shown. Your routine maintenance schedule should include tightening these nuts.

Gears and motor

The blades are moved back and forth by gears at the bottom end of the shaft. These gears should be lubricated at least once a year with a heat-resistant grease. If the teeth of the large gear are broken, you may be able to replace the gear by removing it from the shaft. If you can't remove it, take the tool to a professional for repair. Make sure to get a repair estimate first.

If the gears on the motor shaft are damaged, the motor will have to be replaced. This, too, is a job for a professional.

The universal motor has carbon brushes that will spark when they are worn. Instructions for replacing them are given earlier in this chapter. You can also replace the switch.

Grass cutter maintenance

There's not much to do in the way of maintenance on grass cutters powered by rechargeable battery, although you can replace a defective switch or battery charger. You can sharpen and replace the blades; you can lubricate and, perhaps, replace broken gears.

Access to the blades and gears is through the bottom, stationary blade. Usually, two screws hold the blade to the motor housing; both turn out counterclockwise.

One of the gears has an off-center disc that goes into a slot on the moving blade. When the gear rotates, the disc moves the blade from side to side on top of the fixed blade. If these gears are metal, lubricate them annually with a heat-resistant grease.

To sharpen the blades, remove both blades from the housing. Match the blades together and lock them in a vise. With a flat, smoothing file, file across the blades, retaining the original angle on all edges of the blades. If the blades are badly nicked or damaged, replace them.

The battery that powers grass cutters discharges fairly rapidly. As its life runs out, there may be a surge of power and then a sudden drop. This often leads the operator to look for trouble with the blades or in the motor, but the first place to check is always the battery. An easy way to prevent battery rundown is to mount the tool on the recharger whenever it is not in use. The recharger automatically shuts off the power when the battery is fully charged.

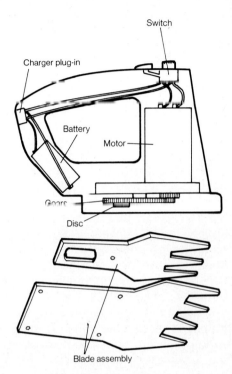

Battery-operated grass cutter. This stubby version of a hedge clipper has similar gearing works and maintenance procedures.

8 Hand Tool Maintenance

Anything a power tool can do, a hand tool can do—and often better. Most power tools, in fact, are just hand tools with motors, not muscle, supplying the driving force. Basic hand tools—shovels, axes, rakes, shears—have not changed much over the years; and although design, balance, and metals have been improved with new technology, the purposes remain the same. A good example is an axe. A 20th-century axe looks about the same as a 16th-century axe and does the same job with, perhaps, a couple of gimmicks added to split wood better and metal rings and wedges to tighten handles in sockets.

Lawn and garden tools are subject to rust and dullness, and you'll encounter both frequently if you dig, rake, hoe, and cut on a regular basis. It is, of course, very easy to put away a dirty, earth-encrusted tool without cleaning it, but this is just how rust gets a toehold to pit and corrode the metal surfaces. Dirt goes along with dullness; if the tool is dirty, most of us are reluctant to sharpen the tool or even see that it needs sharpening. Dull tools make the work harder, and dull tools are unsafe. A sharp tool is a safe tool.

The tools you need

Go into most hardware and home center outlets, wherever lawn and garden tools are sold, and you will be greeted with an array of equipment that will boggle your mind. There are dozens of shovels, rakes, hoes, shears, loppers, scrapers, diggers, hooks—and on and on. By actual

Sharpening chopping tools. Use a whetstone (shown here) or an oilstone frequently. Move the stone *away* from the cutting edge, not toward it. If the edge is nicked badly, grind it smooth, then taper it, and finally hone it with a whetstone.

Sharpening hoes. Cutting edges of hoes must be sharpened occasionally. Use a smooth file to restore the edge, keeping the bevel at about 45 degrees.

count, one hand tool company makes eight different types of shovels and spades, each one designed for a specific lawn or garden purpose.

You'll also find a wide variance in quality with prices to match. The temptation will be to buy cheaper tools rather than the expensive, quality ones. This is a mistake. You should own quality tools because they are designed to do the job better, easier, and faster. It is easier to maintain quality tools than the less expensive products, quality tools last longer, and, most important, they are safer.

If you are just getting started in lawn and garden activities, invest in the tools listed below as you need them.

The difference between shovels and spades

Shovel points (the digging edge) are pointed, round, and square, and each shape is designed for a specific project.

For all-around work, a medium-point shovel is your best first buy; you can use it for dirt, sand, and gravel shoveling as well as for digging. These shovels also have a medium cant for good leverage and workability. (Cant is the degree the handle is elevated when the flat, or back, of the shovel is laid on a flat surface.)

For more specialized projects, a round-nose shovel is a good buy. Some call it a "crumb shovel" because it is wider than a point shovel and can handle more dirt,

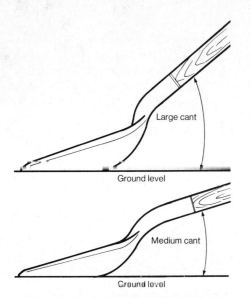

Large cant

Ground level

Medium cant

Ground level

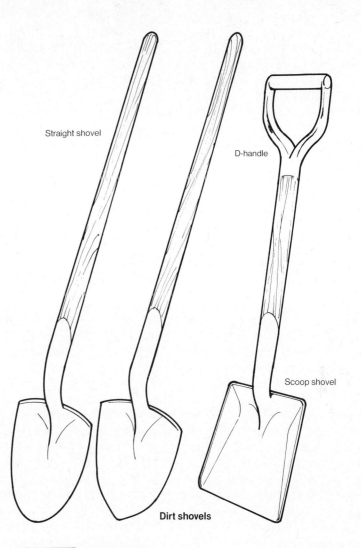

Straight shovel

D-handle

Scoop shovel

Dirt shovels

sand, and loose debris than a spade. You also can use it for digging, but it isn't as efficient as the point shovel or a spade. For ease of handling I recommend a round-nose shovel with lots of cant. More cant lets you stand straighter when shoveling, and standing straight is what you want to do when moving lots of loose debris.

Scoops are wide shovels, some as wide as a snow shovel. They are basically designed for scooping grain; farmers use them for this purpose. You can use scoops as a crumb shovel to move very light and loose debris. Scoops are not made for digging purposes and, therefore, are somewhat limited for many home gardening projects.

You can also buy junior-sized versions of medium-point shovels and scoops. Both deliver smaller loads, but you may prefer to lift less and shovel more.

Most quality shovels and spades have what's called a rolled shoulder or a turned step. This refers to the part you step on while digging.

A *spade* is a straight-line tool; that is, it doesn't have cant. It provides powerful leverage, similar to that of a crowbar or pike. However, use reason when prying. The ferrule (socket) can take the strain, but the wooden handle, although short, will break. The D, or Dee, handle, rather than the T handle, is a good choice. However, if you can find one, the T handle may be more adaptable to your hands.

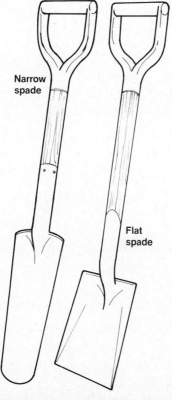

Narrow spade

Flat spade

Spades come in three basic types: medium-blade, tree-planting, and border. The best buy for all-around jobs is a medium-blade (about 8 inches wide by 12 inches long) garden spade. It has a long metal ferrule for the handle; this provides reinforcement for the handle when the spade is used for prying.

A tree-planting spade—or tiling spade, as it's sometimes called—has a long (about 16 to 18 inches) and narrow (about 6 to 8 inches) blade. This is the gardening tool to use for cutting borders around flower beds, for digging trenches, and for digging deep, small-diameter holes for balled tree roots. Like its medium-blade cousin, the tree-planting spade has a long metal ferrule at the bottom of the handle so you can pry the earth without danger of cracking the wooden handle.

A border spade, when you really become specialized, is a junior-sized version of the medium-blade garden spade. It's very lightweight.

Sharpening spades

The cutting edges of spades become dulled by the soil. Rocks and gravel chunks also nick and dull edges. Although you don't have to sharpen these tools every time you use them, it's a good idea to touch up the edges about every fourth time you dig and cut with them. Use a smooth cut file (No. 10) for this, running the file along the beveled edge at a slight angle. Maintain the bevel at about 45 degrees. The job is easier if the spade can be locked in a bench vise. If you don't have a vise, lay the spade flat, bevel side up, over the edge of a low table. File the bevel away from the spade handle. Have a friend hold the tool steady while you work the file.

If the spade is badly nicked along the edges, use a power grinder to remove the nicks by grinding the edge smooth and straight. Do not overheat the metal with the grinding wheel or you may take the temper out of the steel. When the edge is straight, regrind the bevel (to 45 degrees) and touch up the final grinding cut with a smooth file.

Cleaning spades and shovels

Clean spades and shovels after every job. You can remove most dirt simply by washing the tool with a garden hose; use a wire brush on stubborn dirt. Then coat the metal surfaces with regular motor oil or with a combination penetrating oil and cleaner that comes in a spray can. If you will follow this simple cleaning procedure every time, the tools should last you a lifetime.

Wooden handles also need some maintenance. Keep them smooth with sandpaper and protect them with a light coating of linseed oil applied with a cloth. Don't remove the varnish coating on handles when the handles are brand new. After this finish has worn down, remove any remaining varnish and give the handle a linseed oil treatment.

Broken handles

Don't try to repair a broken handle. Always—no exceptions—*replace* a broken handle with a new one. The repair job never will be satisfactory, and, worse, the nails, screws, bolts, and other repair parts may injure your hands if your hands slip on the handle. New handles are easy to locate in hardware, home center, and nursery outlets. They are inexpensive, and installing a new handle is much easier than trying to repair a cracked or broken one.

To replace a handle, you will need a wood rasp to remove excess wood from the new handle so that it fits the socket or ferrule. You also will need a smooth file, to remove the rivet holding the handle in the ferrule, and a hand brace and bit or a power drill, to punch a hole in the handle to accept a new rivet or bolt. If you use a rivet, a ball-peen hammer is the best tool to peen the rivet, that is, to make a head on it.

Some handles are simply wedged into sockets or ferrules. You may need a wood bit to drill out the old handle, or you may be able to knock it out by tapping the rolled shoulder of the tool with a hammer while the handle stub is locked in a bench vise. Do not remove the wood by burning it out; the heat from the fire will destroy the temper of the steel.

Garden forks

Digging forks are miniature plows, each tine representing a plow bottom. Forks loosen the soil and cultivate it for plants, shrubs, trees, and other vegetation.

A medium fork with an 8-inch-wide head and 12-inch-long tines is the best all-around tool; it should have a D handle so you can get a good grip.

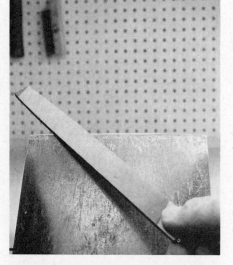

Sharpening digging tools. Keep the cutting edges of spades tool and shovels sharp. Use a smooth metal file to restore and sharpen the beveled edge. File away from the handle, moving across the edge at an angle.

Cleaning digging tools. Use a wire brush after each use for a fast cleaning. Then coat the metal with light household or a penetrating oil to deter rust. Wipe gently with a cloth.

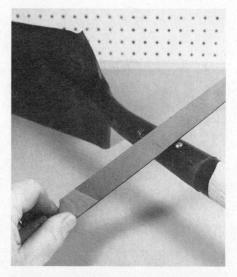

Replacing tool handles. Never repair a broken or split tool handle. Replace it by filing off the head of the rivet that holds the handle in the ferrule and pulling the damaged handle out.

If the soil in your area is rocky or heavy clay, choose a heavy-duty model engineered to handle weight. These forks are usually square, and the ferrule is longer.

A border fork is a small version of the medium fork; it weighs less and is easier to handle, especially in close quarters. Don't expect to work much dirt at a time with it, however.

Hay and manure forks are, as the names imply, specialized tools. A hay fork is ideal for working compost, although a medium fork will do the job with about the same amount of effort.

Repairing garden forks

All tines are pointed; some tines have sharpened edges along their length. Tines seldom need sharpening, but if they become dulled, a touch-up with a smooth file along the edges is adequate.

Bent tines will be more of a problem than dull ones. The tines bend near the shoulder of the fork, rather than on the points. Therefore, to straighten them, apply pressure at this location. It's very difficult to work the bend straight by moving the point.

Lock the tine in a bench vise and use the handle to bend it back to its original shape. If you don't have a vise, use a pipe wrench. You can add leverage to the pipe wrench by slipping its handle into a length of galvanized steel water pipe.

General maintenance of garden forks

Clean forks after each use by washing off the debris under a garden hose; use a wire brush on stubborn dirt or rust. Then lightly oil the tines and other metal parts.

Replace the handle if it breaks; do not repair it. The correct procedure is described above (page 136).

Trowels

Garden trowels fall into three types: standard, V blade, and dibble.

The standard is an all-around planting and transplanting tool, usually made of steel or stainless steel

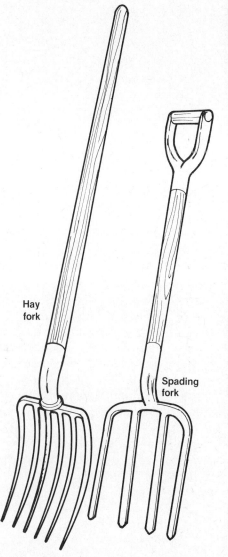

Hay fork

Spading fork

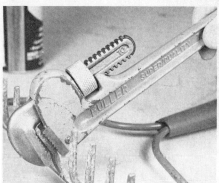

Straightening tines. If they're not cast metal, bent tines can be straightened with a pipe wrench or in a vise. Apply the pressure at the bend as shown, not at the tip of the tine. You can get more leverage with the wrench by slipping a length of pipe over the handle.

1. Maintaining forks. Spading forks rust quickly. Use a wire brush to clean away both dirt and rust; a wire brush mounted on a power drill does the job even faster. When the metal is shiny bright, coat all surfaces lightly with oil or penetrating oil.

2. Fork tines seldom need sharpening; some, in fact, are self-sharpening. However, if they do become dull, resharpen the edges with a smooth file.

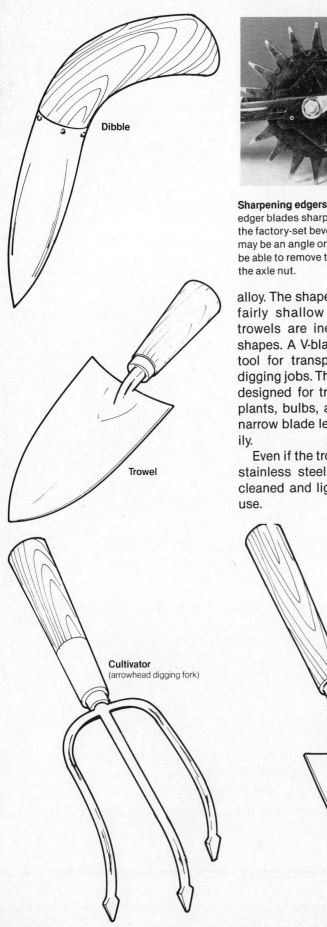

Dibble

Trowel

Cultivator
(arrowhead digging fork)

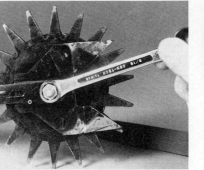

Sharpening edgers. Keep hand-operated edger blades sharp by filing them. Maintain the factory-set bevel on the blade edge; it may be an angle or straight across. You may be able to remove the cutters by unscrewing the axle nut.

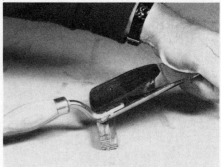

Straightening bent trowels. Hand trowels and other small digging tools may bend at the ferrule if you use them for prying. To straighten them, put the ferrule on a small block of wood and press down carefully on both the handle and blade.

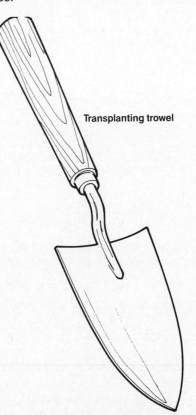

Transplanting trowel

alloy. The shape of the blade may be fairly shallow or deep-set. Since trowels are inexpensive, buy both shapes. A V-blade trowel is the best tool for transplanting and general digging jobs. The dibble is especially designed for transplanting bedding plants, bulbs, and flowers. Its long, narrow blade lets you dig holes easily.

Even if the trowel blade is made of stainless steel, the tool should be cleaned and lightly oiled after each use.

The blade may be sharpened; use a smooth file and follow the contour of the bevel. If the trowel becomes bent, usually at the ferrule, you can bend it back into position by pressing it firmly over a block of wood. Quality trowels are more difficult to bend than the less expensive ones. Don't use any trowel to pry hard earth. Use it only in soft and loose dirt. Leave the heavy work to a spading fork or spade.

Hand cultivators

Hand cultivators are essential tools if you do any garden planting at all. Cultivators do two jobs: they break up the soil close to the plants and they weed. Cultivators usually have three tines, and there are two types. One type has pointed tines, similar to an icepick; the other has tines that are arrowhead-shaped. The arrowhead configuration is best for weeding; the icepick configuration is best for cultivating. Both, however, will do a fair job at either.

You seldom need to sharpen cultivator tines. However, if the edges become dull, you can renew them with a smooth file, stroking the file along the beveled edges. If the tines become bent, straighten them with pliers. If the head becomes bent at the ferrule—and it will if you use the tool as a pry—you may be able to straighten it by bending it back over a block of wood.

Handles can be kept smooth with sandpaper and linseed oil. You sel-

Cultivators

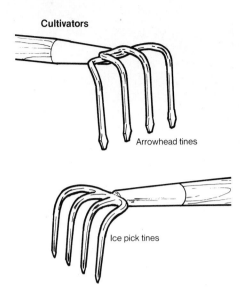

Arrowhead tines

Ice pick tines

dom need to replace a handle. If you do, price the handle first. It may be less expensive to buy a new tool than the new handle.

Hand tools for raking

You're probably most familiar with two types of rakes: flat or bowhead tine rakes and lawn brooms made from bamboo or plastic strips.

For general lawn raking purposes, flat and bowhead rakes are hard to handle because they dig down into the turf grass and dirt. But they're both right at home in the garden. They are designed to level and smooth the soil, prepare a seedbed, and break up the large chunks of soil. The differences in design are these:

■ Bowhead rakes have more spring in the handle since the handle is connected to two bowed pieces of flexible carbon steel (or cast iron in less expensive rakes).

■ Flathead rakes are mounted straight onto the handle with a metal ferrule. They are usually lighter in weight than bowhead rakes, although the weight difference between the two really isn't critical.

Two other rakes should be added to your collection when your garden requires them: a cultivator and a potato rake, or fork. The cultivator is

a grown-up version of the hand cultivator; it has long, curved tines that dig deep to loosen and break up soil. The potato fork looks almost the same as the cultivator, but it usually has five tines instead of four.

Two specialty rakes are available; you may be able to rent them instead of buying. One is the thatcher (see below), which digs down into turf grass to remove the thatch that covers the ground and blocks the soil from sun and rain.

The leveling rake is a wide aluminum tool with many short tines; the tool is used to level soil for planting. If you are establishing a new lawn from scratch, it would pay you to rent this tool since it covers lots of ground easily and quickly.

Lawn brooms are in the rake family, but they are designed for leaf removal, not for moving dirt. They are manufactured from bamboo, plastic, and wire, which makes them lightweight and very easy to use—just like a broom.

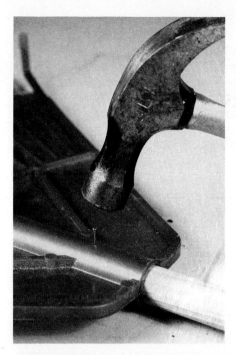

Securing handles. Plastic lawn brooms lose handles fast because the plastic is flexible and the handle won't stay put. Try driving a small brad through the plastic into the handle to hold it. Be careful not to split the wood with the brad.

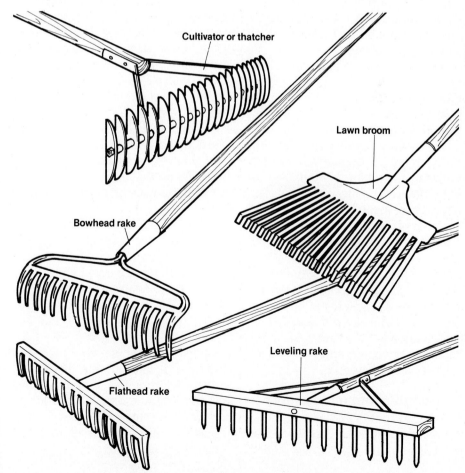

Cultivator or thatcher

Lawn broom

Bowhead rake

Flathead rake

Leveling rake

Repairing and maintaining raking tools

Keep rakes clean. Use a garden hose to wash away debris, and use a steel brush or a wire brush in a power drill to clean down to bare metal. Then lightly oil the metal parts to deter rust.

Tines seldom bend, but if they do and they're made of carbon steel, you may be able to bend the tines back into their original position by locking them in a bench vise and bending the metal back into shape. Try a pipe wrench if you don't have a vise. Don't try to bend cast iron tines; they'll just snap off under the pressure.

Saws

Never use a woodworking saw—rip or crosscut—to remove tree branches and cut down small saplings; its blade and teeth are not designed for this purpose, and you can ruin a good saw in minutes. Instead, use a saw intended for pruning. These tools are made with curved, straight, or bow-shaped blades; all are easy to handle and will rapidly cut limbs and even trees of almost any diameter.

Pruning saws cut on the backstroke since you can generate more power pulling than pushing. Therefore, the saw teeth are slanted backward toward the handle.

The narrow-bladed saws are best for trimming trees since they can slip between branches without disturbing those you don't want to cut. The large saws, those that look like giant versions of woodworking saws or carpenter's saws, are used to fell trees.

For most all-around work, bow saws are a good choice. They are lightweight, have plenty of handle to grip, and cut quickly and cleanly. The blades are easily replaced—as on a hacksaw or coping saw—and, best yet, they are inexpensive.

Sharpening and maintaining saws

It's best to have a professional sharpen pruning saw blades. But if

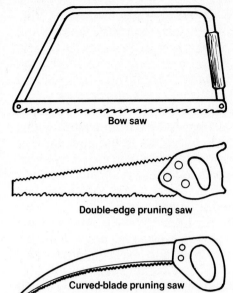

Bow saw

Double-edge pruning saw

Curved-blade pruning saw

you want to do this job yourself, first steady the blade by sandwiching it between two thin boards. Oak flooring strips work best, but you can use 1 × 4s or even flat trim molding (ranch baseboard, for example). Lock this threesome in a bench vise or clamp it together. Then use a cant (triangular) file with a smooth cut to work on the beveled edges of the saw teeth. Follow the bevels carefully with the flat of the file, keeping the cutting edge of the file square to the bevel. Push the file in one direction only, lifting it off the metal at the end of each stroke.

File each beveled edge five or six times, using a firm, steady stroke. After you've filed each edge down one side of the blade, reverse the saw and file each edge on the other side.

If the saw is flat-ground, that is, if the teeth are not beveled but square across the edge, you can file it square to sharpen it somewhat.

Don't try to sharpen a replaceable blade; a new one is so inexpensive that it's really not worth your time to sharpen it.

Filing a saw can set your teeth on edge. The squeak of the file going across the metal is like chalk going across a blackboard. Block this noise with earplugs.

Saw blades need lots of maintenance. Tree sap rusts and gums the

blades. Remove sap by wiping turpentine across the metal with a soft cloth. Then lightly oil the blade.

To remove rust from saw blades, apply light penetrating oil and scrub with a pad of steel wool. Keep wooden handles secure by tightening the fasteners with a screwdriver. Give the handles a coat of linseed oil at the end of each working season.

Cutting tools

Cutting tools with knife edges instead of saw teeth are used for many purposes.

You should have these two prime cutters in your tool collection: an

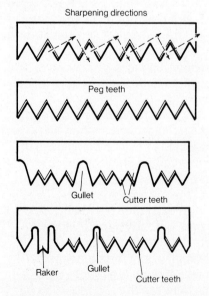

1. Sharpening saw blades. To prepare blades for sharpening, place them between two lengths of board. Then clamp the sandwich in a vise or with a couple of C clamps. The wood stiffens the blade so it may be sharpened easier.

Sharpening directions

Peg teeth

Gullet   Cutter teeth

Raker   Gullet   Cutter teeth

2. Lawn and garden saws have three basic styles of tooth configuration. When sharpening a blade with a cant (triangular) or flat file, work down one side with the bevel; then turn the saw around and work down the other.

1. Maintaining saws. Keep saw blades rust-free by scouring them with a light abrasive block or steel wool. Use turpentine or mineral spirits to remove sap. Lubricate the blades after each cleaning with household or penetrating oil.

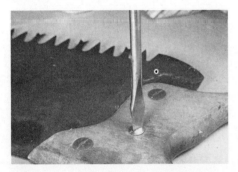

2. Keep saw handle bolts tight. Keep wooden handles smooth with medium-grit sandpaper and seal them with linseed oil.

Sharpening clippers. Hedge clippers are giant, heavy-duty scissors. Do not sharpen a serrated cutting edge. Sharpen the other edge with a smooth file, maintaining the factory-set bevel. If the clippers don't have a serrated edge, you can sharpen both edges.

anvil-blade pruner and a bypass-blade lopper. Anvil-type cutters have a heavy blade set at right angles to the cutting blade; this blade has a groove running down the center into which the cutting blade presses to

cut. Bypass-type cutters have a heavy, blunt jaw past which the cutting blade slides.

Pruners cut flower stems and small (1/4- to 1/2-inch) branches. Loppers, with their long handles, cut larger limbs flush with a tree or shrub trunk. Most loppers are advertised to handle up to 2-inch diameters, but this bite is a little more than most loppers can chew. Use a saw when the diameter reaches about 1 inch. Otherwise you risk breaking the handles.

Other designs you may want to consider include bypass pruners, anvil loppers, anvil loppers with ratchet and gear actions, and grass shears.

1. Sharpening shears. Grass shears usually can be taken apart by removing the pivot bolt with a wrench and slipping the spring and the cutting blade off the pivot.

2. With a whetstone or oilstone, lightly touch up the cutting blade of a grass shears; be sure you maintain the factory bevel.

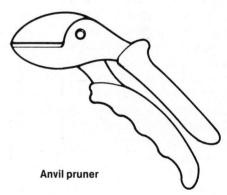

Sharpening pruners. This bypass pruner has a sharp cutting edge that bypasses a blunt jaw. Use a hand-held whetstone to maintain the cutting edge; hone with the bevel angle.

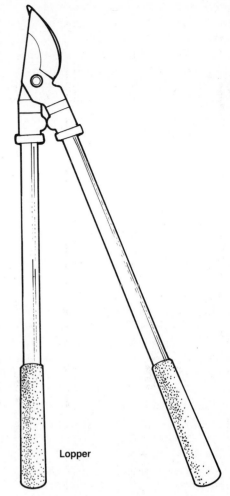

Lopper

Anvil pruner

Sharpening and maintaining cutting tools

If pruner or lopper cutting blades become nicked or chopped, use a grinder to even the edges. Don't overheat the metal or you'll destroy the temper. Then grind and file a new cutting edge, keeping the bevel at about 45 degrees.

Use a whetstone or an oilstone to sharpen the tool. A hand-held whetstone is probably better because it is difficult to take pruners and loppers apart for sharpening.

If the cutting blade can be removed from the tool, lock it in a bench vise and work the whetstone from the pivot point to the tip of the blade. Some anvil cutting blades have two bevels. One, as mentioned, is about 45 degrees; the other is 85 degrees. It is more important that the 45-degree bevel Is maIntained than the 85-degree one, but sharpen both if you can.

Don't sharpen the blunt jaw of a bypass cutter, of course; don't sharpeh an anvil blade, either, but keep its groove clean with a bradawl.

The two weak points on pruners and loppers are the pivot point and the handles. If you try to cut branches too large for the tools to sever easily, the blades tend to jam and bend at the pivot. Once sprung out of shape, the blades won't match up and, therefore, won't cut properly; the cutting edges just chew the bark and wood. If this happens, junk the tools and buy new ones.

Wooden handles on large loppers can crack or even break where the metal ferrule meets the wood if you attempt to take very large bites. The handles can be replaced easily; follow the procedures detailed above for replacing spade and rake handles (page 136).

The pole pruner is a specialized type of pruner that is mounted on a long pole so you can reach high in a tree to remove branches. The blades are worked by a rope that you pull or that is connected to a spring-loaded lever. The hook into which the cutting blade goes is a type of anvil. The blade is best sharpened with a whetstone, although you may be able to remove the blade by unscrewing the pivot bolt. The blade is sharpened the same way as hand pruner blades.

Some pole pruners have a saw attachment; the saw blade can usually be taken off for sharpening by removing the bolt and nut. Use a cant or triangular smooth file to sharpen the tightly spaced teeth. Locking the blade between two pieces of wood for added support while filing main-

tains the original bevel on the edges of the teeth.

The operating levers on pole pruners seldom go bad; broken pulleys and rope can be replaced quickly and easily.

General maintenance of all this equipment—hand pruners, loppers, and pole pruners—should include cleaning off the dirt and tree sap after each use. Wipe the cutting blades with light household or motor oil to deter rust; lubricate all pivot points and the moving parts (levers and pulleys) of pole pruners.

All about sprayers

The first thing to know about sprayers is that they must be used responsibly. See the section on Safety First with Chemicals (page 22).

For spreading pesticides and herbicides, a pump or compression sprayer does a good, all-around job. You can also buy hose sprayers and trombone models to do the same job. They are usually less expensive than compression sprayers, but they're also less efficient.

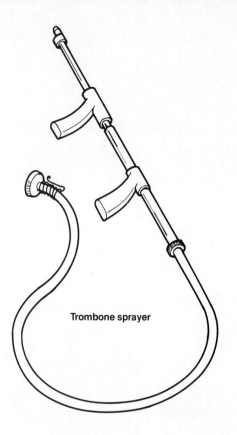

Trombone sprayer

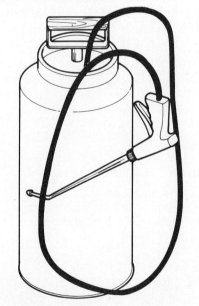

Compression sprayer

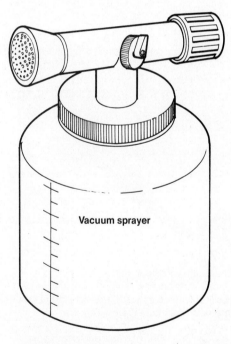

Vacuum sprayer

Repair and maintenance. Pesticides and herbicides corrode metal, and corrosion is the biggest problem you will have with any sprayer that has metal parts. It is essential that you promptly clean the tanks and hoses of sprayers with fresh water

just as soon as you are finished working with them. Then lightly lubricate the metal parts with household or motor oil to help prevent rust and corrosion.

Sprayers malfunction when the nozzles become clogged with dirt

1. Maintaining sprayers. Power failure in battery sprayers may be caused by corroded spade terminals (lower left), which should be cleaned with fine steel wool and then lightly lubricated. Check hose connections and supply tubes for bad gaskets, and loose clamps.

and debris. If the nozzle is neglected, corrosion will be a problem. Keep nozzles functioning by cleaning the holes with a large-diameter needle, a pin, or a paperclip. Do not use a toothpick or a sharp wooden stick; if it breaks off in the nozzle you'll have an awful time getting it out.

Compression sprayers have pumps similar to tire pumps. If the pump fails to build up pressure, remove the top of the pump (pry it off with a screwdriver) and pull out the plunger. At the bottom of the plunger is a cup that has a leather, nylon, or rubber O-ring washer around its rim. When this washer becomes worn the sprayer loses its pressure build-up capacity. You can see the wear on the washer. If the washer is leather, you may be able to soften it back into service by soaking it in lightweight household oil. Worn nylon and rubber washers must be replaced.

Replacement is simply take-off-the-old, put-on-the-new. Most home centers and hardware outlets will have a washer that will fit; take the old one with you to the store for matching purposes.

If the pump builds up pressure but it leaks out of the cylinder, try replacing the rubber seal at the bottom of the pump housing where it fits against the tank. If this washer isn't the problem, you'll probably have to replace the pump. But try cleaning the pump with detergent and water

2. Corrosion is the biggest enemy of compression sprayers where metal pump parts are submerged in chemicals. Clean all parts thoroughly with water after use and between chemical changes. Remove corrosion with steel wool; lightly oil the metal parts before storage.

and replacing the seal before you give up.

Leaks along the air hose may be caused by a loose connection. Make sure all nuts are turned up tight, but be careful not to overtighten and strip the threads. If the leak is in the hose itself—a pinhole leak, for example—try wrapping plastic electrician's tape around the hose. (You can locate the leak by submerging the hose in water and watching for bubbles.) This is a *temporary* repair only; *replace the hose as soon as possible.* The connections can be clamped with a standard worm clamp.

Any spray pattern problem usually can be traced to a blocked or partly blocked spray nozzle. Use a needle or paperclip to clean the holes; do not use a toothpick or sharpened stick.

Hose sprayers use water flow to generate a vacuum that pulls the chemicals out of their container and sprays them out through the hose. Troubles with these sprayers can usually be traced to clogged nozzles, to a worn rubber gasket that connects the hose to the sprayer, or to a

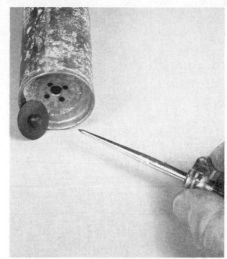

3. Lack of pressure in compression sprayers is often caused by damage to the seal that keeps chemicals out at the bottom of the pump. You can pop this seal out with a bradawl or an icepick to replace it.

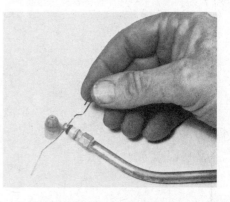

1. Maintaining sprayer nozzles. Clogged nozzles are the big problem with all kinds of garden sprayers. Use a needle or paperclip to clean the nozzles. Buff away any surface corrosion with steel wool.

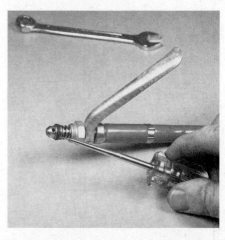

2. Leaks in sprayer nozzles are generally caused by worn or broken O-ring washers at the tip of the nozzle. Use standard plumbing O-rings for replacement. You can pry out worn rings with a bradawl.

malfunctioning on/off lever, which is usually made of plastic.

When a sprayer doesn't perform properly, clean the nozzle with a needle and replace the rubber washer or gasket with a new one made for hoses. You probably can't repair the on/off lever; if it fails, replace the sprayer. The cost is not prohibitive.

Slide sprayers—also called trombone sprayers—have the same problems as the other types. Clean the nozzle with a needle, keep the sliding metal parts free from corrosion with fine steel wool, and oil lightly after each use and before off-season storage.

Dusters: the dry sprayers

Instead of liquid chemicals, dusters spray powdered chemicals. Dusters are operated with a hand pump or crank; they're made from both metal and plastic, and the cost is small.

Dusters are best used to treat foliage, such as rose bushes and other plants, where the chemicals may be applied at close range in still air. Some manufacturers market a duster with chemicals loaded in a cardboard container; you throw away the package after the chemicals have been applied.

Repair and maintenance of dusters

Repairs of the hand pump duster are limited to the pump itself; the pump, similar to a tire pump, has a leather, plastic, or nylon O-ring washer at the end of the plunger that generates compressed air. This washer can sometimes be replaced by removing the cap at the handle and withdrawing the plunger. A screw may hold the washer to the bottom of the plunger. Standard plumbing washers can be used as replacements for worn pump washers.

Dusters must be cleaned after each use. If parts move stiffly, lubricate them with graphite.

And remember; *always* wear a respirator when you use a duster.

Garden hoses

There are three basic types of garden hose: rubber, vinyl-nylon, and two-ply

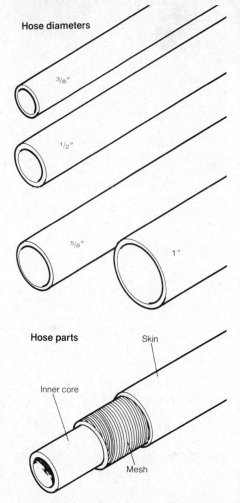

Hose diameters

3/8"
1/2"
5/8"
1"

Hose parts

Skin

Inner core

Mesh

vinyl. The most long-lasting of the lot is rubber, followed by vinyl-nylon and two-ply vinyl. Hose sizes, like plumbing pipe sizes, are determined by the inside diameters; the common ones are 3/8, 1/2, 5/8, and 1 inch.

Hose couplings and connections are made of brass or plastic. Couplings join lengths of hose; connections join the hose to an outlet or a piece of equipment. All types are made in a full range of sizes to match the hose sizes. Couplings and connections are usually packaged individually, and you must be careful when buying to get the part you want; couplings and connections look very much alike.

Care and maintenance of hoses

Kinking causes most hose problems since it leads to leaks and damages the metal connections. Thus, the important maintenance rules are just common sense: don't kink hoses

and don't run over them in vehicles. Also, keep hoses drained and out of the sun when they are not in use; store them properly during the off season. A hose reel—either on wheels or wall-mounted—is best for storage since the drumlike surface protects the hose. Don't hang hoses over nails or shelf brackets; this will kink them.

Nozzles with shut-offs should not be left on unused hoses with the water turned on. The water pressure that builds up in the hose, about 60 pounds per square inch, can weaken the walls of the hose, causing leaks.

Pinhole leaks can be mended temporarily by wrapping the leak tightly with plastic electrician's tape. Extend the wrapping about 2 inches each way from the leak. Although

1. Repairing hoses. For temporary repair of pinhole leaks in garden hoses, wrap the leak with a spiral of plastic electrician's tape. For a permanent repair, however, install a hose coupling at the leak.

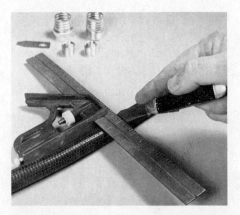

2. Repair hose leaks permanently by cutting the bad spot out of the hose. Keep the cut as square as possible and use an ultra-sharp knife to cut the edges clean. If they're ragged, the connection may leak. *(continued)*

some people recommend plugging the hole with a toothpick, this is a waste of time; the tape will handle the repair until the hose can be cut and properly repaired with a straight coupling. The photographs show how to repair leaks permanently and how to replace damaged couplings.

3. The repair coupling is in four parts—two to each hose section. The larger male and female components slip over the outside of the hose. Then the smaller inserts are screwed inside the hose with a metal key furnished with the coupling kit. When tight, the inserts force the hose against the male and female parts, securing both tightly.

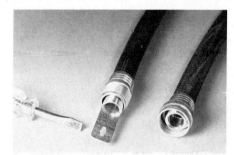

4. Another type of metal coupling consists of male and female parts that are first slipped inside the sections of hose. Then the metal prongs are crimped down tightly around the hose ends.

Nozzles

Nozzles are water distributors; they'll produce full blasts or soft, rainlike spray. Quality nozzles are made of brass metal; inexpensive counterparts are made of aluminum, zinc-coated brass, or plastic. All of these usually provide fully adjustable water patterns, some by turning the nozzle, others by turning a knurled knob.

You also can buy sweeper and cleaning nozzles in both brass and plastic; these are patterned after fire-hose nozzles to do what the names imply: sweep or clean away debris with water.

Pistol-grip nozzles have a trigger

to pull for water adjustment. There is really no big advantage to this type over the straight nozzle that you twist; the pistol grip might even be more difficult to use if it doesn't have a trigger lock.

Repair and maintenance of nozzles

Quality brass nozzles may be disassembled for repairs if the nozzle fails to deliver the proper spray pattern or if it develops a leak. At the outer end of the nozzle insert are O-ring washers; when they become worn, leaks develop. Remove the O-ring with an icepick or bradawl and insert the new washer over the shaft. Standard plumbing washers may be used for this job.

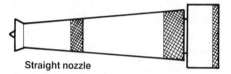

Straight nozzle

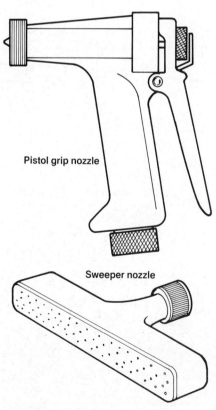

Pistol grip nozzle

Sweeper nozzle

If the nozzle leaks where it connects to the hose, try replacing the washer in the base of the nozzle.

For preventive maintenance, give

Maintaining hose nozzles. Quality brass nozzles may be disassembled so you can replace worn-out washers that degrade the spray pattern. Flip off O-rings with a bradawl and slip new ones into place.

the insert a light coating of petroleum jelly at the end of each watering season. This lubrication helps deter corrosion of the inner working parts.

Accessories for hoses include spray attachments, shower or mist heads, and long-tube root watering devices. All of these connect to the male end of the hose. Repairs to these devices usually involve keeping the spray holes open with a needle or paperclip.

Sprinklers

There are three basic types of sprinkler: impulse, fixed, and oscillating. All are supplied with water by hoses.

Impulse sprinklers operate by means of a spring-loaded deflector pad that bounces in and out of the stream of water from the nozzle, thus scattering the water and turning the nozzle with a ratchet. The machine can be adjusted so the spray pattern goes full circle or half circle.

Fixed sprinklers, as the name implies, do not move, and the area they water can't be altered except by changing the water pressure. They have few maintenance problems. Just keep the spray ports open with a needle or a paperclip.

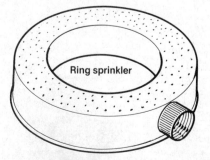

Ring sprinkler

The soaker hose is first cousin to a fixed sprinkler. It's basically an ordinary hose with small holes punched through its three-layer wall to let the water out in a measured run. These hoses are ideal for watering gardens set in rows.

Oscillating sprinklers, which are mounted on skids like sled runners, have a long pipe that carries a series of individual sprinkler heads. Water pressure drives a geared wheel that flips the pipe back and forth to distribute the water that spurts from the heads. Quality oscillating sprinklers have heads that can be adjusted to change the water patterns, along with other controls to limit the height and width of the water spray.

A revolving sprinkler is similar to the oscillating type, but the sprinkler arm in this type revolves continuously around a fixed axis instead of flipping back and forth. Water pressure from the hose furnishes the drive power.

Sprinkler maintenance and repair

Both oscillating and revolving sprinklers are almost maintenance-free since the parts are plastic, brass, or aluminum. Keep the spray ports open with a needle or paperclip. Other parts, if damaged, usually can't be repaired. The cost of replacing the sprinkler is not prohibitive.

Maintenance of impulse sprinklers is limited to cleaning the spray nozzle annually and lubricating the deflector arm occasionally with a waterproof lubricant.

If the nozzle or spring fails, you probably won't find a replacement part in a local store, but you may be able to order the part from the manufacturer. The store probably has the address you need; in fact, the store might even order the part for you. However, most sprinklers, and some sprayers, are molded and riveted together so repairs are impossible to make. Fortunately, the cost of replacement usually isn't great, and if the equipment gets even a small amount of maintenance attention it will last for many years without failing.

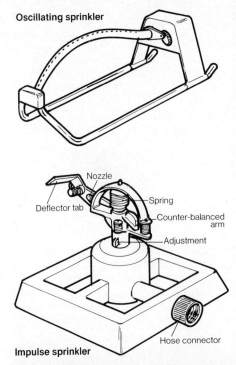

Oscillating sprinkler

Nozzle
Deflector tab
Spring
Counter-balanced arm
Adjustment
Hose connector

Impulse sprinkler

Underground sprinklers

Underground sprinkling systems are, of course, the ultimate luxury in lawn and garden watering equipment. They can be costly to buy and have installed, although some manufacturers are offering do-it-yourself models at a price affordable for most homeowners. Both types are hooked to the house's water supply with a special pipe connection or at a hose bib (outdoor silcock).

Underground systems generally suffer from corrosion on connections and clogged spray nozzles. The nozzles can be cleaned with a needle; corrosion on metal parts may be removed with steel wool and jellied metal cleaner. If buried connections break or leak in the ground, it may take time to find the leak, but a permanent patch of wet, soggy turf is

Maintaining sprinklers. Sprinklers, from the most simple to the most complicated, have one problem in common: the nozzles become clogged. Keep them open with a paperclip or needle. Some nozzle ports may be removed counterclockwise with a wrench for cleaning. Then lay out all parts in the order of disassembly so the components go back together in the right order. If you can't find the right replacement parts, plumbing parts sometimes can be substituted.

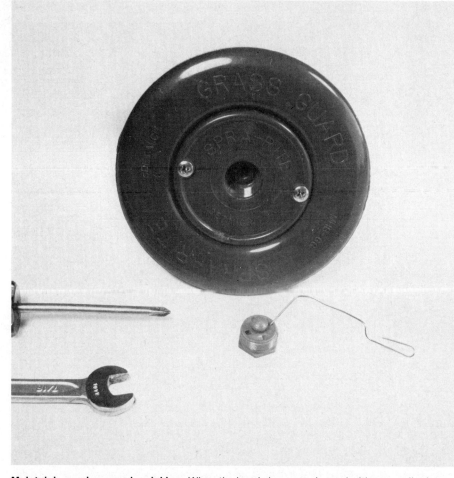

Maintaining underground sprinklers. When the heads become clogged with grass clippings, try using a water blast from the main valve to free them. If this fails, remove the nozzle head with a wrench or screwdriver and clean the ports with wire or a paperclip. Replace damaged nozzles.

Spreaders

These two-wheeled cartlike bins are used to spread fertilizer and seed on lawns and gardens.

Hose them out after every project, dry and lightly oil metal surfaces, and keep the levers and wheels lubricated. With this care, most spreaders, even the inexpensive ones, will last a lifetime.

A spreader is much easier to use than a sprayer when you are applying fertilizers. The weight of the fertilizer is borne by the wheels, not on your shoulder. A spreader can be used on breezy days when a sprayer can't be used. One problem with a spreader, however, is marking the area where you have been. This can be done with a lime marker attached to one of the spreader's wheels or by using moveable stakes. You simply move the stake across the area as you complete a spreader run.

A calibrated drop spreader distributes fertilizers more accurately than either a hand-crank or wheeled broadcast spreader. The controls on a calibrated spreader adjust the rate

the clue. Repairs are easy. First dig down and around the sprinkler head to expose the connection. Then remove the failed connection and replace it with either a straight coupling or a tee fitting. Flexible plastic ABS tubing is generally used for underground systems; it is assembled with worm clamps.

If a spray head is damaged by a lawnmower, when the head isn't set deep enough or the mower is set too low, it will have to be replaced. This will involve unscrewing clamps or couplings, replacing the head, and reconnecting it. Be sure to turn off the water supply before you start working.

Some underground sprinkler systems are equipped with antisyphon devices that keep water in the system from flowing back into the house water supply. Antisyphons are usually connected inside the house

where the water supply and the sprinkler system connect. The antisyphons seldom fail, but you may have to replace them every fifteen years or so.

Timers connected to underground sprinklers to activate the sprinklers at certain times throughout a twenty-four-hour period usually are complicated devices. If the timer isn't working, check for a blown fuse or a tripped circuit breaker at the main electrical entrance panel. Or check a separate fuse system near the sprinkler controls. If this isn't the answer, call in a professional to make repairs.

As the watering season proceeds, occasionally check the level of the sprinkler heads. If water has eroded the ground around them, causing them to protrude or lean over, dig around the heads and reposition them with additional dirt.

1. Operating spreaders correctly. Always adjust spreader settings to match the recommended number on the package of material you're spreading. For example, this bag of grass seed calls for a 9¼ setting. The correct setting lets materials flow freely, keeps distribution ports open, and spreads the right amount of material. *(continued)*

of flow for seed or fertilizer; these controls should be matched to the control numbers provided on the seed or fertilizer package. Some spreaders may be recalibrated with a metal gauge that helps you check the spreader's accuracy and set it to manufacturer's specifications. Adjustments are easy.

Repair and maintenance of spreaders

Quality spreaders require some maintenance but almost no repairs. Replacements for broken or damaged parts usually can be ordered from the manufacturer. Wheels, control levers, and flow bars or discs are simply bolted onto the axle or handle. If parts become corroded or rusted, you should immediately remove this rust with fine steel wool and give the bare metal at least two coats of metal paint. This will stop further corrosion.

Always empty the hopper after each use. Use a garden hose and a nozzle set at full blast to rinse the hopper and other parts of the spreader. Open the spreader setting to its widest point and let the spreader dry thoroughly; you can even blot the water with a soft cloth.

With oil, lubricate the bottom of the hopper surface, the spring and rod inside the control housing or the gears, and the axles at the wheels.

Give the same treatment to hand broadcast spreaders, even though most of them are made of plastic. The plastic won't corrode, but the metal gear parts will.

It's all right to leave fertilizers in the hopper overnight if you're going to use the spreader the next day. But overnight is the limit.

2. Quality spreaders can be recalibrated to factory specifications by loosening the hopper pin and moving the metal slide covering the ports. A setting tool is available, usually free, from dealers and the manufacturers.

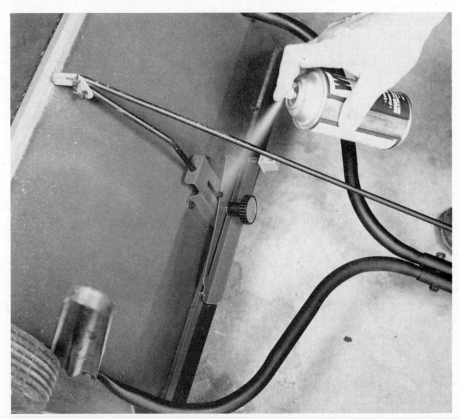

3. Spreaders must be thoroughly washed and dried after each use. Lubricate all moving parts after each clean-up to help prevent rust and corrosion. When you repaint bare metal, use a metal primer and a metal topcoat for best results.

Hand Tool Maintenance   149

Ladders

Quality ladders are classed as to weight loads. For example, a household ladder has a load or weight rating of 200 pounds. A commercial ladder has a weight rating of 225 pounds. An industrial ladder has a rating of 250 pounds. I recommend the commercial or the industrial ladder. It has to support your weight plus the weight of the tools and equipment you carry on it.

If your ladder is wooden, do not paint it; paint hides defects. If you want to treat the wood, use a clear wood sealer or penetrating sealer. Linseed oil is a good sealer for ladders.

If the rails or rungs of any ladder become weakened or split or broken, junk the ladder immediately and buy a new one. *Repaired ladders are dangerous*.

You can test the rungs by laying the ladder flat on the ground and walking on the rungs; most defects will show up under this test.

Working with tools and materials safely

Many safety factors have been built into lawn and garden power tools. For example, most of them are double insulated to prevent electrical shock. You'll also find chain guards, safety tips, power cord protectors, shields, and so on. Most hand tools, however, don't have these devices because they move slowly or are not self-powered. But don't be deluded: hand tools can be dangerous if you don't work carefully. Here is a list of safety precautions to take when using hand tools and equipment in the lawn and garden. I urge you to follow them.

■ A sharp tool is safer than a dull tool. Dull tools require more muscle effort, and the harder you try to work the tool the less safe it becomes.

■ Wear safety goggles when sharpening tools, especially when grinding edges with a power grinding wheel.

■ Wear safety goggles when you chop and prune branches. Flying chips can hurt when they hit you, and they can damage eyes. Wear safety goggles when sawing overhead; they'll keep the sawdust out of your eyes.

■ When you sharpen tools with a hand-held whetstone, work the stone *away* from the cutting edge, not toward it. This way, if you slip your hands won't get cut.

■ When working with rakes, hoes, cultivators, and other tools with sharp, pointed edges or tines, lay the tool down so the points face the ground.

■ Don't work with tools that have broken, split, or repaired handles.

Replace any defective handle.

■ Lean stepladders against a solid surface, such as a tree, whenever possible. Avoid working with the stepladder open. Make sure the bottom legs of the ladder are on solid, level footing. A short piece of 2 × 8 makes a good support bridge if the ground is soft. The 2 × 8 also can be propped at either end to make the ladder level.

■ Always lean extension ladders against a *solid* surface. The correct angle of an extension ladder is important, too. It should be pulled back from the vertical about one fourth of its length. For example, the bottom of a 20-foot extension ladder should be pulled out about 5 feet.

Both legs of the ladder must rest on a solid surface. The 2 × 8 trick detailed above will work for extension ladders. If the ground is hard, stake the bottom rung of the ladder to the ground so the ladder doesn't slide out from under you. Another method is to set both feet of the ladder into small slits dug in the ground.

■ Have a helper stand on the bottom rung while you work above. This will prevent the ladder from sliding on hard ground.

■ Always walk up and down a ladder with both hands. Have a helper hand you tools and equipment or tie the tools and equipment to a rope and pull them up (or lower them) when you are in position.

■ When working on the ladder, keep your hips between the rails. *Do not overreach*. Instead, move the ladder over to the work.

9 Tools for Repairing and Maintaining Equipment

The chances are that you already own many of the tools needed to keep lawn and garden equipment in top running order. Many of them are the same you use for home maintenance and improvement jobs. If you don't own tools, you'll be happy to know that the ones you need for lawn and garden equipment are not specialized. In this chapter you'll find these tools described as "necessary" or as "nice to have if your budget permits." With a few exceptions, most of them are hand tools. I urge you to buy quality tools and to take good care of them. If you do, they should last you a lifetime.

Hammers

For working on machines the best hammer to buy is a ball-peen, or machinist, hammer. It has a shorter neck than a carpenter's hammer, and the metal is tempered for striking metal objects such as punches and cold chisels.

The best all-around weight is 16 ounces, although you can buy ball-peens that are heavier or lighter. The handles are usually wood; fiberglass handles are seldom available in retail stores.

A dead blow hammer is nice to have, but not essential. This type is made from polyurethane with a metal canister inserted in the head. When the hammer hits a solid object, such as the cylinder head cover on an engine, the head won't bounce back. Hence the name, dead blow.

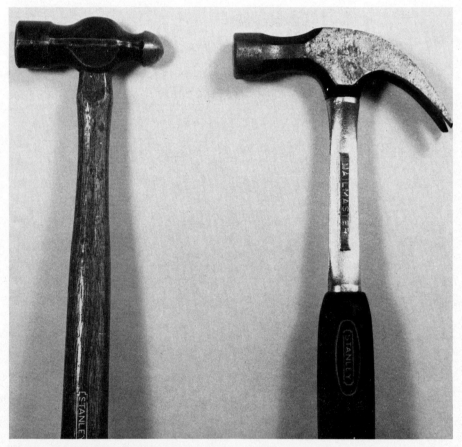

Basic pounding tools. Your tool cabinet should include a ball-peen (left) and a 16-ounce claw hammer. The ball-peen is the preferred machinist tool for working with small engines and lawn and garden accessories. Wear safety goggles when you use pounding tools, since tiny slivers of metal can fly off striking surfaces.

The plastic is tough stuff and it won't be damaged when it strikes sharp objects. The head and handle are one-piece molded parts.

Screwdrivers

There are two basic types of these necessary tools—standard slot and Phillips head—and you need both. In fact, you need at least three sizes of each type, since screwheads vary in size. You also should buy offset screwdrivers, with both standard and Phillips heads, for use in tight quarters where the long-bladed types can't go.

The choice between wooden- or plastic-handle screwdrivers is a toss-up. Both have about the same degree of nonslip grip; either will slip when

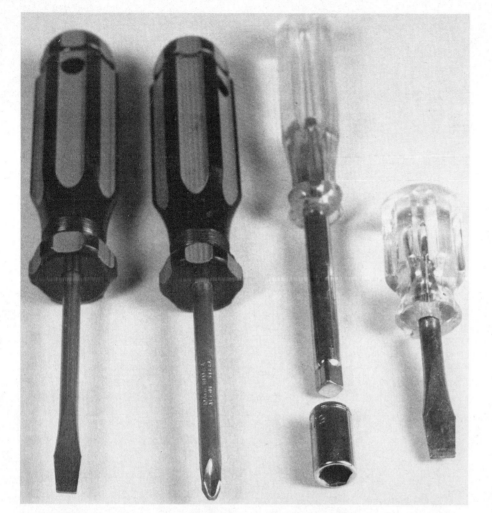

Basic screw and bolt turning tools. The ones you'll need include (left to right) standard slot and Phillips-head screwdrivers. Buy an assortment of three sizes each. Next, handy to have are a nut or socket driver and a stubby standard slot and Phillips driver.

the handle becomes coated with grease.

Many quality screwdrivers have a flat, square, or hexagonal shape built into the bolster of the tool, which is directly below the handle. You can connect a wrench at this point for more torque or turning power.

Phillips-head screwdrivers fit cross-slotted screws. They are sized by points: the larger the point size the smaller the tip of the driver. I recommend small (10 point), medium (8 point), and large (2 point); these will handle most screw sizes on lawn and garden equipment.

Offset screwdrivers have blades mounted at right angles to the shaft at both ends. They are made with standard slots or Phillips heads in various sizes. You also can buy ratchet offset screwdrivers for quarter-turn (or less) increments.

Pliers

Three types are necessary: slip-joint, channel-lock, and Vise-Grip. Although somewhat limited in use, needle-nose pliers should be included if your budget permits.

Slip-joint pliers have two open positions; an elongated slot in one handle slips on a pivot pin mounted on the other. The jaws of quality pliers are tempered steel, and there is a wire-cutter at the base of the jaws. The primary purposes of this tool are to loosen and tighten small nuts and bolts, to bend and cut throttle wires, and to crimp and bend metal parts.

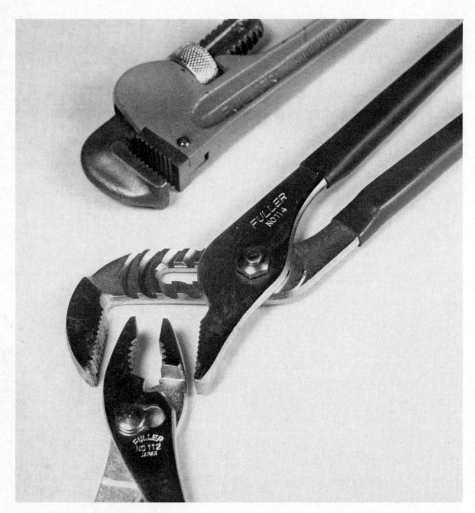

Adjustable turning tools. Regular slip-joint pliers (bottom) and channel lock pliers (center) are basic maintenance tools. Add a 10- or 12-inch pipe wrench (top) when you can.

Socket sets

For mechanical work, sockets are absolutely essential for turning nuts and bolts. Sockets can save you plenty of time, and the wide variety of sizes available ensures a fit regardless of the bolt or nut to be driven or drawn.

Socket sets are the best buys. The least expensive quality sets include an assortment of six to eight different sockets, a ratchet driver, and a socket extension. For a little more money, you can buy sets with more sizes of sockets, a ratchet driver, a breaker bar, universal joints, and a selection of extensions. These sets often have spark plug sockets and deep wall sockets for use with long studs (threaded bolts).

The most common types are 6- and 12-point sockets, the points being the number of gripping edges inside of the sockets. The sockets are designed to fit either hex or square fasteners. While 6-point sockets may be difficult to find, 12-point sockets are plentiful. If you can, buy the 6-point tools since the torque is stronger.

Sockets have $1/4$-, $3/8$-, and $1/2$-inch drives, the drive being the opening at the top of the socket where it is attached to the ratchet or other driving handle. I recommend the $3/8$-inch drive, with a set of sockets ranging in size from $1/4$ to 1 inch in $1/32$-inch increments. The second choice would be $1/2$-inch drives with sockets from $3/8$ to $1 1/2$ inches in $1/32$- or $1/16$-inch increments. The larger-size drive gives you much more torque for the money.

Breaker bars have forged handles with a square in the end. The square usually can pivot 180 degrees. Breaker bars are used to drive sockets when lots of torque is needed to crack frozen bolts and nuts.

Nice to have are speeders, extensions, and U-joints. Speeders are similar to hand braces with an offset handle that is cranked to drive and draw bolts. The sockets fit on one end of the speeder. You probably won't use this tool much in lawn equipment repair, but it is handy to

Channel-lock pliers have parallel jaws that may be opened to various widths using tongues and grooves, or channels, near the pivot pin. Because the tool expands to fit many sizes of nuts and bolts, it has countless uses for lawn and garden equipment maintenance. Channel-lock pliers come in various sizes. The medium size is necessary for general work; small and large sizes are nice to have as your budget permits. You'll use all three sizes frequently.

Vise-Grip pliers ("Vise-Grip" is a tradename) can be opened to the desired width, placed on a nut or part, and then locked in position. By flicking a handle release, the lock disengages instantly. Once locked, Vise-Grip jaws hold like a bulldog on a mailman's leg, with plenty of torque for turning or bending. In fact, one disadvantage of the tool is that its

grip can damage boltheads if you are not careful. The pliers may be used as clamps and as holding devices while metal is soldered or welded together.

Vise-Grips come in various sizes; the medium range is best for all-around work. However, buy a large and small size if possible since the pliers are often used in pairs.

As the name suggests, needle-nose pliers have long, needlelike jaws. These jaws are excellent for reaching into small holes and crevices. Most needle-nose, or long-nose, pliers have wire cutters at the base of the jaws.

Look for these qualitites when buying pliers: smooth operating handles and jaws, firm and even pressure from both jaws, chrome plating, high-carbon steel, and forged manufacture.

have for lawn equipment and for any auto repairs that you might tackle.

Extensions are mounted between socket and driver to reach a nut or bolt recessed behind a component part. A 3- or 6-inch extension will be long enough for most lawn equipment jobs.

U-joints fit between the ratchet and the socket or the ratchet, extension, and socket, in order to let you tilt the unit up to 45 degrees. The U is often included in the more expensive socket sets; the cost is not prohibitive if you buy it separately, although you may not use it frequently.

Adjustable wrenches

The necessary adjustable wrench does many jobs; the jaws of the wrench may be moved to fit nuts and bolts by simply turning a knurled screw in the handle of the wrench. Only one jaw moves; the other one is fixed, and this fixed jaw is the one you must apply the wrenching pressure against.

Standard adjustable wrench sizes are 4, 6, 8, 10, and 12 inches. The three middle sizes are likely to be used most, although the 12-inch wrench can be handy in removing large nuts and turning large bolts.

Box and open-end wrenches

A box wrench has closed (circle) openings on both ends. An open-end wrench has an open pair of fixed jaws on one or both ends of the wrench handle. A combination wrench has one end open and the other end boxed. Your best buy is a combination set. The open end will handle square nuts and bolts; the box end will turn hex nuts and bolts. Both are necessary for engine and tool repair and maintenance.

There is, however, an advantage to buying either open or boxed ends and not a combination: the single tool will usually give you a wider selection of sizes.

Hex wrenches

These tools are designed for screws and bolts that have recessed heads in a hex shape. You will find such fasteners in the hubs of pulleys and on some mufflers.

Hex wrenches are usually sold in a set, and they are very inexpensive and are necessary for engine and tool repair. You can also buy individual hex wrenches.

Torque wrenches

If you get involved in engine overhaul work, a torque wrench is a necessity. Otherwise, it's just a nice specialty tool to own. A beam torque wrench, for example, costs about $20.

The tool has a thin metal shaft connected to a handle assembly. When you apply pressure to a fastener, the thin shaft bends and moves the needle of a gauge mounted on the handle. The gauge gives you a reading of the torque applied to the fastener expressed in pounds, for example, 10, 15, or 20 pounds of pressure.

Saws

A quality hacksaw for cutting through frozen nuts and bolts, throttle wire, stuck mufflers, and wheel bolts is a must tool for lawn and garden repairs.

The blades are made especially for cutting metal. You can buy them with teeth ranging from fine to coarse, and I recommend that you keep an assortment of these inexpensive blades on hand.

Remember that hacksaws cut on the forward stroke, so be sure to mount the blades accordingly. You can, of course, mount the blade backwards if pulling, not pushing, the blade is easier for the job at hand.

Sharpening devices

There are two basic tools to own: stones, (whetstones, oilstones, and

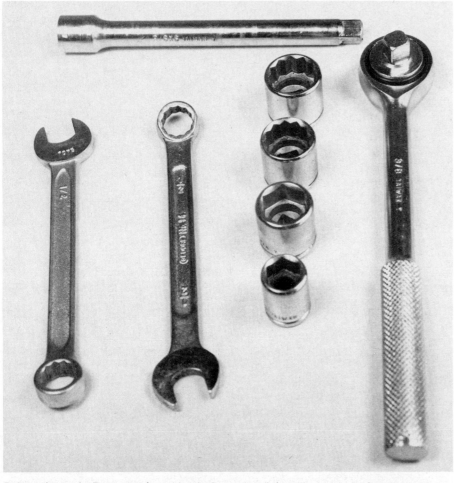

Bolt-turning tools. Buy a set of combination wrenches (left) and a good set of sockets with a ratchet handle (right) and an extension (top).

slipstones) for sharpening hand tools, and special jigs, for sharpening the chains on chain saws. The equipment you own will determine which sharpening devices you need to purchase.

Oilstones are mounted in a box; you stroke the edge of the object to be sharpened over the surface of the stone. Whetstones and slipstones are hand stones; that is, they are stroked over the edges of the tools to be sharpened. Both are used for fine sharpening, for putting an extremely sharp cutting edge on the metal.

Also useful in sharpening are power grinding wheels (consider these nice to have) and single- and double-cut files, which are the hand-tool equivalents of grinders. Basically, they are shaping, rather than sharpening, tools. Grinders and files are used to remove nicks and dents along the cutting edges before the tools are fine-sharpened.

Awls

Necessary for your tool kit is a brad-awl, a sharp-pointed tool that resembles an icepick. The awl can be used for locating bolt holes, for aligning parts, for cleaning cracks and crevices, and for retrieving parts dropped in hard-to-reach corners.

Files

You need four kinds of files: smooth cut, double-cut, cant (triangular), and round. All are very inexpensive and will provide years of service if you keep them clean and lightly oiled so they don't rust.

Files can be used to remove rivets, frozen bolts, rust, and nicks in cutting edges, and to sharpen saws.

Feeler gauges

These bladelike tongues, usually pinned together at one end, are thickness gauges that are used to measure the gaps between spark plug electrodes and breaker points. You'll need a set if you own power equipment. Buy the small-engine set, not the automotive type.

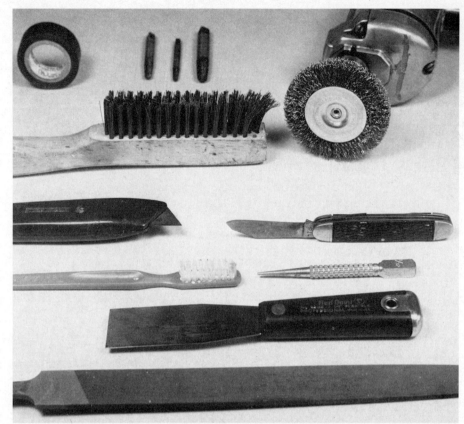

Small tool assortment. You'll need (from the bottom) a smooth or double-cut file, a putty knife, an old toothbrush, a utility knife, a jackknife, a wire brush, and plastic electrician's tape. If your budget permits, buy a variable-speed reversible ³/₈-inch portable electric drill with a wire brush attachment and an assortment of screw and bolt extractors.

The thickness of each blade is stamped in the metal of each blade; sometimes you can put two blades together to get the thickness needed.

Additional tools

Besides the basic tools described above, your lawn and garden maintenance and repair kit should contain the following items. These are not absolute necessities, but you will find all of the items helpful.

putty knife
4-inch wall scraper
ignition file
wire brush
oil can
butt chisel
medium-grit sandpaper
steel wool
nail or center punch
cold chisel
rubber or wooden mallet
gloves

Major repair tools

These specialized tools are designed solely for making minor and major engine tune-ups and for repairing big equipment such as rider mowers and tractors.

■ Flywheel puller or popper. This inexpensive tool is used to remove the flywheel from lawnmowers and other four-cycle engines in order to replace condensors and breaker points (see Page 89 for use).

■ Steel rule. Used to scribe lines and marks with an awl on metal surfaces; it's also used to check metal surfaces for straightness.

■ Compression gauge. Use it to check the compression in engine cylinders.

■ Tachometer. Select one with an rpm range of 1000 to 40,000 (vibration) or 1000 to 5000 (electronic).

Small engine specialty tools. The basic items include a spark plug gap gauge or feeler gauges (bottom right), flywheel poppers and pullers, spark plug socket wrenches, and a short-bladed Phillips-head screwdriver to turn sockets that have side holes in them. This entire assortment costs less than $10.

■ Torque wrench. This is described above; buy one with 0 to 200 lbs. capacity.

■ Ignition timing light or continuity tester.

For advanced engine mechanics, the following tools are usually available as complete sets:

valve guide puller kit
main bearing tool kit
valve seat repair tools
valve seat puller kit
hone set
reamers
reamer guide bushings
plug gauges
pilots
pilot guide bushings
counterbore cutters
crankcase support jacks
starter clutch wrenches
valve spring compressors

piston ring compressors
spark testers
flywheel holders
tang bending tools

Where to write

If you're stuck with an engine problem, need a replacement part or tool you can't find in your community, or want information about a specialized lawn and garden tool or equipment, this listing of manufacturers may help. Write or call the Public Information Director or Service Representative of the company.

Acme Lawn & Garden Division
1217 West 12th Street
P.O. Box 4090
Kansas City, MO 64101
(sprayers, chemicals)

Aircap Manufacturers
Highway 45 South
P.O. Box 1070
Tupelo, MS 38801
(lawnmowers, snow throwers)

Arnold Industries, Inc.
3011 Council Street
Toledo, OH 43606
(lawnmower replacement parts)

Briggs & Stratton Corp.
P.O. Box 702
Milwaukee, WI 53201
(gasoline and diesel engines)

Champion Spark Plug Co.
P.O. Box 910
Toledo, OH 43661
(spark plugs)

Gilson Brothers Co.
P.O. Box 152
Plymouth, WI 53073
(tillers, mowers, shredders)

Homelite Division of Textron, Inc.
Box 7047
14401 Carowinds Boulevard
Charlotte, NC 28217
(mowers, chain saws, blowers, snow throwers)

Kohler Co., Engine Division
Kohler, WI 53044
(engines)

McCulloch Corp.
P.O. Box 92180
Los Angeles, CA 90009
(chain saws and accessories)

McLane Manufacturing, Inc.
7110 East Rosecrans Boulevard
Paramount, CA 90723
(reel mowers)

Michigan Production Grinding Co.
P.O. Box 628
North State Street
Pioneer, OH 43554
(lawnmower blades)

Oregon Consumer Group
4909 S.E. International Way
Portland, OR 97222
(a division of Omark Industries: chain saw maintenance accessories)

Outdoor Power Equipment Institute
1901 L Street N.W.
Suite 700
Washington, D.C. 20036
(association of tool manufacturers)

Rotary Corp.
Box 405
Highway 23 North
Glennville, GA 30427
(power tool replacement parts)

Tecumseh Products Co.
Engines and Peerless Divisions
900 North Street
Grafton, WI 53024
(engines)

Yen Enterprises, Inc.
One Public Square
Suite 400
Cleveland, OH 44113
(tools for repairs)

Glossary

Aggregate. Sand, gravel, or pebbles that are combined with cement and water to make concrete or mortar.

Alternator. An electrical device that generates alternating current.

Ampere, or amp. A unit for measuring the flow of electrical current.

Anchor bolt. A bolt that fastens the sill plate to a concrete or masonry foundation, wall, or floor.

Antisyphon. A valve inserted in a water line to prevent backflow.

Anvil. In garden tools, a flat blade against which a sharp blade is pressed.

Armature. The copper wire windings on the rotating shaft of a universal electric motor.

Auger. On a snow thrower, the spiral blade that moves the snow.

Backfill. To fill a trench around a foundation with earth.

Backlap. To sharpen the blades of a reel mower by applying a grinding compound to the blades and turning them backwards.

Belt drive. A V-shaped continuous belt that transfers engine power to the wheels, blades, or tines of a machine.

Broadcast. To scatter seed.

Brush. In electric motors or generators, a piece of conducting material, usually carbon, that presses against the commutator to collect current.

Butt joint. Two pieces of lumber joined together without overlapping or cutting.

Cam. A wheel-like projection on a shaft that moves an adjacent part.

Camshaft. A rotating shaft with cams that operates levers, such as the tappets in an engine.

C clamp. A screw clamp with jaws shaped like a C.

Cement. A binding substance, usually oxidized clay or limestone, that combines with aggregate and water to make concrete or mortar.

Chain brake. A device on a chain saw that stops the rotation of the chain.

Chain drive. On lawn and garden equipment, a bicycle-type chain that transfers engine power to the wheels, blades, or tines.

Chain saw rails. The shoulders of a groove cut in the chain bar in which the chain travels.

Clearance. A space between two moving parts, or between a moving and a stationary part.

Clevis. A U-shaped connector at the end of a rod or chain to which another part can be bolted or pinned.

Clutch. A mechanical device that connects an engine crankshaft to a gearbox or a drive shaft; it is engaged or disengaged by a clutch lever.

Coil. A wire wound around a core; in an engine ignition system, the coil is used to boost voltage.

Commutator. A cylinder of brass bars on the rotating shaft of a universal motor against which the brushes press to collect current.

Concrete. A stone-like building material made of cement and aggregate, combined with water.

Condenser. An electrical component that stores electrical energy; also called *capacitor.*

Cord. A unit of measurement of cut firewood; usually 8′ × 4′ × 4′.

Cotter pin. A pin with a split end that is put through a hole and then spread apart, to hold parts together.

Crankshaft. A rotating shaft, driven by the piston(s), that delivers engine power to gears or a drive shaft.

Cripple stud. A cut-off, vertical framing member, commonly a 2 × 4, used above or below a window or door opening.

Crosscut saw. A saw with teeth designed to cut across the grain of wood.

Curing. The chemical process that hardens concrete or mortar; water is necessary for proper curing.

Cutting bar. The blade across the bottom of a reel mower.

d. Abbreviation of *denarius,* Latin for *penny;* an old English term that indicates size based on weight. A 16d nail is larger than a 14d nail, etc.

Diaphragm. A flexible disk, such as found in a carburetor.

Dibble. A small, pointed hand tool used to punch a hole in soil to receive a seed or seedling.

Double insulation. In an electric tool, internal circuitry that prevents electric shock to the user.

Drip edge, or drip cap. A metal strip installed around a roof edge to lead rain away from shingles and fascia.

Electrode. A conductor, such as the metal tips on a spark plug, through which current enters or leaves an electrical device.

Electrolyte. The liquid in a wet battery, usually distilled water and acid, that conducts the current.

Electronic ignition. An ignition system for gasoline engines that uses solid-state components rather than a separate condenser and points.

Face-nailing. Driving a nail perpendicular to the surface.

Fascia. The flat member of an eave, which faces outward; the horizontal trim that covers rafter ends.

Feeler gauge. A metal strip, or set of strips, used to measure a narrow gap, such as between points in an ignition system.

Ferrule. A metal part that secures the handle of a tool to the working part.

Fin. A thin, metal projection, as on a cylinder head, that provides heat transfer and, thus, cooling.

Float. A flat, rectangular wood or metal tool used to smooth newly-placed concrete.

Flood. In an engine, to overfill the carburetor with fuel, so that the engine stalls.

Flywheel key. A soft, metal slug that couples the flywheel to the crankshaft; when strain is placed on the flywheel the key breaks, releasing the crankshaft and preventing damage to the machine.

Flywheel puller. A tool used to remove a flywheel from a crankshaft.

Footing, integral. A support for a concrete foundation extending below and around the foundation; the slab and the footing are placed together.

Four-cycle. A type of internal combustion engine that delivers one power stroke for every four piston strokes.

Galvanized. Steel or iron coated with zinc to prevent rust.

Gasket. A metal, rubber, or plastic sheet placed in or around a joint, such as between a cylinder and cylinder head, to make it air- or water-tight.

Gear case. A box-like housing in which meshed gears are protected and lubricated.

Governor. A device, usually coupled with the throttle, to limit the speed of an engine.

Gum. In engines, the residue left by evaporating gasoline.

Header. A horizontal framing member, commonly a 2 × 4, fastened between studs.

hp. Horsepower; a measurement of the power output of an engine.

Hydrometer. A device to withdraw electrolyte from a wet battery and measure its specific gravity to determine battery condition.

Idle. An engine that has been disconnected from its load, as by disengaging the clutch, is described as "running idle."

Idler pulley. A movable pulley that, when engaged, tensions the drive belt, so that the belt operates the machine.

Ignition. A system that ignites a combustible mixture, such as the gasoline vapors in a cylinder, with an electric spark.

Impeller. A paddle-wheel component that moves material through a duct.

Interlock switch. A safety switch in the electrical circuit of a power tool that prevents operation unless a component, such as a discharge chute, is properly engaged.

Jamb. The framing or trim pieces at the top and sides of a window or door.

Kerf. The cut made by a saw blade.

Magneto. An electrical component that converts mechanical energy to electrical energy by means of electromagnetic induction.

Module. In building construction, a standard unit of material, such as a $4' \times 8'$ sheet of plywood, that determines the dimensions of the structure. In an electronic ignition system, a self-contained component that controls the spark.

Mulch. Decomposed plant material, used as fertilizer.

Mulching. Applying mulch to gardens or lawns.

Mulching blades. A pair of blades mounted on a rotary lawnmower that cuts grass into fine bits, which do not need to be raked, but turn into mulch.

Nail set. A pointed tool used to drive nail heads to or below the surface.

oc. On center; describes the distance between two adjacent framing members, such as studs, measured from the center of one to the center of the next.

Oilstone. A stone mounted in a box, across which cutting edges are drawn to sharpen them; oil may be used.

O-ring. A circular washer found in nozzles, sprayers, etc.

Overseeding. Applying grass seed to a lawn that is already established.

pH factor. A number that describes the relative acidity or alkalinity of a substance, such as soil.

Pinion gear. A small gear wheel that engages a larger gear wheel.

Pitch. In roof construction, the difference in height between one side of a roof and another; the slope is usually measured in inches-per-foot.

Pitted. In an engine, cylinder heads, valves, and spark plug electrodes that have been damaged by holes or depressions burned in by improper combustion.

Placement. The process of pouring, screeding, and finishing a concrete construction.

Plate. A horizontal framing member, commonly a 2×4; a sill plate is usually fastened to the foundation; a top plate is fastened to the studs.

Plugging. Strengthening a lawn by planting small cuts of already-growing grass and soil.

Plumb. Vertical; forming a right-angle with the horizontal.

Pocket cut. A cut opened in the middle of a board or plywood sheet with a circular saw.

Points; breaker points. In a gasoline engine, the pair of electrodes that open and close, controlling the ignition system.

Poppet. A valve, such as used in a gasoline engine, consisting of a disk mounted on the end of a stem.

Prehung. A door or window delivered with frame, hinges, and jambs.

PTO. Power take off; on a rider mower, for example, a device to connect an accessory, such as a hydraulic lift, to the engine.

Pulse passage. In small gasoline engines, an opening to the crankcase.

Rafter. A horizontal framing member of a roof, commonly a 2×4; the rafters are attached to the top plates of the wall framing.

Reel mower. A mower with a set of vertically rotating blades that cuts grass against a stationary, horizontal blade.

Reed valve. In two-cycle engines, a thin metal plate mounted between the carburetor and the crankcase.

Regulator, or rectifier. A solid-state electronic component that converts alternating current to direct current.

Respirator. A filter worn over the mouth and nose to stop pollution.

Rhizome. A root-like underground stem that sends out new roots and shoots.

Ring gear. A gear that engages the circumference of a flywheel.

Rip saw. A saw with teeth designed to cut along the grain of wood.

Rotary mower. A mower with one or more horizontally mounted blades.

rpm. Revolutions per minute; a measurement that describes the speed of a turning wheel or shaft.

Screed. A long, flat piece of wood or metal used to level and smooth newly-placed concrete.

Screwdriver. The different designs include: Phillips x, Allen ◯, slot /, and Robertson ■.

Sheathing. The bottom or first layer of covering placed over the rafters or studs.

Shim. A thin strip of metal or wood that is used to make or fill a gap between adjacent parts.

Sill. In wood construction, the lowest horizontal part of a window, door, or frame.

Sill bolt. A bolt imbedded in the foundation, to which the sill plate is attached.

Sillcock. An outdoor faucet mounted on the wall, usually just above the foundation.

Sill plate. In wood construction, the lowest horizontal framing member, commonly a 2×4, attached directly to the foundation.

Soffit. In wood construction, the covering of the underside of the rafters or eaves.

Solenoid. A coiled wire, that, when electrified, becomes an electromagnet; often used to activate a switch.

Spade connector. In wiring, a flat, rectangular connector that slips over a similar connector to make a circuit.

Spark gap. The space between electrodes, such as at the bottom of a spark plug, across which a spark discharge takes place.

Sprigging. Strengthening a lawn by planting small clumps of healthy grass.

Sprocket. A wheel with teeth to guide a chain, such as the nose sprocket at the tip of the bar on a chain saw.

Stator. The stationary component of an electric motor.

Stool. In wood construction, a horizontal framing member, commonly a 2×4, placed between studs under a window.

Stud. In wood construction, a vertical framing member, commonly a 2×4.

Tang. The end of a hand tool, such as a file or spade fork, to which a handle may be attached.

Tappet. The rod, moved by a cam, that operates a valve, such as the poppet valve in a gasoline engine.

Tachometer. A device to measure the rpm of a shaft or engine.

Temper. The strength and hardness of metal.

Template. A full-sized pattern.

Thatch. Dead grass and clippings forming a mat at the base of grass.

Tie-strap. The part of a chain saw that holds the links together.

Tine. A pointed or sharpened prong on a digging or raking tool.

Toenail. To drive a nail at an angle so that it enters two pieces of wood being joined.

Top plate. In wood construction, the highest horizontal framing member, commonly a 2×4.

Torque. Turning power produced by a rotating shaft, such as the crankshaft of an engine.

Torque wrench. A wrench used to install bolts, as in a cylinder head, which has a gauge that indicates the torque applied to the bolt, expressed in foot-pounds.

Two-cycle. A type of gasoline engine that delivers one power stroke for every two piston strokes.

Universal motor. An electric motor that operates on both alternating and direct current.

Vapor lock. In a gasoline engine, a condition caused by overheating of the fuel, in which bubbles obstruct the fuel flow and the engine stalls.

Whetstone. A stone used to sharpen cutting tools by drawing it across the blade.

Wire size. An arbitrary number indicating the diameter of electric wire; the larger the number, the smaller the diameter of the wire.

Index

Contributors
Addresses
Picture Credits

Arrow Group Industries, Inc.
Pompton Plains, NJ
54, 55

Bolens Corporation
Port Washington, WI

Briggs & Stratton Corporation
P.O. Box 702
Milwaukee, WI 53201

Dennis Welsh
Carlisle & Anderson
Hamilton, VA

Dynamark Corporation
875 N. Michigan Avenue
Chicago, ILL 60611

Echo, Inc.
Des Moines, IA

Nick Fannick
NIOSH

Gilson Brothers Company
Plymouth, WI

Gilmour Manufacturing Company
Somerset, PA

Homelite Division of Textron, Inc.
Box 7047
14401 Carowinds Boulevard
Charlotte, NC 28217

Jerry Horton
Purcelville, VA

Kohler Company
Engine Division
Kohler, WI 53044

McCulloch Corporation
5400 Alla Road
Los Angeles, CA 90066

O.M. Scott & Sons
Marysville, OH

Sabre/Townsend Saw Chain Co.
P.O. Box 6396
Columbia, SC 29260

Scott's Lumber & Garden Center
Linthicum, MD

Neil Steinberg
The Photoworks
Leesburg, VA

Bonita G. Taffe
Johns Hopkins University

Tecumseh Products, Co.
Engines and Peerless Divisions
900 North Street
Grafton, WI 53024

Metric Conversions

METRIC CONVERSION TABLES

To convert from	To Convert to Metric To	Multiply by	To convert from	To Convert from Metric To	Multiply by
	Length			**Length**	
inches	centimeters	2.54	millimeters	inches	0.03937
inches	meters	0.0254	centimeters	inches	0.3937
feet	centimeters	30.48	meters	feet	3.2808
yards	meters	0.9144	meters	yards	1.094
miles	kilometers	1.609	kilometers	miles	0.62137
	Area			**Area**	
square inches	square centimeters	6.452	square centimeters	square inches	0.155
square feet	square meters	0.0929	square meters	square feet	10.765
square yards	square meters	0.836	square meters	square yards	1.196
square miles	square kilometers	2.589998	square kilometers	square miles	0.3861
acres	hectares	0.40468	hectares	acres	2.471
	Mass			**Mass**	
ounces	grams	28.34952	grams	ounces	0.03527
pounds	kilograms	0.453592	kilograms	pounds	2.20462
tons (short) (2000 lbs.)	metric ton (tonnes)	0.907185	metric tons (tonnes) (1000 kg.)	tons (short)	1.10231
	Volume			**Volume**	
fluid ounces	milliliters	29.57353	milliliters	fluid ounces	0.0338
pints	liters	0.47318	liters	pints	2.11338
quarts	liters	0.946333	liters	quarts	1.05669
gallons	liters	3.7853	liters	gallons	0.2642
cubic feet	cubic meters	0.028317	cubic meters	cubic feet	35.3145
cubic yards	cubic meters	0.76456	cubic meters	cubic yards	1.30795

DECIMAL EQUIVALENTS

1/64 = .015625	1/4 = .250	1/2 = .500	3/4 = .750
1/32 = .03125	17/64 = .265625	33/64 = .515625	49/64 = .765625
3/64 = .046875	9/32 = .28125	17/32 = .53125	25/32 = .78125
	19/64 = .296875	35/64 = .546875	51/64 = .796875
1/16 = .0625	5/16 = .3125	9/16 = .5626	13/16 = .8125
5/64 = .078125	21/64 = .328125	37/64 = .578125	53/64 = .828125
3/32 = .09375	11/32 = .34375	19/32 = .59375	27/32 = .84375
7/64 = .109375	23/64 = .359375	39/64 = .609375	55/64 = .859375
1/8 = .125	3/8 = .375	5/8 = .625	7/8 = .875
9/64 = .140325	25/64 = .390525	11/34 = .340625	57/64 = .890625
5/32 = .15625	13/32 = .40625	21/32 = .65625	29/32 = .90625
11/64 = .171875	27/64 = .421875	43/64 = .671875	59/64 = .921875
3/16 = .1875	7/16 = .4375	11/16 = .6875	15/16 = .9375
13/64 = .203125	29/64 = .453125	45/64 = .703125	61/64 = .953125
7/32 = .21875	15/32 = .46875	23/32 = .71875	31/32 = .96875
15/64 = .234375	31/64 = .484375	47/64 = .734374	63/64 = .984375